D0862273

The Wild Oats Project

The Wild Oats Project

One Woman's Midlife Quest for
Passion at Any Cost

ROBIN RINALDI

SARAH CRICHTON BOOKS

FARRAR, STRAUS AND GIROUX   NEW YORK

Sarah Crichton Books
Farrar, Straus and Giroux
18 West 18th Street, New York 10011

Copyright © 2015 by Robin Rinaldi
All rights reserved
Printed in the United States of America
First edition, 2015

Library of Congress Cataloging-in-Publication Data
Rinaldi, Robin.
    The Wild Oats project : one woman's midlife quest for passion at any
cost / Robin Rinaldi.
        pages   cm
    ISBN 978-0-374-29021-4 (hardback) — ISBN 978-0-374-71081-1
(e-book)
    1. Women—Sexual behavior.   2. Middle-aged women.   3. Open
marriage.   4. Midlife crisis.   I. Title.

HQ29 .R56 2015
306.7082—dc23

                                                          2014029303

Designed by Abby Kagan

Farrar, Straus and Giroux books may be purchased for educational, business, or
promotional use. For information on bulk purchases, please contact the
Macmillan Corporate and Premium Sales Department at 1-800-221-7945,
extension 5442, or write to specialmarkets@macmillan.com.

www.fsgbooks.com
www.twitter.com/fsgbooks • www.facebook.com/fsgbooks

1 3 5 7 9 10 8 6 4 2

FOR RUBY

Contents

Author's Note

This is a true story, but like all memoir, it is only one person's side of the truth. I have changed the names and identifying characteristics of most of the people who appear in these pages.

PART ONE

Death of the Good Girl

Sooner murder an infant in its cradle than
nurse unacted desires.

—WILLIAM BLAKE,
"The Marriage of Heaven and Hell"

1

The Threshold

IT WAS A RARE BALMY EVENING in San Francisco. Raindrops splattered the long windows of the second-floor bar overlooking the Castro, blurring its neon signs and the headlights below. As the city's offices emptied for the weekend, the bar filled, the DJ upped the volume, and the waiter delivered the first round of sweating margaritas. I was the only woman, and the only straight person, in the room. Chris, a friend I affectionately called my gay husband, was chatting with his buddies as I reached into my pocket, grabbed my phone, and hit Paul's name.

I did it without forethought. The few sips of margarita probably helped me along, but in truth, that night was the perfect storm. It was early, my husband knew I was out with my gay friend, and I wasn't due home for hours. That Friday night in July 2007, some part of me—hidden yet willful enough to pick up the phone—felt it had license to do whatever it wanted. While I went about my business, it was tracking, with silent precision, the changes in my marriage down to the day.

What are you up to? I texted.

Just on my couch watching TV.

Can I come over?

Nothing for five minutes. In that span, I vacillated between anticipating the thrill of a yes and the relief of a no.

Yes. 2140 Jackson.

The indigo characters "2140 Jackson" threw off a crystalline charge that snaked up my arm and lit my chest from inside, as if I'd been sent the combination to a bank vault, or plucked the enemy's secret code off the wires.

Needing encouragement, I pulled Chris aside and showed him the text. He was aware of my recent crush on Paul. He also knew and liked my husband, Scott, but in his world—the microcosm of gay male life in San Francisco—couples who'd been together seventeen years, like Scott and I had, didn't necessarily read disaster into casual flings. Many of Chris's friends indulged their attraction to others now and then without seeming to damage their primary relationship.

He looked from the phone to me. "Are you sure?"

"No, I'm not sure at all," I said, my eyes darting toward the door. I slid into my raincoat.

"Listen," he said, holding my elbow like a football coach instructing a rookie on the sidelines. "Go slow. You can stop anytime you want."

"All right. I need to go."

"Text me later to let me know you're okay."

The sidewalk was a sea of umbrellas. I made my way to the curb and shot my hand up, prepared to wait twenty minutes for one of San Francisco's limited number of cabs. A driver immediately flashed his headlights and pulled over. I gave him the address.

I opened the fogged window and looked up at the starless, heavy sky. The pavement shone with moisture as we ascended Divisadero Street, the long hill that separates the eastern and western halves of the city. As the rooftops swished by, I mentally retraced my steps, taking one last chance to reconsider before I ruined my life.

I'd known Paul, five years my junior, for a few years. He'd always flirted, which had seemed harmless enough until about six months ago. I'd invited him and several others to a party hosted by the magazine where I worked, one of those five-star-hotel soirees where the free booze makes everyone giddy. I'd been chatting away when Paul interrupted, lightly placing his fingertips on my forearm. "I think you might be the most beautiful woman I've ever seen," he'd said, eyeing me without apology. Because he'd met Scott, and because I knew him to be something of a good-natured ladies' man, I tried not to take his compliment to heart. I was used to being called cute, sometimes pretty. No man had ever called me beautiful. I quickened to it despite myself.

And then, two months ago, as I was packing to leave Mexico after a vacation, Paul sprang to mind unexpectedly. I remembered the precise moment. I was folding my bikini into my suitcase and noting with sadness how rapidly my bikini-wearing days were coming to a close. *Even so*, I told myself, *Paul would kill to see me in this.*

Finally, there was another cab ride, just three weeks ago. Paul and I had shared a taxi after impromptu drinks with friends. Once we were ensconced in the cab alone, all I needed to do was sit back and wait. I gave in to the hush that fell over the backseat. I gazed out the window, feeling him watch me. The second I turned to look at him, he lunged, pinning me to the vinyl. His lips on mine. His big hand around the back of my neck. What thrilled me as much as the kiss was how he didn't ask, how his eyes narrowed, animal-like, honing in on my mouth. It lasted only a few seconds. When the taxi stopped in front of my house I quickly pulled away and ran inside, mentally repeating, *It was just a kiss.*

As Divisadero's rambling storefronts approached and then

receded amid the wet sounds of the night, I glanced at the driver's heavy brow in the rearview mirror. I should ask him to pull over. This was a midlife crisis, a cliché. I'd get out, walk through Pacific Heights, and clear my head. I should tell him to turn back toward the Castro and my cozy flat, where my husband waited with a book and a glass of wine.

Perhaps at this early juncture you're already picturing him, imagining some rationale for my behavior: that he was a jerk, that our marriage was sexless. Inconveniently for me, neither was true. Scott had his limits but he loved me, and I loved him.

On the other hand, you might also be thinking this particular cab ride was a simple matter of my being a slut. In fact, with the exception of one very traditional friend, I was the least experienced forty-three-year-old woman I knew, a first-born, over-responsible good girl who'd practiced monogamy my entire life. By "good girl," I don't mean prudish. I'd slept with a few guys—four, to be exact, including Scott—and I enjoyed sex. Neither do I mean especially kind or generous. What I mean is that I was terrified of misbehaving, of causing harm to anyone. My bad deeds didn't come easily and my good deeds were fueled by an overwhelming need for approval. I internalized instead of acting out. Until now.

As the driver turned off Divisadero and headed down Jackson, my phone buzzed with a text message.

Should I open a bottle of wine?

Without hesitating I typed *Definitely.* My stomach churned with anticipation. I was sailing on a strange new momentum, and the simple fact of its energy, the revelation that some kind of internal velocity was still possible, brought such a surprised joy that I easily let it carry me.

The residential streets at the edge of Pacific Heights were dark and quiet in the rain. I paid the cabbie and stood on Paul's front porch. In the distance, a foghorn bellowed its repetitive warning out in the cold black bay. I raised my hand to the door-bell and paused. I knew that the events of my marriage didn't grant permission for this. And yet a renegade voice cheered me on, assuring me I was past the point of needing permission, that indeed it was time to bend a few rules and see where that got us. Lubricated by half a margarita and a cascade of adrenaline, my brain's shadowy and bright chambers held both sides of the argument in balance.

But my body had lost all interest in Aristotelian logic. It had somehow broken from its usual confines to act on its own for the first time in—how long? I couldn't even remember. Perhaps for the first time ever.

I watched as my finger pushed the doorbell.

Thus began my journey away from the straight and narrow. This chronicle of that journey can be read as either a manifesto of freedom or a cautionary tale. For me, it's a little of both. I'll try to tell it as straight as I can and let you decide for yourself.

2

Refugee (Sacramento)

I RESISTED SCOTT for months. He asked me to a concert, then to dinner, and when I said no to both of those, to dinner with a mutual friend. I sat shaking through the whole thing because I knew from the moment we'd met three years earlier that he would alter the course of my life. The setting of that first meeting, a sprawling software company in the parched suburbs of Sacramento, belied the sense of destiny unfolding in its midst. His sandy hair brushed the collar of his button-down shirt. I reached out to shake his hand and it flashed through me: sunshine, forest, a peace as deep and still as a summer lake.

On paper, it didn't look promising. He had a girlfriend studying in Spain, though they were technically free to see others. He'd been my boss until recently and we still worked together. His last girlfriend had been married and her husband had approved of the arrangement. I was an open wound and he was invulnerable, the last thing I needed.

In the flesh, I was losing ground. After work, our team would gather for drinks and he'd regale us with stories of hitchhiking from Indiana to California, nearly getting stabbed by a dwarf in Colorado, falling from a beam several stories up on a construction site in Texas. He would certainly have died, he said, if a mysterious voice, an older male with a southern accent, hadn't suddenly spoken in his mind.

"What did he say?" I asked.

"He said, 'There's a purlin over your left shoulder.' I grabbed it just as the beam fell away."

"What's a purlin?"

"It's like a rafter."

That was notable. He knew the names of things: flowers, trees, parts of machines. And he knew how things worked. On Monday mornings, when we'd all report on our weekends, he'd talk about replacing the transmission in his antique Volvo or laying linoleum in his kitchen at midnight.

He'd grown up along the dunes of Lake Michigan, tall and strong-featured thanks to his German-Scottish blood, cheeks ruddied with a trace of Native American. He looked ten years younger, my age. He owned a tidy little house with hardwood floors, bereft of all furniture except a table and chairs, so full of framed prints it resembled a gallery. He had a cat named Kato and a garden where he grew tomatoes and peaches. He wrote surrealistic short stories with titles like "Mother of Ten Thousand Beings." He quoted Walt Whitman and Epicurus. He kept his old *Boy Scout Handbook* on his crowded bookshelf, tucked between Bertrand Russell's *Why I Am Not a Christian* and William Burroughs's *The Western Lands*. Those three inches of bookshelf sum him up: midwestern, self-sovereign, and below it all, something feral.

He had an MBA and began investing in his mid-twenties. By the time we met it seemed there was nothing he hadn't done, from living out of his car in the Indiana woods to dropping psychedelics to mastering the real estate and stock markets. In the three years we spent as friends before dating, I watched women send him flowers and bake him cookies.

Finally he asked me to drive out to the Sierra foothills for a Saturday picnic. The girl who went to twelve-step meetings wanted to say no; the girl who longed to see the world and learn how to live in it kept drawing nearer.

"I'll go," I told him, "as long as you agree to turn back if I want to." That's how I was then: twenty-six years old and afraid of cars, afraid of men, afraid of any town or highway I didn't know by heart.

"Of course," he said. "We can always have the picnic in my backyard."

When you grow up in a defunct mining town near Scranton, Pennsylvania, your eye trains on every drop of beauty it can find. The apples deepening to red on the trees, the sun rising milky and pink through the clouds, the dilapidated charm of sooty brick and rusted iron set against blue mountains in all directions. On a Paris street, surrounded by grandeur, you might barely note the smell of rain. It might register as merely pleasant, an addendum. On a summer night in northeastern Pennsylvania, after you've swum all day and are lazing in the backseat as your friend drives past abandoned coal breakers and fluorescent pizza joints, one leg hanging out the window, the entire surface of your teenage skin taut with sunburn and chlorine, you learn the essence of rain.

I didn't even notice my father's drinking until I was in high school and he was downing vodka for breakfast. The more pressing problems to my child mind were that he was a bookie, a dangerous secret that could get him thrown in jail, and that he was always threatening to kill my mother. That my mother couldn't go to the grocery store alone or drive on the highway. A weaker woman would have retreated to bed altogether or been carted off to the hospital for nerves, but some engine kept my mother functioning at the very threshold of overwhelm, frying pork chops, vacuuming, doling out hugs and medicine despite her panic attacks. My parents were twenty-two years older than me.

The hate I came to feel for my father never erased my biological adoration of him. My absolute dependence on my mother never erased the fact that she was also my child, coming to me for advice and rides to the doctor. The love I felt for my three younger brothers, that marrow love you feel for an infant with your own DNA that makes you want to eat them and protect them at the same time, didn't stop me running from the house every day to flee the noise and chaos of their constant boy-fury.

Each morning I headed out under the fat clouds, past the apple tree to school to gather perfect grades. Afternoons I went to the ballet studio, where I manipulated my body into demanding, artificial positions. Nights I drove to the woods with my friends, where I listened to Led Zeppelin, drank pony bottles of Michelob, smoked the occasional joint, and learned the numerous ways in which a girl could dabble in foreplay without plummeting into intercourse. Each dawn represented another catastrophe I somehow made it through unscathed.

I spent the rest of my life marveling at how joyful I felt during my turbulent childhood, so connected to the mountains, the little town, my friends and wounded family. How it was only after the childhood ended that I collapsed under its weight.

I blamed it on the cloudless, infinite sky above Sacramento, as one-dimensional as the prosaic suburbs fanning out below it. I came there with a boyfriend when I was twenty to escape, and it worked for a few years while I graduated college and secured a good job as a technical writer. It was a stark letdown from the California of my imagination but it was also three thousand miles from the emotional magnet of home, where my dad was entering rehab, my mom was checking herself into a treatment center for anxiety, my grandfather was dying, and a divorce was in process.

When my grief erupted, it felt like I might tumble off the face of the earth. The flat sky and mountainless expanse of the Sacramento Valley couldn't contain me. Places and routines lost all familiarity. I suddenly belonged nowhere: not to my boyfriend or my job, not in California or Pennsylvania, not even in my own skin. Streets, buildings, sidewalks appeared as if painted on a sheer curtain. I lived in continual fear of the moment when an omnipotent hand might sweep the curtain aside and push me into the void behind it. When that happened I had to run from my desk, pull over on the highway. Sobs burst from me that were more screams than sobs.

My company's employee assistance counselor said I was processing the post-traumatic stress of growing up in a violent, alcoholic family. On the phone, my mother agreed. She told me to call a therapist and get myself to a twelve-step meeting. I was twenty-four. My teenage dreams of becoming a journalist and traveling through Europe would have to wait while I fixed myself. I attended five Adult Children of Alcoholics meetings a week, bought all the self-help books, and showed up religiously for therapy. By day I wrote mind-numbing software manuals; by night I penned angry letters to my father for his abuse and my mother for enlisting my help to put up with it instead of getting us all out of there.

My boyfriend had to go, not because he'd done anything wrong but because I was clearly dependent on him and needed to live alone. I would be celibate for a year. I found a garden-level apartment on a leafy street in Midtown Sacramento—the city at least had trees, I'd give it that—and set about trying to grow into a healthy adult. For two years I didn't allow myself a beer or a glass of wine. I was dead set on avoiding the textbook pitfalls of young women with backgrounds like mine: abusive relationships, addiction, promiscuous sex, and the mental hospital.

That's the girl who agreed to go on a picnic with Scott, seven months into her year of intentional celibacy.

Scott drove us past the little town of Sutter Creek and parked the car near a sign that read "Electra Road." We walked awhile on a trail. He spread a blanket next to a small brook and put out cheese, bread, fruit. I hadn't been out in nature for years—I'd traveled in a circle from apartment to cubicle to therapist's office or self-help meeting nearly every day of the week for the past eighteen months. The woods were both silent and, when I listened closely, brimming with the sounds of water, leaves, insects.

He told me about his dad, a radio announcer who'd built the family's homes in his spare time, and his mom, a woman who'd loved flowers and making things with her own hands, and who'd died three years earlier at only fifty-eight from colon cancer. From his backpack Scott took a printout of a story he'd written called "The Replicant." Lying on his stomach, he propped himself onto his elbows and began reading. The story told of a grown son who downloaded his dying mother's memories into a robot. After her death, he'd turn the robot on whenever he missed his mother, then turn it off when he left the house. Upon returning from work one day and seeing the robot motionless and silent in the corner, he was stricken with guilt and sorrow for leaving it alone.

Scott suddenly dropped the pages and hung his head, tears bursting from him so unexpectedly, I didn't even think before wrapping my arms around him.

"Sorry," he said, pulling himself together. "I've never shown that story to anyone before."

"Don't be sorry," I said. It was too good to be true—that this worldly man was more emotional than he seemed, not so different from me after all. My fear evaporated. A few minutes later, we were kissing. He rolled me onto my back and slipped his hand down my shorts. His body was so long, his shoulders so broad, I was cast completely in shadow. He climbed on top of me. "Not here," I said. "Someone might come by."

We drove home listening to Bonnie Raitt. When we got to his house, he dragged a mattress out from his guest room to the living room floor. Perhaps he avoided the bedroom because of the framed photo of his Spain-dwelling girlfriend on the bureau.

In the months to follow, we drove all over Northern California's back roads. He showed me the high Sierras, the small foothill towns like Volcano and Nevada City, the ramshackle bars and outposts on the Sacramento River Delta. We drove down mountain roads and around hairpin curves listening to an audiotape of the poetry of William Butler Yeats. I learned every word of "Sailing to Byzantium." Scott got me reading T. S. Eliot's *Four Quartets*, William Blake's "Proverbs of Hell," and Walt Whitman's *Song of Myself.* I began to feel like I might just get a chance to live after all.

One Sunday afternoon, on our way down Highway 1 where it hugs the Mendocino coast, Scott ejected the Yeats tape and inserted Brian Eno and John Cale's *Wrong Way Up.* Eno began singing "Spinning Away"—*One by one, all the stars appear, as the great winds of the planet spiral in*—a lone violin string tugging an octave above the lyrics. I stood up on the passenger seat, stuck my upper body out the sunroof, and threw my arms back, letting the sea wind hit my face until the road became too curvy to keep balanced. I plopped back down in the seat, laughing, and looked over at Scott. He said, "I'm so happy I feel like my heart could burst right out of my chest."

In my memory, that statement stands as the most passionate

one he ever uttered, and the tears he shed at Electra Road were the last for nearly a decade. But I shunned the general dating wisdom of the time, which advised seeking out a verbal, "emotionally available" man. I wanted Scott and no one else. Though I often wished he would offer more of the vulnerability I saw on our first date, his reticence only ended up pulling me in deeper. He was solid and large, and against this solidity I surrendered body, heart, and soul.

We would come to call that day at Electra Road our anniversary. We'd use it ten years later as our wedding date.

During those ten years, Scott was the still point around which I revolved. I fed him passion and he fed me stability. It also felt, at times, like I was a crash test dummy and he was a wall, and the only way to obtain information, or a reaction, or any kind of headway, was to ram into him. You could look at photos of us talking at a party or lying on a couch and see instantly why we put up with each other, a depth of mutual adoration evident in our eyes and bodies that surprised even me when I saw it captured in freeze-frame. You could note that for those ten years, and throughout the entire marriage that followed, we never entered or departed each other's company without kissing. I showed my love by asking him to live together three years in and then haranguing him to propose seven years in; he showed his by eventually giving in to my requests. Many others had tried to secure Scott's monogamy and failed.

When Scott did finally propose, over a Valentine's Day dinner at my favorite restaurant, my reaction astounded me. There was no ring yet, just a letter he'd typed—about the origins of Valentine's Day—in which he'd buried the words "Marry Me" in a slightly different, slightly larger font. As the letters coalesced before my eyes, I began to cry from happiness. Within moments, though, a cloud swooped in, a chill that caused me to say, unbelievably, "Can I think about it?"

Soon I announced that I needed space. I'd become too dependent on him; I needed to live alone one more time before we married, just to make sure I still could. By this time I was finally working as a journalist at a newspaper downtown. I rented a tiny apartment near the paper and routinely went to sit in its kitchen at lunchtime, silently staring out the third-floor window at the tops of palm trees. But I spent very few nights there. Away from Scott and the house we'd shared for years, my hands shook. Ordinary activity fatigued me, as if I were moving through something viscous. Was it the pathological anxiety of being alone—something I wanted to purge myself of—or the more acute anxiety of threatening my relationship with the person I loved most? I couldn't tell and I got sick of trying. When the six-month lease was up, I was ready to set a wedding date.

From the convoluted way we got engaged, such a far cry from the scenes in movies and Tiffany ads, it was easy to assume we weren't meant for each other. But I knew that our commitment fears originated outside of our relationship. I wasn't sure where Scott's came from—possibly a fiancée who'd broken it off when he was only twenty, possibly a subsequent girlfriend who'd betrayed him. It mattered little, because once he made a commitment he'd work on it and succeed at it every day, just like he worked on running a certain number of miles and saving a certain amount of his paycheck.

My fear of commitment was much more obvious in origin. I tried to picture a man so ideal that marrying him would feel natural. I couldn't. One of my clearest memories was of a morning in eighth grade, on my way out the door to school. My father was on the couch, sleeping off a hangover. My mother stood at the kitchen counter, wiping it. There was a crying infant on her hip, a two-year-old crashing a toy against the floor, and an eight-year-old downing cereal at the table. She looked up at me, exhausted but determined, and said, "Robin, don't ever get married. And if by chance you do get married, then whatever you do, don't have kids."

I wasn't planning on it. And since marriage occupied so little importance in my youthful mind, it was a no-brainer, when my foreign boyfriend's student visa ran out soon after we got to California, to drive to Nevada with him and marry him on the spot. We were in love, monogamous, and living together, so I couldn't see the harm. But deep down I knew it wasn't forever. His family and friends called me his wife, but to my own family and friends I continued to refer to him as my boyfriend.

With Scott it was different. I was thirty-five and this was for real. I was ready and willing to push past my mother's indictment of marriage. The only hitch was that I'd never done what I'd imagined most women my age had done: date a variety of men, sleep around a little, have a one-night stand. An incomplete, restless feeling came over me every so often, and I occasionally brought it up with Scott, but even when he'd once given me permission to fool around on a weekend trip to New Orleans with my friends, I couldn't go through with it. I wasn't built for casual sex. Scott and I had a healthy sex life, a bit vanilla perhaps, but it worked. From what I'd gathered, my sexual peak was still a few years away, and since monogamy looked to be my natural state, why not just cross that bridge when we came to it? There were all kinds of things married couples could try. Tantra, for instance. New positions. Toys. We had time for all that.

No, there was no way I could give up a man like Scott just to get a few more lovers under my belt, lovers I probably wouldn't even enjoy. I would sacrifice breadth for depth. Scott was the only man I could conceive of marrying, and certainly the only one I could ever have a child with. We had our share of issues, but there was also a deeper battle going on inside me: fear versus hope. I clung to hope.

3

The Leap

I STOOD ON PAUL'S PORCH at the edge of Pacific Heights, listening to the rain and the foghorn, willing him to answer the doorbell quickly. He did. Though in his late thirties, he had a baby face—smooth pink cheeks framing emerald-green eyes. His rumpled shorts and T-shirt hung over thick bone and muscle.

He drew me into a hug. I lay my head on his shoulder, hiding beneath the humid tangle of my hair. "Kiss me," he ordered, and though lusty commands were half the reason I was there, I was too shy to instantly obey. Instead I took off my raincoat and walked to his couch, where he'd opened a bottle of Cabernet. We took a sip, and as soon as I put the glass back down on the coffee table, he was on me. His kisses were lingering and firm. His hands—one against the small of my back, the other on my collarbone, then the tie of my halter top, then my breast—emitted a slow, insistent pressure to which I simply yielded.

The entire time, he whispered steadily into my ear. "I want to fuck you from behind, then turn you over and suck on your tits until you come. When I fuck you will you keep your dress on?"

"Yes."

"Will you keep these boots on while I bend you over?"

"Yes."

He leaned back and unzipped his pants, taking out his penis. "Do you like it?"

"Yes."

"Will you suck it?"

"Yes."

He stuck his finger in my mouth and I sucked that instead.

"When you suck it, can I come in your mouth?"

I nodded yes.

"Will you swallow?"

I looked him in the eye and nodded more slowly. I was drunk on dopamine, ecstatic. It was more than just his touch. It was all the pent-up words I'd craved for years. Words my husband didn't say, that I couldn't make myself say to him.

He took his finger from my mouth and put it between my legs, pushing it high up into me against the front wall. I arched back and my eyes watered. Reflexively I gasped, "Stop, Paul, stop," but what I meant was that if this didn't stop, I would go skidding over a precipice and never return. And even though I was verbally, instinctively pressing the brakes, I had no intention of stopping. I wanted him to hook his middle finger into my center and hurl me over, landing me in a heap of bones at the bottom.

We went on like this for two hours, just hands and words. I wasn't avoiding intercourse out of some misguided theory that what we were doing didn't constitute cheating. I was simply taking it one step at a time, and since our foreplay produced more heady intoxication than I could ever remember from an act of coitus, I didn't mind waiting.

It was almost 11:00 p.m. when we finally sat up, fastened our clothes, and called a cab. We sipped our long-ignored wine and chatted about his relationship problems while we waited. Paul had recently begun dating a woman I'd met a few times, but things between them were vague and rocky.

"I don't want to ruin your marriage," he said.

"You won't," I lied.

"Are you afraid I'll fall in love with you?" he asked. This was exactly why I'd chosen Paul, for the good heart evident beneath the bad-boy demeanor. I knew without a doubt that he was salt of the earth, someone I could actually call in an emergency. That's how I categorized people: those I could and could not depend on in a crisis.

"No," I said. "I'm more likely to fall in love with you. That's what I do."

When the cabbie phoned to say he was outside, I stood on syrupy legs. As I bent to gather up my purse, Paul slapped my ass, hard.

"Ow!" I yelled, turning to him. We both laughed and he winked. Then he walked me down the long hallway, opened the door, kissed me on the cheek, and freed me into the damp night.

4

Wife (Philadelphia)

GEORGE WAS THE WISEST PERSON I'd ever met. Trim, in his six-ties, with a thick head of salt-and-pepper hair, he was always dressed immaculately in creased slacks, button-down shirt, shiny oxford shoes, and a silk tie. George was not the kind of therapist who listened for forty-five minutes and then announced that time was up. He routinely doled out practical advice that I could tell he'd learned from his own life. I wrote the best nuggets down so I wouldn't forget them.

"Let yourself experience the distance your conflicts create, so that you'll have the space to fall in love again."

"You are not responsible *for* your pain but you are responsible *to* it."

"Apply Occam's Razor: Always use the simplest possible explanation."

George could often get Scott to admit feelings that remained otherwise inaccessible to me. We sought him out for premarital counseling to talk about kids. Scott had never wanted them, and I couldn't say that I did either. I'd entered adulthood with my mother's anti-childbearing warning firmly in place. Yet telltale signs of a biological clock began to emerge. Right from the start I told Scott that if I accidentally got pregnant, I'd have the baby. I'd already survived one abortion at nineteen and didn't feel I could handle, or justify, another. "I'll support whatever you decide," he'd said. "It's your body."

Shortly after we began living together, two of his friends got vasectomies. He scheduled a consultation for one as well at Planned Parenthood. When we showed up and the counselor asked if I was on board, I instinctually said no, so he canceled without a word. By the time we got engaged, I'd had nearly a decade of therapy, and the further I got from the chaos of my upbringing, the more I noticed myself drawn to children. At parties that included kids, I often excused myself from small talk to huddle on the floor with a toddler. If a friend was being run ragged by her infant's crying jag, I habitually scooped the baby up and began bouncing and rocking it, as I had my brothers. I suspected my maternal instinct might intensify once we married, and worried about how far Scott would dig in his heels.

George was not one to let emotional explorations go on forever. He was there to help us decide whether and how to move forward. After several weeks of hashing it over, he put down his pen and said, "I think we've talked this out as far as we can. Scott, I have to say, you're one of the most understated people I've ever met. And Robin's the opposite. You remind me, Robin, of that old commercial for gelato: 'So Italian, so intense.' Remember that?" We all smiled.

"Yep, that's her," Scott said.

"But you balance each other out, and, more important, you love each other. In most couples, there's the partner whose job is to rock the boat and instigate change and the partner who keeps the boat steady."

I took Scott's hand while we waited for the punch line.

"I don't know whether you two will end up having kids. But

my feeling, Robin, is that if you eventually want children badly enough, Scott will get on board."

That was exactly what I wanted to hear. After all, he'd eventually gotten on board with every new phase I'd initiated. I'd remained in Sacramento much longer than I'd wanted, because of Scott's job and the house he owned, but after many years of my waiting it out he'd agreed to move back east.

Scott bowed his head, mulled it over for a second, then looked up at me and arched his eyebrows as if to say, *Well, that's that.*

George put his notepad on the floor next to his chair, signaling an end to the session. He folded his hands in his lap, smiled warmly, and said, "There's no way you two are getting out of this without getting married first."

His unexpected, world-wise conclusion soothed me into a sense of clarity. It seemed as close to a commitment as a driven and doubtful woman like me could possibly hope to come.

After we married, ten years to the day from that first picnic, we quit our jobs, bought a small RV, and drove around the country for a while. Eventually, we landed in downtown Philadelphia on the second floor of a three-story brownstone with soaring ceilings, built-in bookshelves, and a five-foot-high marble fireplace. Scott got a job as a project manager in the IT department of an international law firm, and I landed a job as a food columnist at the weekly paper, which meant we ate at a new restaurant once a week. In the stainless steel kitchenette, Scott delved into his home-brewing hobby, emptying cans of malt over the stove, boiling honey and fruit juice to make mead.

If the anticipation of marriage had frightened me, the experience of it agreed with me. I liked calling Scott my husband and being referred to as his wife. I loved receiving Christmas cards and invitations addressed to "Mr. and Mrs. Mansfield," even though I hadn't officially changed my name. My favorite thing was to cook him dinner and, while it was simmering, bring him a drink or ask if he needed anything.

Living just two hours from the family I had fled sixteen years before submerged me in a whole new layer of anxieties. I suddenly had a hard time navigating bridges, supermarket aisles, large pedestrian intersections, and especially the Pennsylvania Turnpike, a road with few exits, unlit at night, that cut a swath through endless forest from Philadelphia north to Scranton. At the halfway point loomed the Lehigh Tunnel, two lanes blasted into an imposing mountain. As soon as the car entered the fluorescent-lit passageway, my heart hammered violently, my skin prickled, and my vision faltered. I had to count my breaths to get from one end to the other.

But the fear was worth it, because amid the same sensory cues that could press in around me claustrophobically—the smell of fresh-cut grass in summer, the sight of red and orange leaves bundled into a patchwork so thick it obscured the tree trunks, the silent blanket of winter snow—I found relics of my soul. Little by little, I was returned to myself. We spent more time with our five-year-old nephew, and out in California, my best friend, Susan, decided to have a child and began the process of finding a sperm donor. No sooner had my pieces begun to coalesce into something resembling a crooked, weary whole than they began vibrating with the urge to reproduce.

At night, the talks would begin. "Just tell me why you don't want to try," I'd start.

"I've just never felt the need. I don't want to spend Saturdays at soccer games. I want to do other things with my time." He measured each sentence out in reasoned strokes, using only the necessary amount of words.

"I can do most of the work," I'd say, some distant, rational part of me shocked at such an offering. "Once the baby is born, you'll fall in love with it. I'm not asking you to go to great lengths with fertility. I just want to take the birth control away." We'd been religiously using a combination of cervical cap and spermicide forever.

I approached the topic from every angle—the purpose it would bring, the sense of connection, the emotional and physical challenges, the spiritual growth. Given my background, my latent desire to create a family with Scott felt weighted with significance. It attested to the enormous trust we shared, a trust it had taken more than a decade to build. Yet he always responded with some version of a calm shrug.

"We don't have to give up our lives just because we have a kid," I'd say. "People with kids still travel. They write symphonies and novels." My verbal style was the opposite of Scott's. Every sentence I uttered stripped away another degree of self-control. Each word seemed to land on him with less impact than its predecessor.

One day after Scott left for work, our neighbor Catherine, a political consultant who was my age and seeing a fertility doctor with her husband, showed up at our door in her tailored business suit, a briefcase slung over her shoulder and a plain brown paper bag in hand.

"I want you to have this," she said. We had talked once or twice about babies and age. I peered inside the bag to find three plastic urine specimen cups, their bright yellow tops secured with white labels that read "Sterile."

"Fresh sperm stays viable for thirty minutes," she said. "All you have to do is collect it and get it to a lab. They can separate out saliva from the sperm, too."

It took a few seconds for that last piece of information to register. I laughed. "Are you kidding?"

"No, I'm not," she said, her eyes shining with resolve.

I lowered my voice. "I don't think I could do that."

"Robin, you'll resent him forever if you don't make this happen. Do you understand?"

I nodded. "Yeah." I hugged her then, because she reminded me that there was indeed a sisterhood at work behind the dealings of the world. "Thanks, Catherine." She squeezed my arm and strode off to work.

I didn't use Catherine's little sterile cups, though she wasn't the first friend to recommend trickery. Later that day, however, as I hid them away under the bathroom sink, the solution dawned on me. It was so reasonable, so mathematical that I couldn't believe it had taken me this long to see it.

I bolted into my home office and looked up fertility rates by age. When Scott walked in the door that night, I sat him down at the dining room table.

"I did research today," I said. "It takes the average thirty-eight-year-old sixteen months to get pregnant naturally, when she's trying. If we try for sixteen months straight, I have a pretty good chance of getting my way. If we don't try at all, you have a hundred percent chance of getting your way."

Scott leaned a few inches back in the chair, so I sped up the presentation. "So, if we tried for eight months and then stopped, it would be statistically fair. We'd both have a fifty-fifty chance of getting our way."

He furrowed his brow.

"If we don't get pregnant in eight months, we could go back to birth control and I'll never bring it up again. Fifty-fifty. Mother Nature decides, and we accept the outcome."

Scott stood up from the table. The sun had just gone down and bluish light angled into the room. "No!" he boomed, raising his voice for only the third time since we'd met. "How many times do I have to tell you? I don't want to have a kid!"

I watched him ascend the spiral staircase to our bedroom, wondering if it was the airtight logic of the proposal that had enraged him. At the same time, I knew no amount of logic could persuade someone who didn't want children. If the tables were turned and he were pressuring me, I might get angry too.

The fleeting thought arose: *I should leave him. This is never going to change.* Before it fully formed, it dissolved into impossibility, for when I removed Scott from the equation, my desire for a family flew right out the window with him. I couldn't do it myself and I could never trust another man with such an endeavor. Thus we spent the next several years locked inside a dilemma born of extreme stubbornness or extreme love or both: I wanted a child, but only with him. He didn't want a child but wanted to keep me.

I began to awaken at 3:00 a.m. I'd lie in bed listening to Scott breathe. He slept on his left side, facing away from me, and he could fall asleep no matter how stressful the day had been, even immediately after an argument. I always tried hard not to wake him. In our twelve years together, we'd never once made love in the middle of the night.

In my dreams, my body morphed into subhuman form. I tugged at the charred flesh of my arm and it lifted away like snakeskin, revealing new pink growth beneath. My back bloomed into a sea anemone, its spongy white tentacles swaying. My chest became a starburst-shaped succulent, the swollen green leaves tinged in red. Repulsed and awed, I tapped their pointed tips gingerly, wondering if the desert plant had taken the place of my heart, whether its insides flowed with its own milky water or my blood.

I looked up the succulent to find a clue to the dream's meaning. It had a long Latin name and was commonly known as a hen-and-chicks plant.

According to Mama Gena, arguing was not the way to convince a man to do anything. Seduction was. That was just one of the many skills she taught at the School of Womanly Arts in New York, which I'd stumbled across while researching a newspaper assignment. Mama Gena was a leggy middle-aged Manhattanite named Regena Thomashauer. Photos on her website showed her styled in all manner of hot pink minidresses and feather boas. High-powered career women flocked to her classes to learn the ways of flirtation, sensuality, and abundance. She claimed to have studied ancient matriarchal religions and aimed, she said, to put the feminine back in feminism—out with suffering, in with pleasure. Her pupils called themselves sister goddesses.

At an earlier point in my life, phrases like "sister goddess" and "womanly arts" would have sent a serious woman like me running. Feminism wasn't a label I felt free to choose or discard. It was a fundamental shift, a tectonic righting that might have completely changed my mother's life had it appeared just a few years earlier than it did. In college I marched in pro-choice rallies, picketed in front of porn outlets, and made a short documentary on domestic abuse as a senior project. That same strident year, I tossed all my makeup straight into the wastebasket. The minute college was over, I grew just as intent about healing as I had about equal rights. I would die a feminist but I was long overdue for some fun.

My first teleconference class found me sitting on my bed with ten other women from around the country on speakerphone as Regena instructed, "Okay, sister goddesses, time to take off your panties." Thus began a lesson on the anatomy of the vulva and the best way to stroke the clitoris's eight thousand nerve endings—twice as many as in a penis, she noted. Our homework was to "self-pleasure" daily, flirt with everyone we met regardless of gender or age, and continually ask ourselves what small thing we could do to increase our enjoyment. Our mantra was, "I have a pussy."

"From now on you must brag at least once a day," Regena

said. "Ditch the communal bemoaning that usually passes for female bonding. Brag to your girlfriends instead of complaining."

Frivolous as it initially sounded, Regena's advice proved life-changing. As I began to make pleasure the basis for my decisions, I relaxed. I wore brighter colors and laughed more. I took up the habit of smiling at the barista, the cranky cashier, the wrinkled old man sitting on a park bench. I didn't have to try to argue less with Scott; I simply lost interest in it. When a discussion became entangled, I changed the topic. It was like I'd switched my wavelength from the work to the play channel.

Regena was a proponent of "extended massive orgasm," a state of whole-body ecstasy that could theoretically go on for hours, as opposed to a regular climax, which she liked to call a "crotch sneeze." I bought the book she recommended, *The Illustrated Guide to Extended Massive Orgasm*, complete with detailed instructions on the exact spot where my clitoris should be stroked— one o'clock, if you were facing it. It didn't hold my interest. I thought of it as an alternative technique for women who couldn't have, or weren't satisfied with, a real orgasm. Unless I was exhausted or ill, I climaxed with Scott every time we made love, often through intercourse alone. I counted myself as one of the lucky ones.

5

The Return

WHEN THE CAB FROM PAUL'S PULLED UP to my house, it had finally stopped raining. Ours was the smallest building on the block, an oasis of warm yellow stucco tucked between taller homes on Sanchez Street. All the lights were off. I put my key in slowly and turned the lock silently, afraid to drag what I'd just done into our safe space. Scott was asleep. I unzipped my boots and padded into the bathroom to wash my face and hands, then climbed into bed. He barely roused. I lay in the dark recalling the last time a new man had put his hands on me, how it had taken Scott months of patient seduction and gentle backing off before I gave way during that picnic at Electra Road. How he couldn't bring himself to abandon the girlfriend in Spain, so he waited for her to return and let her do the breaking up. How more than one friend, upon meeting him, told me, "He's so self-contained he makes me nervous." How once, early on, when I turned to him and thundered, "I'm so angry!" he stepped closer, took my hand, and said quietly, "You don't seem angry. You seem hurt."

That was the conundrum I lived inside: Was Scott's kindness

inspired by love, or made possible by his nerve-wracking capacity for self-containment?

Scott was facing away from me. I nudged up behind him as usual, hanging my arm over his waist. He didn't stir. I waited for something to happen, some fracture that made it clear things had changed forever. When I was twenty-six, the minute I took my clothes off, my sense of self went with them, and it took days to recover it. That's how it had been with my lovers before Scott, too. Regardless of feminism or birth control, I'd completely absorbed the generational lessons of my Catholic hometown: that every act of sex was something the woman gave and the man took. Now, seventeen years later, the situation had miraculously inverted. *I* was the plunderer. I felt larger instead of smaller, more powerful instead of less so.

My warm bed enveloped me. A hiss echoed far in the back of my mind: *adulteress, adulteress, adulteress.* It was drowned out by my husband's steady breathing, our cat purring peacefully at my feet, and the surprising recognition that my house was still standing, my life still intact.

6

Madonna (San Francisco)

ONE OF THE PHRASES Scott had picked up from his time in the south was "putting lipstick on a pig." That's what he felt about Philadelphia and the East Coast in general: No matter what enticements it offered, nothing could hide the fact that it was an old, ugly sow compared with California.

"I miss the western sunsets," he said.

"But if we move back west, I'll miss my family," I said.

"Philadelphia isn't the place to buy a house."

"I could leave my family more easily if I knew we were going to make our own family."

"I'm not going to give in to ultimatums."

I felt the familiar powerlessness creeping in, immobilizing my chest, wanting to erupt as tears. I kept it in check. I'd dreamed of San Francisco for twenty years, since the first time I'd driven over the Bay Bridge and seen it shimmering all white and kinetic out in the water. I was nearly forty, and Regena was teaching me to focus on the positive, focus on desire.

"Then I want to live in San Francisco," I said.

Within a year of arriving, I found my ideal job—senior editor at a city magazine—and we set out looking to buy our own place. For eight months, we spent weekends traipsing from one open house to the next until we found a Georgian duplex that had been built in 1892 and survived the 1906 earthquake. It was located in the center of town on Sanchez Street, between the Mission and the Castro, and the ground-level flat was for sale. As the real estate agent gave us a tour along with several other couples, I stood in the front room gazing down a long hallway into the sun-drenched kitchen. The hardwood gleamed, the brick fireplace was painted picket-fence white, and the deep tub was lined in marble. My heart skipped with possibility. I tugged Scott's sleeve and leaned in, so no one could hear me. "This is the one."

On the day we were due to sign papers on our five-year adjustable-rate mortgage, I found myself unable to sit still at work. My stomach clenched and I couldn't see straight. I called Scott at the law office, just a mile down Market Street from the magazine, and asked him to meet me for lunch.

"What's wrong, button?" he asked when he sat down.

"I'm afraid if I sign those papers this afternoon, in five years I'll be childless, infertile, and unhappy."

He reached his hand across the table and took mine. "Have faith in us."

I signed. No matter what the scope of the dilemma, it was easier to have faith in us than to imagine the opposite.

One of the first things we did after moving in was to install a stripper's pole in the living room. Some of the sister goddesses who lived in San Francisco raved about their pole-dancing lessons at a place called S Factor, and I figured I'd give it a try. Each Sunday I drove to a class in the Marina, where I learned to walk in six-inch Lucite platforms, spin around the pole in various graceful positions, and perform a sultry lap dance to songs by Hooverphonic and Spiritualized. The studio allowed no men inside, and the dark classroom was lit only with red lamps, eliminating outright most of the lethal self-criticism a roomful of seminaked females would endure in the light of day. Outside in the dressing room, my classmates were average-looking women of all sizes and ethnicities, ranging from their early twenties to their mid-fifties. In the dark studio with the music on, each of them transformed into a vision of sensuality. I began to see that, for how much we all agonized over our features and shapes, beauty didn't actually live there. It didn't dwell, static, in skin and muscle; it emerged in how we moved.

Once I'd mastered the routine, I pulled a chair up several feet from the pole and sat Scott down in it. I started facing away from him, hands against the living room wall, slowly gyrating my hips in wide circles. I turned and flattened my back to the wall, legs wide, bending to a low squat, then crawled to the pole and pulled myself up onto it. I swung around it, hitched my legs overhead and grabbed the top of the pole with my ankles, spiraling down toward the floor, my hair landing first. From there, I slithered over to where Scott sat, kneeled up in front of him, peeled off my shirt, and climbed into his lap.

Scott watched, a sliver of smile signaling bemusement. His hand brushed my leg as I hovered over him, my breasts nearly touching his face. We both held our breath. When the music ended, he said, "Very nice, doll." I picked up my clothes and we went to the bedroom.

Scott exercised religiously and was in better shape than most men half his age, still as muscular and narrow through the waist as when we'd met. Our lovemaking was patient. He took his time kissing me. He spent a long time touching me, lightly at first, barely at all, until I could stand more pressure. He went down on me gently, circling my clitoris until it emerged. He allowed my layers to unfold. By the time we switched places and I took him in my mouth, I was hungry, writhing against his leg until I almost came. Then I inserted a little transparent square of spermicide film and climbed on top of him. His erection was solid and dependable, just like him. I could go as slow as I wanted without worrying that it would flag. What I couldn't do was go fast. It wasn't in our repertoire.

After I came, I got under him. At that point I wanted pressure. I wanted to tell him to fuck me hard but I couldn't get the words out of my mouth. More than anything, I wanted him to look me in the eye. Instead, we silently kept pace, faces buried in each other's shoulders, both saying *I love you*. When he came, he put his mouth over mine. Often, during either my orgasm or his, tears brimmed and fell down my cheeks, leaving me cleansed and centered.

Afterward, Scott got up to go wash off. Then I threw my knees back over my head in a yogic plow pose, hoping to somehow wriggle his sperm past the contraceptive. By the time he returned to the bedroom, I was lying flat again.

"Why don't you look at me during sex?" I asked. We had been together so long and I'd only recently noticed this.

"I can focus on the sensations better with my eyes closed."

I couldn't summon a response to that, so I lay there staring into the guest bathroom a few feet away, where Scott kept his homemade wine. Huge glass jars of cherry-red liquid sat fermenting in the shower stall, burping out carbon dioxide. Guests were always impressed by Scott's array of mead, limoncello, and homemade absinthe. When we weren't away for the weekend, we'd throw dinner parties for the editors, artists, and biotech entrepreneurs we'd quickly befriended since arriving in the city. At some point during the evening, we'd gather in the living room, the stripper's pole looming. I could see the looks on their faces. I imagined the women thinking *They must be having great sex*, the men thinking *That lucky shit*, and a few of each thinking *Oh boy, midlife crisis*.

One night I lit a log in the fireplace, Scott slipped a DVD into the player, and we settled onto the couch with our cat, Cleo. A picture-perfect calico, Cleo had been with us since she was only days old. We'd found her and her littermates orphaned on the side of the road near the software company back in Sacramento and fed her through an eyedropper for many weeks. Now she was fourteen.

The film was *Munich*. Its opening scene showed a close-up of a husband hungrily fucking his wife from behind. A clear, assured voice in my head pronounced: *That's what I want.* The statement was so simple, yet somehow revelatory. Then the camera pulled back to expose the wife's huge pregnant belly, and in that moment the unrequited yearning in my gut knotted itself into a kernel of pure will.

At my annual exam, I asked my doctor to include an FSH count in my blood work. "FSH" stood for follicle-stimulating hormone, a basic measure of fertility; the lower the number, the easier it was to get pregnant. Mine was low for a forty-two-year-old, as low as many women would test in their early thirties. "And you've got a lot of estrogen left," she said, "which means you'd be able to carry to term. Still, it's pretty much now or never."

That sent me in search of a new therapist. Delphyne had a PhD in feminist spirituality and a long mane of thick auburn hair. She wore dark eyeliner and maroon lipstick. She adorned her fingers in gold and jade, and her flowing skirts breached the top of lace-up boots. I suspected many tattoos beneath her clothing.

Week after week, I sat in Delphyne's office looking up at a painting of the Hawaiian fire goddess, Pele, which hung above her door. According to legend, Pele had spewed lava from beneath the sea to form the island of Hawaii and made her home in the caldera of its most active volcano, Kilauea. She was creator and destroyer, a source of both love and violence. The goddess's black hair flowed outward into liquid flames and her orange eyes bored into me, asking where I was going to draw the line. I wanted a baby, yes, but how badly? What was I willing to do for it?

It turned out that Chris, my so-called gay husband, also wanted a child. Knowing my predicament, he offered to artificially inseminate me and share custody. In theory, the deal looked perfect. Chris was a published author, financially secure, and his family supported the idea. I could be a half-time mother, Scott a half-time stepdad. Scott and I would still have lots of energy for hobbies and travel. When I broached the subject, Scott actually said he'd consider it because he didn't want to stop me from experiencing motherhood.

When Delphyne had me sit quietly and envision this scenario, however, it made my heart sink. I couldn't fathom how Scott would consent to let another man inseminate me before he'd do it himself. Grateful as I was to Chris, the baby itself wasn't the goal. It was the process I wanted, and I wanted it with Scott. Was that asking too much? How difficult could it be to convince my own husband to impregnate me? Left and right, teenagers and lesbians alike were bulging in the belly.

While I knew a baby couldn't save a bad marriage, I felt sure it could bolster mine from perfectly decent into something to which I could devote myself. We'd surmounted so much: a long illness in my thirties, our substantial commitment fears, two cross-country moves, and the usual slew of family crises. True, we didn't have wall-banging sex, but when I polled my married friends, I realized how exceptional was the fact that after sixteen years we still had regular sex once or twice a week—sex that lasted forty-five minutes and often ended in joyful tears.

In private, my friends and family occasionally labeled Scott selfish for not wanting children and, by default, my maternal longing unselfish. I didn't buy it. Every woman I knew who'd gotten pregnant had done it one of two ways: by accident or out of an urgent drive to become a mother. I had no illusions about motherhood being easy. But it came with deep emotional and societal rewards, and I saw no one consciously pursuing it without those rewards in mind.

Delphyne exuded dark wisdom. After many weeks spent lobbing seemingly unrelated questions my way—questions about my female friendships in particular, which buzzed about my addled mind like annoying insects—she took another tack. She handed me a tall green candle in a glass jar. She had poured it herself and decorated the jar with an image of Demeter, the Greek goddess of motherhood. Her arms spread wide, the goddess wore a long golden dress and a crown of wheat stalks.

"Take this home and light it," Delphyne told me. "Let it burn until the flame dies. Maybe it will bring you clarity."

I did as instructed, placing the candle on my nightstand, letting it burn through the day and night. By the time the flame went out, my period was several days late.

Scott always left for work by 6:30, so I was alone in the house. The December dawn filtered in through the light well window in the bathroom. I sat on the toilet, my bare legs trembling. Next to me on the sink lay my cell phone and a digital pregnancy test. I uncapped the test and peed onto it—one, two, three, four, five seconds—then shook it off, laid it carefully back down, pulled up my pajamas, and waited. The last time I was pregnant, when I was nineteen, I'd driven from Planned Parenthood in Scranton straight to my mother's house for dinner, containing my tears. On the porch, as I was leaving, I turned to her and said, "I have to talk to you." The fall dusk hung crisp around us. My youngest brothers had just run back inside, yelling and wrestling. My fourteen-year-old brother was at football practice. My dad was out gambling, drinking, or fucking. That was good. Relief permeated the house in his absence.

She looked at me squarely. "You're pregnant."

I gave a little gasp. "How did you know?"

"You're not keeping it. Make the arrangements, and I'll take you."

She didn't have to tell me that. I'd already made up my mind. Two weeks later she drove me to New York and held me while I cried in the recovery room, groggy and doubled over with cramps. I remember walking up to the clinic, my mother behind me, and stopping at the entrance. I stared at the glass door as if it were made of bolted steel, thinking *I can't do this*. I remember the counselor in pink scrubs who sat with me in the low-lit surgery waiting room, saying, "You're going to sleep like a baby tonight, you just wait." I remember, right before going under, the doctor's hand inside me and his voice announcing, "Seven weeks," as if from the next room. I knew only two things: that I was not strong enough to carry a child and then give it away, and that I would rather die than trap myself in my hometown with a baby and no college degree. The kindly counselor turned out to be right. On the way home we stopped at my favorite restaurant, where my mother ordered me a steak, and afterward I slept for twelve hours. We told everyone we'd gone to Atlantic City for the day, to gamble.

As I sat on the toilet waiting, I still harbored potent fears of motherhood—surrendering control of my body, giving up all my mental space and sense of self, and, worst of all, the possibility of suffocating so much under a child's constant needs that I hurt or abandoned her. Now, though, I was equally afraid of not being pregnant—of the existential default in which I skirted life's surface, locked mentally into a thousand possibilities while never committing to any, experiencing the world through a jumble of restless potential.

The test beeped. I picked it up and there in tiny sans serif font it said: "Pregnant." With a capital "P."

My fingers shook as I dialed my best friend, Susan, in Los Angeles.

"Am I waking you?" I asked.

"No, I'm just getting Amelia ready for school. Did you do it?"

"Yes. It's positive."

"Oh my god. Wow. How do you feel?"

"I don't know," I said, but even as I spoke, I looked up in the bathroom mirror and saw a smile. And then words came. "Oh my god, Susan, I won. I can't believe it. I won."

I wasn't sure what I meant. What, exactly, did I win? The power struggle with Scott? The last and greatest trophy of modern womanhood: college degree, enviable job, handsome husband, beautiful house, and now, just in the nick of time, baby? Or something much deeper than any of that, namely the battle of hope—maybe I could create a happy family, a happy life— over memory?

"All right, take a breath," Susan said. "Call your doctor right now and tell her you want a blood test to confirm it."

Susan knew the drill. When she was forty, with no boyfriend in sight, she went to a sperm bank and chose Number 58499, a grad student who was studying music and willing to meet the baby when she turned eighteen. Since then, Susan had dedicated her waking life to being a single, working mother. The woman who once jetted off to Belize and Venezuela now spent every free moment cooking, cleaning, chauffeuring, and bathing, all while nursing what seemed like a never-ending string of viruses Amelia brought home from preschool. I never worried about Susan, though, because I remembered one afternoon when she'd just come from an insemination and had to lie with her legs up for several hours. We were on the phone, and, trying to be helpful, I said something like, "No matter what happens, it'll be okay."

"No, it won't," she replied. "If I don't have a baby, I'm really not all that interested in being on this planet."

If Susan's maternal instinct was a roar, mine was a whisper. It had slowly and quietly fought its way to life against my mother's warnings like a weed in a sidewalk crack. Subterranean and tenuous, its sole chance of manifestation was the old-fashioned method: in my bed, with my husband, the only human being I'd ever fully trusted.

And now, beyond all odds, it would get its chance.

I slipped on a skirt and boots, ran my hand over my abdomen, and headed out to work under a mauve-blue sky. The winter wind braced my cheeks, and a hundred little surges unfurled inside me like tendrils, accompanied by a checklist of anticipation. I would eat well. I would be offered seats on buses. I would join a hallowed sisterhood, one that even my mother had come to honor in time. Scott and I would be guided by primal forces larger than our fears. This baby would change us in the best possible ways: fulfilling my need to be needed, snapping Scott from his philosophical heights down to the mire of fragile flesh. Parenthood would sculpt me into someone less selfish, Scott into someone less cold. We would have something important to do with the next twenty years of our lives, and when we were old, grandchildren would sit at our table.

I had a feeling it was a girl. I already knew her name. Ruby.

As I headed underground into the subway, I brimmed with an unfamiliar kind of happiness, a joy that traced its way back through pain and circumstance to the source of things, and that simultaneously cleared a path to the future. A feeling that finally, my life would come to fruition.

I've never had a morning like it, before or since.

I didn't expect Scott to immediately rejoice, but I also didn't imagine how stricken he'd be. By the time I got home from work that night, he looked so depressed that all my earlier excitement was sucked from me as if into a vacuum. The only other time I'd seen him so listless was when his dad had been diagnosed with cancer.

"You know when a flower blooms," he said, "if you cut the stamen off, the part that holds the sperm, the flower lasts longer. Once the flower reproduces, it dies. I don't want to die. I want my own life."

The strangest thing happened as he spoke. As if I'd taken a psychedelic drug, his features softened and his shoulder-length hair appeared to grow a half inch longer, transforming him, for a brief second, into a woman. I reactively took a step backward.

"You won't die," I countered. "You'll grow into someone new, someone larger."

"I don't want to grow into someone new."

"Why?" I pleaded, beginning to cry. "Why!"

He took my forearm and led me to the hallway, where hung a framed, enlarged photo he'd taken the year before on a trip to his hometown in Indiana. It showed an abandoned train track receding into the blurred nighttime distance, surrounded on both sides by the bare, wintry branches of overgrown trees. It was lonesome and surreal.

"Because of that." He pointed to the photo.

"What do you mean?" I asked. Because of the months he spent drifting after high school, living out of his car in the Indiana woods? Because of some existential ache at his core? Was he finally confiding to me, a full six years into my earnest and tearful questioning, the reason he couldn't bring himself to have children?

"What do you mean, Scott?"

"Just . . . that," he said, looking at the photo. This often happened: At the moment of divulgence, we trailed off into a dead end. I waited but he remained silent. I had no idea whether he was hiding something or simply in the dark himself.

After a full minute I quietly said, "All those months talking to George about this before we got married. Do you remember him saying that if I wanted a child badly enough, you'd get on board?"

He shook his head. "George was wrong."

That's when I gave up. If it had just been me and Scott, locked motionless in that hallway, I might have kept fighting until menopause, but luckily the deeper reality finally hit me. This wasn't at all like talking him into cohabitation or marriage, because it wasn't merely my happiness or his at stake. There was a third person to consider here, a powerless person whom it was my job to protect. I could well be bringing into this world a child unwanted by its father. That might change in the ninth month or the ninth year, but suddenly, the thought of risking it made me sick—perhaps the only shred of selflessness in my desire to be a mother.

By the time I went to my doctor the next day, half of me was hoping it was all a mistake. She sent me into the restroom with a pee cup and the results mirrored my inner turmoil: negative. "I don't get it," I told her. "It wasn't like I had to interpret a pink line. The test was digital. It said 'Pregnant.'"

"You might be pregnant," she said. "Or it could have been a false positive. Or, you might've had what we call a chemical pregnancy, which is really just a very early miscarriage. We need a blood test." She sent me to a lab downtown, and after drawing my blood they told me it would take five days to get the results.

I scheduled a couple's appointment with Delphyne on the fifth day. Scott had joined me for a few sessions in the previous months. My plan was to call the doctor, then walk immediately to Delphyne's so I didn't have to be alone with the answer. But I already knew the answer, which the doctor merely confirmed. No pregnancy. Whether I had miscarried or gotten a false positive, I'd never know.

I walked the four blocks to Delphyne's and sank into her couch. Scott was already there. I put my right hand on the cushion and he placed his left one over mine, as usual. Pele the fire goddess looked down on us with her murderous eyes.

"I'm not pregnant after all," I told them. A column of thick, dry air, ancient and immovable, lodged in my throat. It made breathing an effort.

I don't remember the next fifty minutes. All I know is that at one point, Scott said, "I'm going to get a vasectomy. I've been wanting Robin to suggest it, and she hasn't, but I'm going to get one anyway." I looked up from the spot on the floor where I'd been fixing my gaze and, still holding his hand, said, "I agree. Get a vasectomy. I support you. And I'm going to do whatever I want, and you need to support me. Starting now, we're in this for our own individual goals, not for anything larger."

He stared at me, forlorn. I let the grief suffuse my skin, muscle, all the way to the bone. I let it nail me to the couch without a fight. And yet, deep inside my skull, back where the brain attaches to the spine, something shivered to life. Relief. Freedom. The happy family a long shot I needed no longer concern myself with.

"All bets are off," I said, looking back at the floor. And I must have meant it, because seven months later I found myself knocking on Paul's door.

7

The Epiphany

IT TOOK FORTY-EIGHT HOURS for the reality that I'd cheated to hit me. Scott and I went to Napa to research a travel story I was writing, and after a day of vineyard-hopping, we checked in to a plush bed-and-breakfast in Yountville. As Scott dozed off, I lay in bed next to him reading a magazine and came across an ad for diamond anniversary rings that showed a couple meeting, marrying, having children and grandchildren. A few pages later I flipped to an ad for a mattress, on which a gorgeous couple sprawled with their three young children. Next up, a profile of Catherine Zeta-Jones, describing her life in Bermuda, how she was "crazy in love" with her husband and how she quizzed him on having kids before agreeing to marry him.

I closed the magazine and tried to sleep. My limbs buzzed and my head started pounding. I massaged my temples, as if that could stop the gathering onslaught. I knew that women's magazines were not the place to go looking for truth. But the storm that had been looming since the moment I rang Paul's doorbell was so inevitable that it took only a few pretty pictures to invite its descent.

I curled up on my side. The pain knifing my forehead was more than physical. I blamed myself, not just for Paul—for everything. For marrying Scott when I knew he didn't want kids. For not having slept with more men before I married. For wanting both passionate sex and motherhood while doubting I could handle what either of them would require of me. For masquerading as a carefree little tart with Paul when in reality I was a damaged weakling. No wonder my marriage was floundering. I was pathetic.

I sat up, switched on the light, and dug through my purse for ibuprofen in vain.

Scott rolled toward me. "What's wrong, kitty?"

"My head's killing me. I need some medicine." I missed the days when I could tell him anything. No matter how difficult the confession, we could count on the honesty to add one more layer to our strong foundation. Even if I hadn't been keeping a deadly secret, that habit had ceased a few years back.

He got dressed, drove us to a convenience store, and went in to get me Advil. Two minutes after I swallowed the pills, the pain migrated to my stomach. I broke out in a sweat, my vision spinning. I opened the passenger side window and hung my head out. Back at the hotel I shook on the toilet, holding on to the sink and breathing slowly so as not to pass out.

"Are you okay?" Scott asked from the other side of the closed door.

"Yes," I moaned. "I'll be out soon." Twenty minutes later I shuffled to bed, clammy and exhausted.

The next morning, I awoke to a fully formed certainty flickering in the space behind my eyes. It said: *I refuse to go to my grave with no children and only four lovers. If I can't have one, I must have the other.*

When we arrived home, Scott dropped me off in front of the house and went to park the car. As I approached the door, I bent down to pick up a scrap of cardboard lying in the entryway. No more than an inch long, it looked as if it had been ripped off the corner of a cereal box. I unfurled it, turned it over, and saw written in minuscule, perfect script: "Find for the defendant: not guilty," like a note a juror had written during the trial of an innocent person.

I looked around, wondering who wrote it, why, and how it had blown into my doorway and landed at my feet. I'd always been a believer in synchronicity, the symbol that appears at the moment it's needed, a reassurance that life is proceeding according to plan.

Find for the defendant: not guilty. I was indeed guilty: of lying, stubbornness, and, worst of all, betrayal. I wasn't deluded enough to read the note as absolution of my actions. What I took from it was absolution of my desire. Make that plural: all my desires. To marry Scott despite his imperfections and mine. To have his child though he didn't want it. To try to harness my sexual energy within the marriage. To now turn that energy elsewhere. My competing desires for security and newness, domesticity and passion. My selfish desire to nurture. My desire to fuck as well as make love.

I might not get what I wanted, but I wasn't going to stop wanting. I was done talking through my dilemmas. It was time to follow my instincts and see what wisdom I could gather up through my body.

As I pocketed the little slip of cardboard and put my key in the door, I heard Scott's beloved Walt Whitman singing down across the ages: *"Urge and urge and urge, always the procreant urge of the world."*

Four days later, Scott went to his vasectomy appointment alone.

8

Whore

AFTER THE VASECTOMY, Delphyne constructed a ritual in which Scott and I each wrote down our vision of the future. She asked us to imagine, among other things, how we could stay in our marriage without losing too much of ourselves. That's how I broke the news to Scott that I wanted an open marriage.

"If we sleep with someone and the sex isn't good, we've threatened our marriage for nothing," he said. "And if the sex is good, we'll want to repeat it, and the more we repeat it, the more invested we'll become." He knew this from the five years he'd spent with a married girlfriend.

I believed him. An open marriage was risky and emotionally messy. And given both his history and my restlessness over the years, this wasn't the first time we'd discussed it. In the past we'd quickly dismissed the idea. This time I just kept repeating the words that came to me in Napa, but out loud: "I won't go to my grave with no children and four lovers. I refuse." Sometimes it was "I won't"; sometimes it was "I can't."

On the train downtown in the morning, I found myself staring at men. Just imagining their hands on me during the twelve-minute commute was enough to keep my whole day ambling along pleasantly. When a stocky Russian-speaking repairman came to fix our kitchen window, I sat at the table pretending to work while secretly drinking in the shape of his arms, the sound of his voice.

We lit candles, read our answers to Delphyne's questions, and buried the pages in our backyard under the bright pink flowers of a weeping fuchsia tree. I saw a chasm opening up ahead of us and I could imagine no way to close it short of turning back time. Together or alone, it had to be crossed.

It took months to construe what an open marriage might look like. Rule number one was obvious: We would practice safe sex. Everything else was up for debate. We talked about constraining the "side action," as Scott called it, to out-of-town trips, but decided that was too unwieldy. Instead, I would get an apartment. I'd spend weekdays at the apartment and weekends with Scott. We agreed that we wouldn't sleep with friends or acquaintances we both knew. To allay our fears, we cracked the occasional joke about free love and began half-seriously calling it the Wild Oats Project.

Of course, I'd already set my sights on Paul. I told myself I'd make him a temporary exception to the no-friends rule, my set of training wheels before venturing out into a sea of strangers. So a full two months before I had secured an apartment, I planned a business trip to Denver for a weekend when I knew Paul would be there. Paul had no idea until two weeks prior; I practically chased him down.

I left on Friday night from the office, taking the train to the airport, which was strangely quiet. I ordered a glass of wine on the plane and relished its sharp warmth, spreading from my chest down through my legs, smoothing out the edges where my skin met my clothes and settling me into the seat. I fingered the gold medal my mom had given me on my wedding day. It hung on a long chain, in the shape of a four-leaf clover. Jesus was carved into the top leaf; the Virgin Mary, St. John, and St. Christopher into the other three; and on the flip side was engraved in small type, "I am a Catholic. Please call a priest." I hadn't practiced Catholicism for a long time, and I probably wouldn't ask for a priest if I were dying, though I wouldn't send one away either. I only wore the medal when I flew, just like I only said Our Fathers when I flew, or when someone I loved fell direly ill. The rest of the time I did yoga and burned incense and prayed to pagan and Hindu deities.

The moment we touched down, Paul texted from a bar. *Have you landed yet? Text me when you get to the hotel. Are you nearly there? You said 25 minutes it feels like 45.* I could sense him getting drunker with each message and I understood why. He felt guilty about Scott and was only doing this because I'd instigated it. Paul's plan had been to steal one kiss from his married friend in a cab, not to spend a weekend with her.

I got to my room and began unpacking. He texted that he was a few blocks away, downstairs in the lobby, in the elevator, and by the time I opened the door he was already rounding the corner. He wore a black jacket and dark jeans, his hands thrust into their pockets like a nervous kid. His green eyes gleamed from flushed cheeks, and his smile betrayed a hunger that, for a split second, pierced my heart with sadness.

"Paulie," I said, reaching out to hug him. He pinned me against the wall and began kissing me. I laughed and said, "Let's go into the room." He pushed me back onto the bed, threw off his jacket, and climbed on me, holding down my arms, looking at me a few seconds before diving in to my neck.

"I love you," he whispered, running his hand over my sweater, then under my skirt. "Would you run away with me if you could?" It was mostly the liquor talking, yet I sucked up his words like oxygen. If he produced two plane tickets that moment, I probably would have run away with him. His body on top of me was all I'd wanted for months. His erection was like stone beneath his jeans. I unzipped them and reached in to touch it. "Get a condom," I said.

"I don't have one."

I pushed his chest up and away from me. "You didn't bring condoms?"

"No, I wasn't sure I'd actually show up." I believed that.

"You need to go get some."

He pressed his mouth to mine, tried to put himself inside me.

"Listen," I said, holding his face immobile in my hands. "We need a condom."

He paused, then kissed me again.

"Are you kidding me?" I said, louder this time, rolling out from under him and sitting up. "I'll kick your ass. Go get a condom." I pointed to the door.

He sat up and looked at me, catching his breath. The vulnerability on his face was more than I could bear. It made me want to cry. We sat in silence a few seconds, his way of saying we could stop if I wanted to. I knew I should leave and go get the condoms but I couldn't tear myself away from his body or the urgency it was trying to contain. Then time was up, and he was on me again.

In truth, I was sick of protecting things. I wanted the joy of being overcome.

He entered me, lifting my knee in one hand while grabbing my breast with the other. He pounded, then pushed all the way up and held it there. It hurt, a good kind of hurt. As I relaxed into it, it felt better and better. After a while I rolled onto my stomach and raised my hips in the air. He pulled them back and plunged forward—in and in and in until a dizzy, blissful trance descended on me. He grabbed my hair and wrapped the length of it around his palm like rope, arching my chin toward the ceiling. That's how he came, my head yanked back in one fist while he pulled himself out of me at the last second with the other.

Afterward he went and got a warm towel and wiped me off, and we turned the lights out and tried to sleep. He tossed fitfully, seeming to struggle in dreams. I lay half-awake and unnaturally still all night, his body a magnet, a force field I dared not touch in the quiet. I was only allowed access in the fire of drunken passion. In the morning we ordered breakfast: eggs for him and oatmeal for me. I could barely choke it down. I felt ill with a kind of dark ecstasy. I'd never behaved so destructively, and yet in the shadows through which I descended I caught a glimmer of something, a recognition.

After breakfast, Paul left, saying he'd return that night to pick me up for dinner. I closed the door and got back into bed. Beneath me I felt something cold. My medal. The chain was lying on the mattress, snapped in half.

I picked it up, and a little surge of horror chilled up my spine and evaporated. Ten Commandments, gone. Marriage vows, gone.

I slept with Paul again that night—this time with condoms, at least—and the night after that, and on Monday morning he drove me to the airport. We also went out to eat and had drinks with his work friends, all just restful distractions to punctuate the main event taking place in the hotel bedroom. Scott knew Paul was in Denver and that we had plans to have dinner; we talked and texted several times over the weekend. All those years I'd spent as a faithful girlfriend, then a faithful wife, I'd imagined lying to be an impossible feat. It turned out I had quite a capacity for it, at least in the moment. I had yet to learn how lies turn cancerous in the long run.

When I got back to the office straight off the plane on Monday morning, there was an email from Scott asking if I'd slept with Paul.

"No," I typed. "We're friends, that's all." I knew he'd have too much discipline and dignity to ask twice.

Two rules made, two rules broken, like sand castles at high tide.

That should do it, I thought as I hit Send, launching my lie into the ether to kick off our progressive and enlightened open marriage. That should do away with the good girl once and for all.

PART TWO

The Wild Oats Project

There is more wisdom in your body than
in your deepest philosophy.
—FRIEDRICH NIETZSCHE, *Thus Spoke Zarathustra*

9

Mission Dolores

BY THE TIME my forty-fourth birthday arrived two months later, I'd found a studio in Mission Dolores to sublet during the week. Its renter, Joie, spent weekdays with her boyfriend in the Haight. From Monday morning until Friday night, Scott and I would have an open marriage with three rules in place—no serious involvements, no unsafe sex, no sleeping with mutual friends. From Friday night until Monday morning, we'd be together and monogamous. Though I'd already broken two rules with Paul, I resolved to start over and try to stick to them from here on out. It was a relief to have the open marriage officially in motion, to have some semblance of equality and boundaries around it.

Several of Scott's long-term friends and their wives still lived in Sacramento, forming a little community of couples. We'd vacationed and spent holidays with them over the years. Most were on their second marriage by this point; almost all of them were more conservative than us. Thanksgiving dinners often turned into raging debates, yet Scott and I considered them family. As the move-out date approached, Scott told the guys about it over a weekend camping trip. When he got home on Sunday he relayed their general response: Why was he allowing it? Why didn't he just leave?

"What did you tell them?" I asked.

"Same thing I tell myself. It's a terrible idea, but since you're determined, what's the harm of trying to see if we can come out the other side? I've had two affairs with married women, I've cheated on girlfriends, I have friends who've cheated, and all of that was okay with me. Now I'm going to be a hypocrite and leave you because you want to try the same thing I've accepted in others and myself?"

I was surprised to hear that his acquiescence was built on flawless reasoning instead of simple guilt over the vasectomy. I was a slow learner where Scott was concerned.

By Monday, the wives began emailing me.

"I don't approve of what you're doing," wrote Andrea, the one I was closest to, "but I love you both and want to stay as neutral as possible."

"You have not asked for my feedback," wrote Marilyn, an attorney, "so I will refrain from giving it."

Heather was less diplomatic. "If you want a child so badly, why don't you get divorced and adopt one? This is no substitute for children, which you knew Scott didn't want when you married him. After I got divorced, I met lots of men and had lots of adventures, but now that I have Cody, I wouldn't trade my marriage for all the adventure in the world. Where are all those people now? Where will they be when I get cancer? Nowhere. Cody will be there."

I saw Heather's point. At forty-four, I had unequivocally crossed into middle age. Menopause, declining parents, illness, and death loomed like increasingly dark signposts along the path. Scott was the perfect partner for the rocky changes ahead and for the quiet companionship of old age, just as he'd been the perfect partner for the oversensitive, underparented girl I'd been in my twenties.

I sat looking at my friends' names at the top of my inbox, feeling small and unsure. In the cold light of day, could I really do this, risk not only my marriage but my friendships? Even as I wished, momentarily, I could put everything back in its neat little box, I knew that retreat was no longer an option. I'd been striking some version of the who's-going-to-be-there-to-drive-me-to-chemo bargain all my life. I knew without a doubt that this was my last chance to choose differently. If I opted for safety this time, something crucial would die, something without which my marriage, my friendships, and even my physical body were nothing more than mere shells.

On May 1, I took a carload of clothes, books, art supplies, and toiletries to Joie's studio. It was L-shaped, with a double bed in one corner, a modernist couch and audio-video setup in another, and an office area leading into the small kitchen, all flooded with light. She had cleared half the long closet for me. I hung my clothes, lined up my toiletries in the bathroom, and arranged my books by the bedside. The studio sat at one of the best corners in San Francisco: Twentieth and Church, the very top of the hill overlooking Dolores Park, the downtown skyline spiking itself into the horizon. My house, my husband, and my cat were only six blocks down the hill, but they felt a world away.

I'd secured my freedom and now I had to use it. I wasn't about to try my luck at bars every night after working ten hours at the magazine. So on a lunch break, I went to Craigslist and composed an ad under "Casual Encounters":

GOOD GIRL SEEKS EXPERIENCE

I'M A 44-YEAR-OLD PROFESSIONAL, EDUCATED, ATTRACTIVE WOMAN IN AN OPEN MARRIAGE, SEEKING SINGLE MEN AGE 35–50 TO HELP ME EXPLORE MY SEXUALITY.

YOU MUST BE TRUSTWORTHY, SMART, AND SKILLED AT CONVERSATION AS WELL AS IN BED. WE WILL FIRST MEET IN PUBLIC FOR COFFEE OR A DRINK. IF THAT GOES WELL, WE'LL HAVE DINNER, POSSIBLY FOLLOWED BY SEX. OUR TIME TOGETHER WILL BE LIMITED TO THREE DATES, AS I CANNOT BECOME SERIOUSLY INVOLVED. I'M NOT POSTING BECAUSE I'M HORNY OR WANT A FAST HOOK-UP. I SEEK ENCOUNTERS WITH MUTUAL RESPECT AND COMPASSION, EVEN IF THOSE ENCOUNTERS ARE FLEETING.

I hit Continue and checked my email. The confirmation from Craigslist was already there; I clicked it to publish the ad.

Five minutes later, when I tried to view it, it said, "This ad has been flagged for removal by Craigslist users."

Confused, I went to the Help page, where I learned that Craigslist was community moderated. Users could flag posts for one of three reasons: if they were miscategorized, if they violated the terms of use (which included pornographic or hateful content), or if they were posted too frequently. My ad clearly breached none of these rules, so I posted the text of the ad on the Flag Help Forum, asking why it had been removed.

Within minutes, the responses appeared.

"Probably because you are a cheater," one user wrote.

True enough, but he (she?) couldn't know that by looking at my ad. I clicked back to Casual Encounters, hit "m4w" and typed "married" into the search box. There were more than five hundred ads by married men looking for hookups. Then I did the same on the "w4m" page. There were eleven ads: About half of them were married women seeking trysts, the other half women clarifying that they did not want a married man.

"The ad clearly stated that I'm in an open marriage," I posted back on the Flag Help Forum.

"That's just another word for cheating," someone else responded.

I couldn't believe my eyes. This was Casual Encounters, widely known to be a clearinghouse for any imaginable sex act between strangers. Yet it suddenly looked like the Boston town square circa 1642.

I emailed Craigslist staff explaining that I wanted my ad reposted. They never responded.

Back on the Flag Help Forum, an experienced user took the time to explain the situation. "Male readers probably didn't like the tone of your post. Unfortunately, if enough users dislike and flag it, you'll have to reword it in order to get it back up." I searched other women's questions as to why their posts were removed, and learned that male readers frequently flagged posts that didn't include the woman's "stats," meaning her weight.

"You could comply with every term in the book," wrote one user, "but without the info the guys want (good physical stats) you'll keep getting flagged."

Another wrote: "If they can't verify you're the body type they want, they flag, probably on a 90 percent basis. Sorry."

I decided to boycott Craigslist.

I signed up for a Nerve.com account, and reposted the ad there with a few pictures. Since Nerve's site was much more detailed, I also entered information like my favorite books, music, and movies.

Within twenty-four hours, my Nerve inbox filled up with twenty-three prospective suitors, mostly men much younger than me. I'd never been a stunner, and I knew it wasn't my fetching photos that reeled them in. Nor, I guessed, was it my devotion to Wilco or my preference for Milan Kundera novels. It was the fact that I was going to let them get away scot-free after three dates.

But I didn't concern myself with their intentions. All I wanted was their maleness, the very thing they most liked giving. I wanted their smells, their stomachs, their grasping hands and hungry mouths. The more maleness I had, the more female I could be. I sought it out despite the warnings of concerned friends, the obvious pain I was causing my husband, the moral code and defining boundaries of the self I'd known for forty-four years. Come what may, I would be ravished. And then they could leave.

10

Nerve

IF CRAIGSLIST CASUAL ENCOUNTERS was the Walmart of hook-ups, Nerve.com was the hip designer boutique. The men tended to the smart, progressive end of the spectrum, in line with Nerve's sex-friendly, urban content. And Nerve shared its personals with Salon.com, the Bay Area's intellectual bellwether.

Vetting the responses took several days. I grouped men into yes, no, and maybe lists. I had a thing for tall men. All four of the boyfriends in my humble history had been at least six feet. I tried to overcome this bias, adding a few short men to the list of those I decided to meet.

One, a single dad and motorcycle rider dressed head to toe in black, met me at a coffee shop in Hayes Valley. When I asked what he did for a living he shrugged and said, "Lots of things." When I asked how he'd describe himself, he said, "Very private. I don't reveal a lot." One down, twenty-two to go. Nothing turned me off like reticence.

Several men over fifty answered my ad, even though that was my cutoff age. One large and fit man described himself as "Olympian" and promised that he was well endowed and schooled in the tantric arts. "I can take you places you've never been," he assured me. This lured me into an email conversation to set up a date. Just as we were sealing the details, he mentioned that, by the way, he wouldn't be using a condom. "I'm a believer in pleasure, and they are antithetical to my pleasure and my partner's," he wrote. With the Paul weekend still fresh in my mind, I replied, "That's fine, but condoms are not negotiable for me. Good luck." Making even simple boundaries with strange men pleased me as deeply as it had frightened me back in my twenties, the last time I'd been single.

One of the profiles waiting in my Nerve queue featured close-up photos of a rippled torso. My coworker Ellen, as smart as she was beautiful, volunteered to act as my online dating consultant. She informed me that a bare six-pack in someone's profile photos was a red flag: sleazy. But the sculpted abdomen evoked one of my occasional fantasies: the big, hairless brute, wide jawbone set inside a shaved skull, torso covered in tattoos, ass muscles arcing high above thick thighs, every surface of him a rock against which I could writhe or slam.

Mr. Six-pack was a man of few words. His first note said simply, "You look in your twenties, miss." He suggested meeting at the 500 Club, a dive bar in the Mission. He knew what I looked like while I had yet to see his face. Something told me to bring Ellen along, and our mutual friend Jenny came too. They walked in ahead of me and sat at the bar. When I entered, I saw a bald, muscular man, about thirty-five and leather clad, sitting alone in a booth. He met my eyes instantly and slanted his lips into a half smile that said I was exactly what he'd expected.

"Pete?" I said, approaching his table. At least that's what he called himself; he looked like the sort who used aliases. He nodded, one slight dip of the chin. "Nice to meet you," I said, sliding in across from him. I asked the waitress for a gin and tonic and raised my eyebrows at him expectantly.

"So," I said. "Hi."

"Hullo."

I looked around the room, the kind of bar where all the maroon surfaces fade to black under low lighting. "Have you been waiting long?"

"Nope."

There was perhaps a hint of brogue, though I would need more words to tell for sure, and he wasn't offering them.

"I like your jacket," I said.

He glanced down at it. "Thanks."

Sudden anger flashed through me. Who did he think he was, making me do all the work? I might be easy but I wasn't desperate.

"So what do you like to do?" he asked, rubbing a few thick fingers across the stubble on his chin.

"What do you mean?" No answer. "You mean . . . in bed?"

He just smiled, a vengeful smirk.

"I'm open," I said. "I'm in learning mode. Maybe you'll find out soon enough if we get to know each other."

"We don't need to know each other." Right. Let's just throw back our drinks and sneak into the bathroom so you can bang my head against a stall for thirty seconds. In theory, I had nothing against that scenario. With Ellen and Jenny waiting at the bar, the bathroom would actually feel safer than Pete's lair, which I imagined as a bare studio apartment holding only an army cot, a mini-fridge full of Guinness, and heavy barbells. But he wasn't going to get me that easily. He eyed me with glaring impatience.

"I'm going to use the ladies' room," I said. I washed my hands, dabbed on some lip gloss, returned to the table, and remained standing. "I don't think this will work out, Pete, but thanks for meeting." On the way out I motioned for Ellen and Jenny to meet me at the car.

"Oh my god, that guy was a serial killer," Ellen said.

"For sure," Jenny concurred.

After a few more misses I came across Jonathan, a fortysome-thing lawyer from Silicon Valley. Slim, handsome, with tor-toiseshell glasses and a stylish haircut, he had a big smile and quintessential West Coast optimism. We met at Beretta, a crowded restaurant and bar in the Mission. About an hour into the conversation, he put down his drink and asked, "So, how do you think it's going so far?"

"Pretty good," I said. "Nice. What about you?"

"I agree. The sexual chemistry isn't readily apparent, but I suspect if we kissed, there'd be a lot of heat."

I wasn't sure if that was some sort of move, but it worked. We had another drink and he walked me several blocks back to my apartment. At my door, he put his hands around my waist and kissed me skillfully, slowly exploring with his tongue. We stood there making out for a full twenty minutes until he had to run for his train, leaving me dizzy.

On our second date the following week, he came to the stu-dio with a little cooler of snacks: hummus, good cheese, fancy crackers. We unpacked it all in the kitchen as the sun set, poured some wine, and brought it to the living room. He was a Wim Wenders fan and because I told him I'd never seen *Wings of Desire*, he brought it with him. I went to the TV to insert the DVD and he was behind me, kissing my ear before the tray closed.

We stumbled to the bed, where he turned me onto my hands and knees and fucked me from behind, first with his finger and then for real. He never stopped talking, and, as with Paul, the dialogue turned me on as much as the physical act. I was wet before he even touched me and matched his nasty talk word for word. And just like with Paul, I didn't come. It usually took several tries for a new man to learn how to bring me to orgasm, and I had no idea whether any of these lovers would figure it out in the two or three encounters we shared. It didn't even occur to me to coach Paul or Jonathan on how I liked to be touched. I was more concerned with being taken than with orgasming.

Afterward, he sat on the couch in his briefs, opened his laptop, and started playing music, lots of New Wave stuff I'd never much gotten into—Echo and the Bunnymen, Depeche Mode, the Smiths. He asked if he could stay over. I gently said no, and he got dressed to leave, but our goodbye kiss was so hot that he unzipped his pants, fumbled for another condom, pushed me back onto the bed, and fucked me again before going.

I felt satiated when I closed the door behind him. Lover number two. It wasn't just the sex that delighted me. It was the food, music, conversation—the intimate glimpse into another person. Like a castaway rescued from a small island, I could finally sight the edges of the larger world as my little boat trailed along an unfamiliar coastline.

My job at the magazine required late nights and regular weekends, but the perks were many. On one assignment, I flew to Las Vegas and stayed overnight in a luxury hotel decked out in midcentury glamour. The bathroom was as big as a small bedroom. Every surface gleamed black, white, or pewter. On trips like these, editors were treated like VIPs: Everything was free or upgraded, and our names were always on some list that a pretty, long-legged girl was holding at the door. The party on this particular trip was held in the lobby of the hotel, where men in suits and women in heels swirled Champagne and grabbed little puff pastries circulated by tuxedoed waiters. A wide spiral staircase led underground to the darkened dance club. I made my way down and stood near the bottom of the stairs, surveying the dance floor. A lanky, dark-haired man—a boy, really—approached the stairs looking so familiar that I reflexively said "hi" as he passed. I frequently ran into acquaintances on the press-trip circuit.

"Hi," he responded, confused. No, I was wrong. I didn't know him.

Ten minutes later he returned, asking if he could get me a drink.

"Sure," I said. Having been monogamous my entire life, I lacked both the sultry and the icy varieties of bar demeanor apparent in the single women. My default mode was to chat away as if meeting a new friend. I was doing so when, fifteen minutes in, he took advantage of a natural pause to ask, "So, do you want to go upstairs to your room?"

I almost glanced over my shoulder to see if he meant me. I'd never picked up a man in a bar. Moreover, I was wearing my wedding ring. I didn't take it off during the project.

"You realize I'm married?" I asked, stalling.

"Yeah, I see that."

"Just for the record, though, I'm separated right now. Well, part-time. Never mind, it's a long story."

He smiled. "I figured it was something like that."

"How old are you?" I ventured.

"Twenty-three."

Twenty-three. Why was he pursuing a middle-aged married woman in a room full of single hotties? It must have been my scent. My pheromones overpowered theirs exponentially.

"Okay," I said, turning to go up the stairs. "Follow me."

Something about our age difference made me hesitant to have actual sex, and he didn't push it. We made out on the king-sized bed, fully clothed. I rolled him onto his back, got on all fours astride his hips, and slowly went down on him, my default alternative to intercourse ever since high school, when I was determined to preserve my virginity with my boyfriend until graduation. I knew women who enjoyed fellatio and those who avoided it; I was in the former camp. I found penises beautiful—ordinary organs that grew into sculptures made of flesh. I took pleasure in mastering them from up close, watching them expand and harden, tracing the ridges of their warm architecture against the roof of my mouth.

"Can I give you a tip?" he asked after we were done.

"Okay," I said, taken aback.

"Near the end, when the guy is close to coming, ease up a little. It gets really sensitive then."

"Hmmm," I said. "Roger that." All those years of practice and a twenty-three-year-old just gave me blow-job advice. His words should have stung, but I only registered curiosity at his preference, and pride at my detachment. Along with my new easy assertiveness, I took this as evidence that in the two decades since I'd last dated, I'd actually grown up.

Or had I? A pattern was emerging. I liked being on my hands and knees. My affinity for cock notwithstanding, I was quick to go down on a man with vigor but didn't expect him to return the favor. I wasn't sure if I was deprioritizing my own orgasm to please men or to protect myself emotionally. Did I even want to orgasm with a new man?

I intended to find out. I was already noticing how each new encounter brought with it not merely the thrill of lust, which was vital in itself, but a whole host of questions that trailed behind it like fairy dust. I suspected they would take a while to answer.

He got dressed and I walked him to the door. We stood facing each other for an awkward moment. He held his cell phone out.

"You don't have to take my number," I said.

"I was thinking just in case I'm in San Francisco. My brother lives up there."

"Okay." I recited it to him. "Really, though, you don't have to call." He would in fact leave a message a few months later, which I wouldn't return.

I climbed back into bed and texted Scott to say goodnight, fully aware that if he weren't waiting for me back in San Francisco, I might feel as vulnerable as any other woman who'd just gone down on a stranger instead of acting so cavalier about it. On weekdays, when we were apart, we emailed and texted but often didn't speak at night, instinctually keeping an emotional distance from whatever the other might be doing. Part of our agreement was that we wouldn't ask, and didn't want to know, the details of each other's dalliances. Cell phones provided further cover; we could check in from anywhere.

Just texting to say goodnight, I typed to the man who never put me on my hands and knees—in the literal sense, at least.

Scott texted back from wherever he was, *Goodnight, dove.*

11

OneTaste

WHENEVER I MENTIONED my open marriage to anyone in San Francisco, I got one of two reactions. The first was a watered-down version of the warnings our Sacramento friends proffered. San Franciscans didn't judge me, at least not out loud, though I could see the worry on their faces. "Sounds risky," they'd say. Or, "You two seemed so happy."

The second response, usually from a woman, was quiet, wide-eyed reverence. "Wow, that's so brave." It surprised me. I didn't feel brave. What I was doing felt instinctual, inevitable.

Certainly the idea wouldn't have gone over so well in Omaha or Baton Rouge. In San Francisco, however, polyamory wasn't all that rare. Many of the gay men I knew, and even a few straight couples, had open relationships with their long-term partners. Half the city attended Burning Man each September and took "relationship vacations"—what happens at Burning Man stays at Burning Man. San Francisco was home to cuddle parties, group sex hangouts like the Power Exchange, week-night happy hours at the Porn Palace, and sex therapists who called themselves surrogates and climbed into bed with their clients.

To me, the most intriguing of these subcultures was One-Taste, a South of Market "urban commune" that focused around something called orgasmic meditation, a practice that involved quietly stroking a woman's clitoris for fifteen minutes. An article in the weekly paper described how OneTaste's few dozen inhabitants hooked up with relationship "research partners" for weeks or months at a time and frequently slept together in one big loft a few doors down from its courses center. OneTaste's sleek website listed several weekend courses as well as a regular Wednesday-night introductory gathering called InGroup.

I drove over to SoMa on a Wednesday night and pulled up to OneTaste's headquarters, a nondescript two-story building situated between a pizza parlor and a diner on a busy stretch of Folsom Street. A petite brunette behind a reception desk asked me to sign in. The center looked like a yoga studio: clean, sparse, with high ceilings and heavy wooden tables. Black-and-white photos of female nudes hung on the wall. About two dozen people milled around, ranging from their mid-twenties to their mid-forties. When I read about OneTaste I had imagined a gathering of hippies. Instead, most were clean-cut and well dressed, tapping away on smart phones and laptops.

When it was time to begin, a man of about forty named Noah, who looked like he could have been a rabbi in another life, led us up a large staircase to the second floor. Through a thick velvet curtain was another airy studio with a couch up front facing rows of chairs arranged in a semicircle. I took a seat in the second row.

Noah sat down on the couch next to a woman with a blond bob and a permanent smile. She wore black slacks, a black drapey top, and black stilettos. She sat with her legs spread wide, a hand resting on each knee, and announced, "I'm practicing sitting this way, with my pussy open, to see if it feels different than crossing my legs."

No one recoiled at the word "pussy." Thanks to Regena, I was so used to it by then that I'd forgotten it was ever considered vulgar. We went around the room introducing ourselves, then began playing word games, finishing off sentences such as "What I'm feeling right now is _____," "What you'd never guess about me is _____," and "If I were a master of orgasm, I would _____." Noah turned to the high stool perched next to the couch. "This is what we call the hot seat," he said. "It's exactly what it sounds like. You volunteer to sit on it and we get to ask whatever we want. You have three choices: You can tell the truth. You can lie. Or you can pass. We highly recommend telling the truth." Noah explained that the respondent must stop talking when the questioner said "Thank you," even in midsentence. "Who wants to start?" he asked.

A few hands went up. Noah called on a slim young woman in the front row, wearing skinny jeans and a hipster T-shirt. Her long, dark hair fell to the middle of her back. Half the men in the room raised their hands to begin the questions.

The first man asked, "Are you happy?"

She thought for a moment, tilting her chin. "Mmmm, pretty much so."

A second man asked her, "What do you want?"

She shifted in her seat. "I want more passion in my life."

Noah asked, "Do you control men with your beauty?"

"Yes," she said, smiling. Everyone laughed. The room grew palpably cozier.

As the game progressed, more people volunteered, including me. Noah called on me and I sat down on the stool. Nervous and excited, like a kid waiting in line for a roller coaster, I slid my palms under my thighs. Several hands shot up and Noah pointed to a man in back to begin the questions.

He asked, "What is your body language saying right now?"

I looked down at my hidden hands and released them into my lap. "I guess that I'm protecting myself a little, because I don't know any of you."

A woman in front asked, "What are you protecting yourself from?"

"Being judged."

"What's dangerous about being judged?"

The answer seemed obvious, but I played along. I didn't even think about passing or lying.

"I don't want other people flinging their psychological garbage at me."

Noah chimed in. "Do you ever protect yourself from people you do know?"

"Yes."

"Like who?"

I went mentally fuzzy, the way I used to in therapy when the question hit too close to home.

"Probably my husband." My heart rammed my rib cage. All eyes were glued on me.

A man asked, "What do you want?"

"I want intimacy."

Now the brunette from the front desk raised her hand. "What scares you about intimacy?" she asked. She had a regal, avian face atop a long neck.

"Um, no, I said intimacy is what I—"

"Thank you," she interrupted. "Why are you here?"

"Honestly? Because I just started having an open marriage. I'm here to find lovers." My neck and cheeks went hot but I forced myself to stare hard at her, thinking *Bring it on, bitch*.

"What are lovers going to give you that your husband can't?"

"Life experience," I said. "Masculine energy."

"Okay," Noah said, "nicely done," and the group applauded as

I returned to my seat. I felt enlivened and clear, the way I did after a good workout.

At the end of the hour and a half, Noah announced that we'd go around the room cleaning up any emotional charge left over from our interactions. "So if anyone needs to say anything, now's the time." Several seats to my right sat a thin, long-featured man with full lips and a dimpled chin. He said, "When that woman on the hot seat said she wanted lovers, I was really turned on. I wanted to volunteer." His name was Jude and he wore a jean jacket and a striped beanie atop a nearly shaved head. Not many men could have pulled off such a look.

Two chairs away, a woman with wiry curls stiffened. When her turn came she said, "I feel pissed off and violated by men outwardly telling women they lust after them. I come here to feel safe." The air hung heavy with her disapproval. Jude's face momentarily clouded before he regained a yogi-like calmness.

At my turn, I was still registering what Jude had said. "I guess I just want to say thanks to Jude. It feels nice to be wanted." At this, everyone seemed to relax except the angry woman. The anxiety of getting on the hot seat and the discomfort of the woman's reaction only added to the buzz. Jude smiled at me with serene eyes. *Lover number four*, I thought.

I joined OneTaste. For ninety dollars a month, I could take an unlimited number of workshops, each of which cost a few hundred bucks. As Noah signed me up, I said, "I'm probably never going to take off my pants and let a man stroke my clitoris in public." He smiled as if he knew better and said, "That's fine. It's completely up to you."

I didn't need orgasmic meditation. The wordplay at OneTaste was more than enough. *What do you want, what do you fear, what are you protecting yourself from* . . . these were questions I'd been asking Scott for seventeen years, with very little in the way of answers. He had what he wanted. He didn't fear much. Sometimes when drunk, he would become overly talkative and hint at his unedited feelings, but I had trouble following him and if I revisited it the next day, he didn't remember the conversation. When sober, he usually answered my queries with "I've never thought about it" or "You know as much about me as I do about myself."

The first workshop I attended ran from Saturday morning through Sunday night and included about twenty people, split pretty evenly between women and men. Jude was one of them. This time, the instructors were a fresh-faced woman named Grace and a huge bald man named Silas who looked as if he could crush anything in his path between his bare hands.

We played more word games like the ones at InGroup: what I'm feeling right now, what you'd never guess about me, what I hate most. We each stood up and danced spontaneously to a theme song the leaders chose to fit our personality. They assigned me a percussive dance number by Shakira. Half the participants put on blindfolds and the other half rotated among them, listening to the blindfolded people confess feelings they usually kept secret. I sat in front of a man named Andrew as he told me how angry he was at his mother, how she had used manipulation and guilt to shut him down and poured her hatred of men onto him. When I asked him how it felt to divulge this, he placed his hands on his pelvis and said, "I feel a lot of energy gathering right here. It feels good, like I'm growing bigger. It feels like I want to push it outward."

I was seized with a desire for him to rip my clothes off and unleash his mother anger on me. I wasn't allowed to comment.

Grace and Silas described how, in the culture at large, men constantly ogled and lusted after women's bodies, while women weren't taught to objectify men or unleash their own physical cravings onto them—indeed, they were out of touch with their desires. To illustrate and reverse this process, they instructed the men to line up in a long row and lie down on the floor faceup. The women would wander among the men, touching them however we liked, for our own pleasure. The only rules were that we couldn't kiss them or touch their groins, and the men had to keep their eyes closed and their hands at their sides. They put on a slow, sexy song and the women walked over to the line of supine men, approaching them slowly, unsure.

My urge was to start at one end of the line and interact with every man, in the interest of fairness and not hurting anyone's feelings. Then I remembered they weren't allowed to open their eyes, and I was supposed to act on my own impulses instead of worrying how I'd be perceived. I made my way straight for Jude. I knelt down at his head, feeling the shadowy stubble where he'd shaved his hair off. I ran my finger down his cheek and into the Cupid's bow of his upper lip, staring at his mouth with no fear of being caught. I touched his soft T-shirt and felt his ribs underneath. He was very thin. I lifted one of his hands and tugged gently at his fingers before releasing it.

I crawled from Jude over a pile of legs, carefully, to where Andrew lay, then straddled him and moved up to sit astride his stomach. I could feel the warmth of it through our clothes. I touched his chest at the opening of his denim shirt, then bent over and ran my cheek against the hairs poking through. He smelled clean, healthy. I let my hair fall over his face and dragged it along his neck. He moaned quietly. A sudden fear rose in me—what if he got a hard-on?—until I realized that it wouldn't be a problem. I wasn't going to be held accountable. I needn't do anything more than what my body wanted.

I sat up for a moment to digest the novelty of this. It was the first time I could remember acting solely out of my own instincts, without the pressure of performance or obligation, without an awareness of myself as an object of male desire—a desire I must always navigate and often mitigate. Suddenly I was the protagonist. Even during masturbation I thought of myself more as the one reacting instead of the one doing the touching. I glanced left and right, taking in the sight of the other women writhing against the men, running their hands over them. Most of them had their eyes closed and were smiling. They looked free. And hungry.

As the first day of the workshop came to a close, we gathered in a semicircle in front of the couch again. I sat on the floor in front of Andrew, who was in a chair. Though his eyes were closed both times I'd interacted with him, we were already linked, perhaps by scent. I could almost feel his knee a few inches behind my head. As Silas spoke about how to "come down" from the day's high energy by taking a hot bath or watching a relaxing movie, Andrew put his hands on my shoulders and began slowly rubbing them.

"Is this okay?" he bent down and asked in my ear.

I nodded yes, backing up until I was leaning against his shins. His touch was un-urgent. He gave off a highly awake, meditative sense of dwelling fully in the moment, of not planning ahead.

As we were leaving, I passed Jude near the door. "Hi, I'm Robin. We kind of met at InGroup. You liked me."

"I still do," he said. "Come to lunch with me tomorrow." His forwardness surprised me, coming as it did from such an ethereal frame.

At the lunch break the next day, Jude strode straight up to me, put on his denim jacket, and said, "Ready?" We walked a few blocks to a large natural foods market; there wasn't much open in SoMa on a Sunday afternoon.

Jude was vegan. We filled our plates with greens and vegetables from the organic gourmet salad bar, then sat down at a table. Summer sunshine poured in through the market's glass walls. I had topped my salad with chicken and feta cheese.

"How long have you been vegan?" I asked.

"Ever since I saw *Earthlings*."

"Is that a documentary?"

"Yeah. It's brutal. I'll loan it to you if you want, but you have to be prepared."

"What do you do for a living?"

"I'm a healer." In San Francisco, that could serve as one of many euphemisms for unemployed. With Jude it seemed legitimate. He'd attended two different schools in New York, where he'd studied astrology, Hindu philosophy, meditation, and intuitive healing. He did full-on astrological readings with birth charts and conducted weekly fire ceremonies in which participants purged themselves of old problems and negativity. This could easily have put me off if there weren't something street-smart about him. I asked him his last name.

"Liebman," he said. Ah, Jewish. Raised in New Jersey. That explained it.

"You seem very grounded for such a spiritual guy." By this time he was sitting within inches of me.

"It's because I'm a Taurus," he said, staring at my arms and hands.

"Really? Me too. April twenty-second."

"You're kidding," he said, pulling his chin back to focus on me. "That's my birthday."

I'd only met one other man who shared my birthday, back in my twenties. He had felt like a kindred soul, though I'd ultimately declined his advances in favor of Scott.

"I bet we don't share the same year," I said, shining the overly confident smile meant to cover any trace of insecurity. "I'm 1964."

His eyes widened. "Wow . . . I've got myself an older woman."
Twelve years older, to be exact.

Jude was working on a fable-like novella about a gifted boy on a mythical journey. He waited tables at Café Gratitude, San Francisco's infamous vegan restaurant. He wrote and recorded songs and played guitar. He came forward to kiss me and I leaned away.

"My husband and I are actually monogamous on weekends. Then we live apart during the week."

"That's cool. How's Tuesday, then?" He was careful not to touch me on the way back to OneTaste.

That afternoon we were introduced to orgasmic meditation. An Asian woman with long, dark hair walked into the room wearing a red silk robe, accompanied by a middle-aged man with big blue eyes and a sweet face. She disrobed and lay down naked on a massage table that had been set up in the middle of the room. We gathered our chairs in front of the table, looking at her spread legs straight on.

Her knees angled outward, the soles of her feet touching. Her buttery tan skin smoothed out over firm muscle. The man stood beside the table to her right, his left palm placed gently on her pubic bone. Grace stood on the other side, narrating the process.

"Joe will begin by asking May if she's ready to be touched," Grace said. May nodded and closed her eyes, her hands resting on her small, peaked breasts. "Then he'll start with light strokes on the upper left side of her clitoris, as lightly as he can possibly touch her."

Joe dipped his hand into a jar of lube that looked like Vaseline, then bent over and began moving his finger ever so slightly, concentrating. Almost immediately, May began to moan, exhaling a "ya" sound to the beat of Joe's stroke. The air around us condensed. We shifted in our chairs. Gradually, Joe increased his speed, which made her moans louder. "Ya-ya-ya-ya-ya-ya-ya." She sounded like an instrument being plucked. Joe hunched over, gazing slightly askew of the action and listening for nuance like a cello player in an orchestra.

"He's taking her higher now," Grace said. "Upstrokes increase the energy." Every so often, Joe would pause, and May would go momentarily silent until he resumed. Then her moan would recommence, building in intensity until, a little more than ten minutes in, she seemed to climax.

"Now Joe will take her down," Grace pointed out. Joe moved his finger from the top of May's clitoris downward a few times, then inserted his right thumb into her vagina and pushed firmly down on her pubic bone with the heel of his left hand. "His thumb in her introitus and the pressure from his other hand will ground her," Grace concluded.

Joe took a hand towel and gently wiped May's vulva. He helped her sit up and she pulled her robe around her, smiling. Both she and Joe were flushed a deep shade of pink. The class applauded.

In OneTaste language, the pleasure May experienced from the first stroke to the last was "orgasm." Her climax they called "going over." Going over did not end an OM session, which always lasted fifteen minutes, and neither was it the goal. Many women, Grace reported, never went over during OM, while some went over more than once. The goal was simply for both partners to fully experience every sensation. Afterward, they communicated their discoveries. May described how the pleasure swirled into her stomach, and Joe spoke of spirals of energy moving from the tip of his finger up his arm.

It all sounded similar to what I had read in *The Illustrated Guide to Extended Massive Orgasm*, authored by two of Regena's friends, a Bay Area couple named Steve and Vera Bodansky. They too claimed the magic point on the clitoris was in the "upper left quadrant," the one o'clock spot if you were facing it. In Regena's parlance as well, "orgasm" simply meant pleasure, and actual climax was deemphasized, even denigrated as a crotch sneeze.

I appreciated that OneTaste was trying to teach a model of sex that centered on the female. But I didn't want to call all pleasure "orgasm" or my actual orgasms "going over." I liked calling things what they were. Both the practice and the language had been the doing of OneTaste's founder, a woman named Nicole Daedone, whom I'd yet to lay eyes on.

As evening fell and we got up to go, I walked up to Jude.

"My husband is picking me up outside," I said, feeling a little like Cinderella leaving the ball. "I'll see you at my place on Tuesday at seven."

"I'm looking forward to it," he said, watching me walk off.

12

Eight Days

AT THE MAGAZINE, I worked with eight other editors, all of them women, in an open, high-ceilinged space above an Agnès B. shop in the middle of Union Square. The office's mint green walls, sheer white curtains, and flower-box-framed windows made it cheery despite the never-ending piles of accumulated mail. Car horns, sirens, and a handful of foreign languages wafted up from the street below as we quietly typed away to a nonstop alt-rock soundtrack: Gomez, Arcade Fire, the Shins. I sat next to the executive editor, and behind our two desks, layouts in all phases of production hung on horizontal racks. It always lifted my spirits to arrive in the morning, or return from grabbing a coffee at the French bakery around the corner, and see the pages hanging behind my desk. I loved my job and enjoyed my colleagues to a degree I'd never imagined possible. The long hours, constant deadlines, and semi-decent pay were more than offset by creative freedom and camaraderie, and by invitations to every concert, play, new restaurant, and party in town.

We all had iPhones. They beeped continually with text messages and the pervasive marimba of missed calls. On the day of my date with Jude, mine vibrated around lunchtime, his name highlighted in the familiar blue box. It said, *How are you feeling?*

Is there any question a woman wants to hear more than that?

Happy and excited, I wrote. It was midsummer and I had a real date with a man I'd met in person instead of through a computer. Though I was a busy, carnivorous magazine editor and he was a placid, table-waiting vegan, I sensed a potential kinship.

I'm excited too. See you at 7. I'm bringing you something.

I left the office later than I'd planned and ran to Whole Foods, a few blocks away. I'd never cooked for a vegan before. I raced through the aisles, picking up pasta, sundried tomatoes, broccoli, vegan tofu "sausage," and a bottle of organic wine. By the time I emerged with a heavy bag of groceries, I was late for the train, so I spent fifteen minutes hailing a cab.

I raced into the studio at five to seven, hoping Jude would be late, dropped the groceries, washed my face, and dug through Joie's closet for something to wear. We'd already determined that we were the same size and any clothes we left in the closet, the other could borrow. This little routine smoothed the transition between my dual existences. I slipped on a cotton skirt of my own and a black ribbed tank top of Joie's that said, in large white letters, "Hugs For Thugs."

The doorbell rang. Joie's buzzer didn't work, so I ran down to let Jude in. He stood outside the glass door with a backpack over one shoulder and a tiny potted hen-and-chicks plant in the other hand. "This is for you," he said, handing it to me.

"Wow," I said, looking down at it. "This is my favorite kind of plant. I've actually had dreams about it. That's weird, right?"

"I'm a little psychic," he said, coming through the door.

"Thank you so much." My hands and hearing and eyesight quavered as he followed me up the steps. I couldn't believe he'd just handed me a hen-and-chicks plant, out of all the gifts he could have chosen.

He trailed me around the kitchen as I made dinner. I handed him a glass of wine. "I'm not good at talking while I cook, but I can listen, so chat away."

He told me about his parents' divorce, his background in astrology, and how he'd inherited enough money from his grandmother to not have to work full-time, but needed more income so he could help his mother. Mostly we talked about music. He hooked his iPod up to Joie's stereo. I was thrilled to find that the playlist he'd made contained many of my own formative songs: Dire Straits, Talking Heads, Tom Petty and the Heartbreakers.

"You were, like, six years old when this music came out," I said, closing the refrigerator door.

"You are, like, my perfect physical type," he said, inching up so I could feel his breath on my skin. "Your face, your hair, your body, everything."

"I am?" I winced, though I was overjoyed. This was the kind of attention I'd missed in my twenties. Either my early boyfriends were too young to give it, or I was too insecure to hear it. Scott no doubt appreciated me; one of his many nicknames for me was "Sex." But if I asked how he liked my hair, he said, "If you like it, I like it." If I asked whether I looked pretty, he said, "You're *attractive*. You have an energy that draws people in." It disoriented me to have such long-held yearnings instantly fulfilled, and by someone other than Scott.

We sat on Joie's couch eating, sipping wine, and listening to his playlist. Neither his talk of spirit guides nor his non-leather vegan shoes bothered me. I could see the East Coast–raised, guitar-loving Jewish kid underneath the beanie. He took it off and rubbed his elegant musician's fingers over his closely cropped scalp. "I'm insecure about my receding hairline."

"I love it," I said, and he brightened. He unbuttoned his cuffs and rolled up his sleeves, revealing two Gaelic-looking tattoos, one word on each of his forearms. I turned his wrists over to see them as he held his arms out. "Go Love," I read. "Very cool."

"It says, 'Be Love,'" he corrected me.

I stared at his left forearm. "Oh, right. I like 'Go Love' better, though."

I began to slide my hand away but he took my arm and pulled me toward him. "Uh-oh," I said, laughing nervously.

He kissed me softly. I'd never kissed a man with fuller lips than mine. We walked the five feet from the couch to the bed and he lifted my shirt over my head, then gently pushed me back onto the mattress.

"Your breasts are amazing."

"You should have seen them in my twenties," I said, cupping my black push-up bra with my palms.

"You're cocky. I dig that."

"It's just a front."

"I figured," he said, sliding my bra strap down. The opening chords of Roxy Music's "More than This" came out of the speakers, the same song I used to listen to repeatedly with the long-ago man who shared my birthday.

Again with the dirty talk and the penis show, and again I wasn't complaining. He was graceful, full of energy, unafraid to take. "Suck that cock, girl," he said, his hand firm on my head. The length of it on my tongue actually made me contract with pleasure.

"Open those legs up," he commanded, and when I did, he slid his finger up into the same notch Paul had located the first time he touched me, probably my G-spot. It sent an arching jolt up my spine, a shock that filled me with a devouring urge toward annihilation. I could have swallowed him whole like some madwoman. Once we started fucking the pace never changed, as if we'd attached and gone unconscious, leaving our bodies to function as one organism.

Afterward I lay flushed and vibrating. What was a seven-second orgasm compared to this euphoria of mind and body? I didn't need the pleasure that suffused me to wax or climax or wane; I didn't need a bell curve or any kind of path whatsoever through it; I was happy to drift in it. The feminist in me might have wanted to editorialize against this—I vaguely recalled some treatise from my college women's studies class stating that women who claimed to enjoy sex without orgasm were lying to themselves—but she was too tired and well fucked to rally much of an argument.

I'd expended so much effort as a teenager and young woman trying to avoid the shameful female pitfall of "being used." Why had no one ever mentioned the satisfaction of being *useful*, of sharing pleasure and sustenance through my body? As I nodded off, the physiological process of infatuation, the urge to care for Jude and delight him, began to course through my veins.

It wasn't difficult to go from my promiscuous single life in the Mission back to my cozy domestic life in the Castro on Friday. In fact, it comforted me. The excitement of answering Nerve.com ads, hanging out at OneTaste, and juggling flirty texts with Paul and Jude balanced the domesticity that awaited me on weekends. I looked forward to making Scott dinner, waking up in our bed, walking to brunch in our neighborhood. By Monday morning, I was ready to return to my busy job and rotation of lovers. Any disappointments that emerged at home lost their sense of urgency.

For years I'd intermittently pleaded with Scott to romance me. His response had alternated between "I know, I've gotten lazy, I'll do better" and "If you want romance, make it." I'd tried making romance for Scott with the getaways I planned, the womanly arts lessons, the stripper pole. What I couldn't figure out was how to make romance for myself. A woman planning her own romance is like a cat chasing its tail. A decade earlier I'd bought and placed on his nightstand a book of couples' getaways in Northern California. After years of nagging, he had planned one weekend with it.

The morning after I kissed Jude goodbye at Joie's and headed into the office, I got an email from OpenTable informing me that Scott had made a reservation at Michael Mina, the city's most expensive restaurant.

"Michael Mina?!" I typed in response. "And all I had to do was move out!"

"You know I'm a slow study," he wrote. "But I learn eventually."

That Friday after work, I walked to the St. Francis Hotel in Union Square, through the marble lobby and into the temple of gastronomy. Scott was waiting at the table with a glass of wine, reading his BlackBerry. At the height of summer his skin teemed with healthy color. His broad shoulders filled out the lines of a sage green sports jacket.

I kissed his cheek—warm scent of clean earth—and sat down. "What are you reading?" I asked. Our current reading material was our no-fail entrée to conversation.

"*The Barbary Coast*," he said, sliding his BlackBerry into his pocket and taking off his black-framed reading glasses. "This town was absolutely batshit crazy during the Gold Rush."

"How so?"

"Not far from here, right over on Embarcadero, they had saloons with trapdoors in the floor, and these kidnappers would spike a guy's drink, slip him through the trapdoor, and he'd wake up on a ship headed for China. That's where the word 'Shanghaied' comes from."

"Why, though?"

"For free labor. The guy could be stuck on the ship for years. I mean, it was just lawless. This place was the wild frontier."

"It still is."

"Socially, maybe. Politically. But nothing like it was. We're a bunch of babies today compared with back then."

A tuxedoed waiter in white gloves took our order: good French wine, oysters, sashimi, Mina's famous lobster pot pie. As we ate, Scott continued to talk about the Barbary Coast, the characters who ran the boardinghouses, the corrupt politicians who swept the kidnappings under the rug. History animated him, and I'd always resented how he seemed to take more interest in the lives of dead strangers than he did in what was happening between us here and now. Not just dead strangers, come to think of it—living strangers interested him, too. His eyes had stayed dry during our entire wedding ceremony, even when he first saw me in my dress, but I'd expected that. It didn't bother me until a few years later at a friend's wedding, when he pushed back tears as the bride walked in. Somehow their big moment had moved him more than ours. Later that night, after our friend's wedding reception, I had cried myself to sleep.

I'd always tried to engage Scott by asking how he felt about issues that affected him or us: work, money, family, his childhood, his friendships, sex. After a quick recap of his oft-quoted position—and he maintained a thought-out position on every subject, to the point of keeping a file on his laptop called "My World View"—the conversation typically ran dry, leaving me frustrated and locked out. The more I tried, the more wretched I felt. What's worse, I considered this stilted dynamic due to some shortcoming of mine, some lack of either communication or understanding or, failing that, detachment.

At this point, though, I couldn't complain about him focusing on impersonal topics. After all, it wasn't like he could ask me how my week went. In fact, the hushed luxury of the restaurant relaxed and invigorated me. The seventy-five-dollar pot pie was a once-in-a-lifetime dish. Scott looked so handsome in that shade of green.

". . . so this guy rents out a boat, invites about a hundred sailors on board for a party, laces the drinks with opium, right? And dumps these guys by the dozens onto three different ships, all in one night . . ."

My phone vibrated inside the purse resting against my thigh. When I used the ladies' room, I checked it: one text from Paul, one from Jude, and another from a number I didn't recognize.

Hi Robin, it's Andrew, from the OneTaste workshop. You up for a drink next week? He must have gotten my number from the online contact list.

Sure, I typed. *How's Thursday?*

Scott was signing the bill when I returned to the table. I bent over his shoulder to kiss his cheek. Four hundred dollars. Three times the money we'd ever spent on a date. "Thanks so much for doing this, honey," I said. "It was so delicious. I love you."

"You're welcome, darling," he said, returning my kiss and patting my hand on his shoulder. "I love you, too."

After seventeen years I'd finally achieved some detachment. I left Michael Mina a satisfied wife.

On Monday night, Jude came over again, ripe with anticipation and hormones. This time he brought me a shiny new paperback copy of *Autobiography of a Yogi*. I made more vegan pasta and he played more music. The sex was much like the first time: fast, verbal, intense. I lay there afterward thinking about May singing out in orgasm as Joe stroked her.

On Tuesday night, I went to a women's group at OneTaste. We sat cross-legged in a circle on oversized pillows and talked about jealousy, competition, sex, and body image. I learned that women often stroked other women; there was no rule that said the stroker need be a man. When I got home around eleven, I called Jude.

"Hi," he said in his calm, husky voice.

"Hi. Want to come over?"

"I do, but it's late. By the time I got a cab it would be midnight."

Silence.

"Don't be mad," he said.

"I'm not." Three dates in and the trouble was already starting. I couldn't let myself indulge it; my problem-solving energy had to go toward my marriage, not casual lovers. We chatted a bit and hung up.

Five minutes later he texted me, *I'm in a cab. Be there in a half hour.* Happiness.

When he arrived, though, he climbed under the covers, made out with me, and went to sleep. I noticed a fullness slowly growing at the base of my throat that usually meant I was readying to say something uncomfortable.

In the morning, as the light poured in from the northern windows, I asked, "Have you ever done that OMing thing?"

"Yeah, a few times."

"I want to try it."

He smiled. "Get on your back, woman!"

I took the position I'd seen May do, opening my knees wide and crossing my hands over my belly. Jude sat up next to me, crossed his legs lotus-style and laid my right knee over them. He put lube on his left index finger and asked if he could touch me.

"Yes," I said, subtly bracing myself. Receiving a new man's full sexual attention put me on the spot. It was safer to just perform, go down on him, get on top.

My clitoris had always been so sensitive that direct contact would often produce irritation before pleasure. When a man did apply his finger or tongue, I needed it slow and steady. Jude's finger was slow enough but his stroke—or perhaps it was One-Taste's signature stroke—was too light, causing a little internal jump every time he brushed by, sending a familiar coldness down my legs into my feet.

My job was to communicate my sensations and anything I wanted changed. This was difficult. Even when I touched myself I had to withstand a bit of trial and error; each time could be different depending on my mood and my cycle. It was like trying to explain music.

"A little more to the right," I ventured. Then, "Yeah, there. Now a little more pressure." That was better, but within half a minute the sensation changed again. I decided to just relax and observe the process instead of trying to control it. After fifteen minutes, Jude put his thumb inside me, pressed down on my pubic bone, and I got up and dressed for work.

On Thursday, I met Andrew at Dalva, a bar in the Mission known for its great jukebox and back-room poetry slams. He was as tall as Scott and dressed like him, loose jeans and a loose denim shirt, as if he cared little for fashion. Still, his good looks and strong build made him stand out. He was five years younger than me. He ordered bourbon, I ordered wine, and we began the what-do-you-do rundown.

"I'm a senior editor at *7x7*, the city magazine," I said. He seemed less impressed with this than most. "How about you?"

"I'm working on my dissertation at CIIS." That was California Institute of Integral Studies, a local school that mixed academics with mystical spiritual traditions.

"Wow. A PhD? What's the dissertation on?"

"Basically it's on the relationship between Schopenhauer's

theories and the Bhagavad-Gita. That's an oversimplification, but . . ." He shrugged.

"That seems like an immense task."

"It is." He laughed, swirling his bourbon. "I've been working on it for four years. I'm broke."

I had to focus intently to follow the meanderings of Andrew's intellect, and even then, I had trouble repeating or remembering them later. He told me he also studied something called holistic sexuality with a couple who held workshops through CIIS and at the Esalen Institute in Big Sur. He described it as "a way of integrating your spiritual and intellectual energies, which live up here"—he framed his hands around his head—"with your vital and sexual energies, which live down here," moving his hands to his belly.

"So, do you have sex at these workshops?"

"No. Not actual sexual contact. It's more like people placing their hands on you, to help you get in touch with your energy centers. It's about integrating it all inside yourself, not necessarily with another person."

Andrew had grown up in Philadelphia, which gave us a nice common ground. "I lived there for three years and grew up near Scranton," I told him.

"I liked being around you in the workshop because you felt strong," he said. "Solid. Like I could push up against you and you wouldn't break."

"That's what happens when you grow up near Scranton," I joked. "Seriously, though, I'm not very tough. I grew up obsessed with ballet and academics. I was the valedictorian, for god's sake." I must have felt compelled to throw that in, given his mental scope.

He put his drink down and sat up straight. "You were the valedictorian?"

"Yes. It was a small class, though."

"I have a thing for valedictorians."

"What a coincidence. I have a thing for guys who like valedictorians."

We had another drink, then walked down busy Valencia Street
to get some falafel. Andrew needed everything to be cheap, as he
was living on a pauper's budget. After we finished eating I said,
"My studio's only a few blocks away."

Once there, we sat on opposite ends of the couch drinking
wine, our feet up, continuing to talk about the East Coast, our
screwed-up childhoods, and Eastern philosophy.

"Show me an example of what you do in the holistic sexuality
workshop," I said.

He lay back on the couch and put his palms on his chest,
then his solar plexus, then his pelvis, describing how he felt the
energy moving among the three. He used phrases like "I feel
very present to" and "what's moving through me right now," as if
he were less a personality than an observant vessel. He looked
happy to be with me though in no hurry to seduce. We'd been
together more than four hours.

When he was done, he sat up and told me to lie back. He put
one hand on my lower belly and the other on my forehead. "Just
feel the sensation there," he said, pressing my belly, "and then feel
all the thoughts and tension coagulated up here in your head.
Imagine the mental tension dropping down and the primal energy moving up until they meet here." He touched his fingertips
to my sternum.

His hands on me produced the same rush as they had at
OneTaste. Soon we were kissing, then slowly walking to the bed.
He got on top of me, both of us clothed, and pushed down on
my arms. He was by far the largest man I'd been with, even larger
than Scott. Unlike the light-as-air brushstrokes of orgasmic
meditation, his full weight settled me into my body. I spread out,
grounded into the bed. I unbuttoned his shirt and unzipped his

jeans. He lifted my dress off. He didn't talk dirty, but let himself make all sorts of loud organic sounds. When he did speak, it was to say what he wanted or ask what I wanted. He felt fully present, with no mask and no show.

It freed me from some age-old, unspoken dictum. I was underneath pushing against him, when suddenly the pressure inside me overflowed. I rolled on top of him and we looked into each other's eyes, silent and knowing. Without a word, he turned onto his stomach, ass in the air. I mounted it, grabbed his shoulder in one hand and his hair in the other and pulled hard, grinding against his ass. Now we were both moaning loudly. I came with a throaty growl.

I collapsed onto the pillow, stunned. So much for being ravished. All this time I'd been wondering when a new lover would bring me an orgasm, and all I had to do was take it.

13

Glory Road

IN MY SMALL HOMETOWN in the Appalachian Mountains, there is an isosceles triangle anchored by three buildings. The first is on Glory Road, the house I grew up in, where my divorced mother lives. A half mile away, at the apex of the triangle, sits my maternal grandmother's house. And back on Glory Road, just three blocks from my childhood home, is St. Mary's Roman Catholic Church, where my brothers and I all received baptism, First Communion, and confirmation.

A peek inside the first house circa 1970 or 1975 would reveal me lying in a single bed behind thin paneled walls listening to my parents' escalating whispers. It's a weekend in fall. My father's been watching NFL games one after another, chain-smoking and screaming at the television. My brothers are asleep in the adjoining room. The kitchen is mere feet from my door. I can hear my father mutter the word "douchebag" more loudly than the others. A little louder now, I hear "ugly fucking cunt." My mother isn't silent and I know from experience that she isn't cowering. She answers back but I can't make out her words, only his.

He says, "I'll cut your jugular vein so fast, you'll be dead by the time the ambulance gets here."

It's strange, I think, lying in the dark. *I'm not afraid or even all that upset. I must be a very strong girl.* My heart beats normally. I think of other children who, in my place, would whimper or turn the light on. I don't feel the need to do either. I won't fall asleep, though, just in case my mother calls for me. I'll know when it gets to that point. The words almost never spill over into physical violence—at most he'll take it out on the furniture or the doors—but they always hover on the verge of it. "Robin!" she'll scream defiantly, and I'll run to the kitchen and stand between them, talking calmly to my father with both hands up, saying, "Daddy, please, it's Robin. Please, Daddy, please just go to bed." He'll ignore me, reach around me to jab his fingers into my mother's shoulder, still calling her cunt, fucking whore. The words "Daddy, please" will make my chest feel funny, only for a few seconds. Sometimes, if I stay between them long enough, he will eventually retreat to the bedroom. Only a few times will he slap or shove me to get to her.

As I get older, I'll get louder and more brazen, welcoming the rare blow when it comes, inviting it with taunts like "What a big man you are! Pushing women and children around!" That one will get me knocked to the ground. My father's body is large and merciless. It is a wall of cruelty I am destined to collide with. Knowing I can never win doesn't stop me, because it's the fight that counts. He himself has taught me that.

Once, when I am twelve and come between them during a particularly vicious fight, he kicks me across the floor until I am doubled into a fetal position. The next morning when I wake up, I shit blood. I yell for my mother, she in turn howls at him, and when he comes into the bathroom, I see him freeze, go white, as if God Himself had reached down and slapped him in the face.

A month later I have my first panic attack. As I shut my locker and walk down the hallway toward homeroom, the crowd of kids in front of me and in my peripheral vision suddenly tilts and then recedes. I drop out of their world and into a parallel universe. Their voices echo. I can't breathe. In an attempt to steady my vision I focus on the orange brick wall and see its lines turn jagged. I reach out for it so as not to fall, and stand paralyzed in the spinning hallway, waiting to be swallowed up. Is it death, is that what's happening? Somehow I make it to homeroom and lay my head down on my desk. And in the dark space behind my eyes, pressed against the backs of my hands folded on the desk, the terror begins to dissolve like particles, separating from solid black to a fuzzy grain. As it dissipates a warm light begins to take its place, growing brighter, filling me with peace. It is not just light. There is a presence at its center, a consciousness projecting unassailable power and kindness. This presence silently proclaims, *You will be okay. I will take care of you.* Every cell in my body responds with joy. Its assurance gets me through the next five years and stands to this day as the most profound spiritual experience of my life. When, in my senior year, my classmate dies and the panic attacks return, I will wait for the reassuring coda. It will never come again.

Most late-night fights don't end in blows. They end with my father screaming, "Take your kids and get the fuck out! You're all driving me nuts! I can't take care of you anymore!" My mother and I gather up my brothers, all of us in pajamas, and drive to my grandparents' house. We spend the weekend there, sprawled on their living room floor in sleeping bags, watching *Hee Haw* and *Lawrence Welk* with Grandpa, piling into his Chrysler Cordoba to go for ice cream. Grandma makes us eggs for breakfast and spaghetti and meatballs for supper. We go back home late Sunday night or possibly Monday after school. When we get home there might be broken dishes scattered across the floor, or overturned chairs. One time there will be an ax stuck in the thick wood of the front door.

Daddy won't ever apologize. We'll all just carry on, and it's not even hard to carry on. There's school, ballet, football games and football practice, all of it in a town where kids roam in packs and there's no such thing as a stranger. There's a built-in pool in our backyard and all the clothes and toys and cash we could want. There's Dad when he's not in a rage, telling me how smart and pretty I am, how proud he is of me. There's Mom cooking and making my bed. There's both of them always hugging and kissing all four of us and saying that they love us. I believe them. Even on the days when I hate one or both of them, I know it's true.

During one of my mother's visits to California, knowing how children can exaggerate, I ask her, "How often did Daddy kick us out of the house? Was it, like, twenty times? Or fifty?"

She looks at me. "Twenty or fifty? Are you kidding? It was hundreds."

Whatever had protected me as I lay awake listening to my parents fight for eighteen years fell away within weeks of leaving my father's house and moving into a Penn State dormitory two hours from home. Plucked from my environment, I had to rely on myself, and there was no self. The minute I awoke in the morning, burning heat traveled up my spine and bloomed into cold sweat. Vomit filled my throat, causing me to run from bed to toilet. A black ugliness descended over everything. In class, where earning a good grade remained my sole buffer from a complete breakdown, I'd watch the clock in disbelief at how slowly the minutes passed, with no idea how I'd get through the next hour. If I let myself think that I was only eighteen and had to last sixty or seventy more years on earth, I'd wince in pain. Several times a day I'd whip my head around, thinking I heard someone viciously hiss my name. I'd walk home from my night class balancing on a curb like a gymnast, telling myself that if I could make it to the dorm without falling off I'd be okay, but if I toppled even once that meant I was going insane.

I told no one. On weekends at home, my mother occasionally saw me wake up in a nauseous panic and tried her best to give me empty pep talks I couldn't believe. What did she know about being on her own, leaving her family, assimilating into a college of thirty-six thousand new souls? Nothing. I was alone.

I white-knuckled it through six months before giving up and transferring to a satellite campus back in Scranton. Once home, though, in another bizarre twist, I suddenly couldn't bring myself to walk into my parents' house. On the front steps my body tightened as if bracing for impact. By the time I got to the porch, I could barely move. Emotions I couldn't begin to name ricocheted through me like pinballs trapped under glass. With no outlet and no context, I barely contained them through sheer force of will.

My grandparents took me in. I retreated to their small two-story house, always smelling of either bacon or onions. I hid out behind their heavy green curtains. They bought me a used car, took me out for clams on Saturday nights, and made sure I saved twenty-five dollars a week from my waitressing job. I slept in their tiny spare bedroom at the top of the creaky stairs with the wrought-iron railing, all of it scaled down to contain and hold me fast like an overgrown child in a fairy tale. That's where I gathered strength and planned my getaway to California—too young to realize that there was no escaping myself.

It was this same bedroom in my grandmother's house where Scott and I slept on our trips home. Though we'd go to my mom's each day for meals and visits, I hadn't spent the night there in twenty-three years.

My ninety-year-old grandmother protested when Scott sprang up to do the breakfast dishes the minute we had finished her French toast. He brushed her aside, laughing. He sat in my late grandfather's old recliner reading while Grandma and I watched *The Price Is Right* and *The Young and the Restless* with the volume too loud. Framed photos of her children and grandchildren lined every wall and table, among them several of Scott and me: snuggling on the shore of Lake Tahoe in woolen sweaters, leaning into each other in Puerto Vallarta wearing bright summer clothes that showed off our tans. In the oldest one, taken in Venice around my twenty-eighth birthday, we sit arm in arm on a tiny walk-bridge over a canal. Whenever I called my grandmother from California, she unfailingly asked what I planned to cook Scott for dinner that night. It was the time we'd spent in her house over the years that had made family life look worthwhile and possible.

St. Mary's simple cross and sole rosetta window stood solemn watch over the surrounding buildings on Glory Road, the date of its construction chiseled in Roman numerals into its corner-stone. Inside, light filtered and multiplied through two levels of soaring stained glass windows, against a concave altar painted sky blue, from rows of votives flickering beneath a statue of the Virgin Mary. The last time I had stood in front of her, I wore my wedding dress, crying as Scott and I exchanged rings with shaky hands. I'd wanted to get married on a beach but for my grandmother's sake chose the traditional forum. And so I walked down the aisle of St. Mary's that spring evening light-headed and trembling, my lifelong fears compressed to a single point that existed both in real time—a rapidly approaching moment—and in my body, deep inside my chest cavity. To my astonishment, the ritual took this dread and alchemized it, spinning its dark surface into something sublime. I limped shallow-breathed toward the threshold and twenty minutes later emerged beaming, grasping Scott's hand, every cell relaxed.

After our raucous wedding reception, Scott and I had gone straight to sleep, exhausted. The next afternoon, at a beach resort in Jamaica, we napped on a king-sized bed under a gently whirring ceiling fan while a rainstorm outside the screen door rustled palm trees, unleashing the smell of frangipani and grass. In the darkened room, Scott climbed on top of me as usual, but something was different. In the same spot where the day before my heart had strained, a cog turned one smidgen, just enough to unlock it. Scott's touch released an unfamiliar yielding in me. My skin went porous; his woodsy scent swirled straight through it. An orgasm began to build, not in the usual place but up high behind my belly button. It shot through my chest, my throat and limbs, realigning me as it went, touching for the first time some chord buried in my center. It was enough to allay all my previous misgivings about marriage.

Scott and I were in Pennsylvania for the baptism of my brother Rocco's first child. He was three weeks old. I was to be his godmother. My mom had mailed a handful of photos: one of Rocco encircling his wife and the baby in his arms; another of Rocco holding the swaddled infant, my father and two other brothers smiling alongside him; a third of the baby newly washed after emerging from the womb, crimson as an autumn leaf. He's sitting on white towels with knees bowed and tiny fists raised as if in self-defense. A nurse's gloved hand supports his head, which is largely hidden as it is thrown back, the mouth wide and dark, the tongue vibrating in an existential howl.

I didn't intend to ever tell my grandmother about the project, and the baptism wasn't the time to bring it up with my brothers.

But I was too close to my mother to keep it from her. I did it while we were in her kitchen, she unpacking groceries and me loading the dishwasher, gazing out the window above the sink onto the backyard and the old built-in pool, collapsed now and filled with weeds the size of trees.

"So, Scott and I are spending weekdays apart," I began. "I got an apartment."

"Why? Did he do something?" She paused at the refrigerator and turned to me.

"No. Nothing dramatic like that. Just, after the vasectomy . . . I don't know, Ma. I'm not getting any younger. I need to get some things out of my system, and what's to stop me if I'm not going to have kids? A lot of people in San Francisco have open relationships."

"Good," she responded conclusively. She turned back to stocking the fridge. "Good for you. You need to do whatever makes you happy. Scott does what makes him happy."

It was difficult to discern her motivation. After divorcing my dad in her mid-forties, she had spent twelve years living with a hardworking man who eventually drove her crazy with his inability to communicate. Having experienced both extremes of passion, she now lauded the joys of living alone. She shut the refrigerator door, littered with family photos and magnetic twelve-step slogans: "One day at a time," "God grant me the serenity," "Keep it simple." Centered among the inspirational quotes, a shiny purple magnet read: "There are only two things wrong with men: everything they SAY and everything they DO."

"I had a wild phase in my forties," she said as she moved about the kitchen folding up grocery bags. "Every woman needs that at some point."

That night, I met my two oldest friends, Stacey and Maria, at a local bar. We'd known one another since kindergarten.

"So, I need to tell you guys about my midlife crisis. After the vasectomy, I kind of lost it. I told Scott I need to sow my wild oats before it's too late. We're living apart on the weekdays and we're free to see other people. And then I come home on weekends."

They looked unimpressed. Stacey, the more liberal of the two, glanced down at her drink and back up at me. "I'm not surprised, Rob. I love Scott, but he always has to have it his way. He didn't want to live here in town so you went to Philadelphia. He didn't want to stay in Philadelphia so you went back to California. He didn't want kids so you didn't have them."

"I know," I said. "This time, it's going to be my way."

"But I wouldn't do this if I were you," she continued. "It can't end well."

"I know it's risky. But I have to do it."

"You're crazy," Maria interjected, shaking her head. She was still with the man she'd married at nineteen. Though our paths had diverged long ago, I counted on her to give me the no-bullshit reading.

"What else am I supposed to do, then? Neither of us wants to get divorced. But I can't go to my grave a quiet, childless wife with no adventures. I was ready to give up more lovers for a family, but I can't give up both."

"But how is sleeping with a lot of guys going to make you feel better about not having kids?"

"It's not going to make me feel better about kids. Sleeping with a lot of guys is going to make me feel better on my *deathbed*. I'm going to feel like I lived, like I didn't spend my life in a box. If I had kids and grandkids around my deathbed, I wouldn't need that. Kids are proof that you've lived."

"But then why did you get married?"

"Because I loved him, and I hoped we'd have kids!" I said a bit too loudly. "I mean, seriously, Maria, tell me you'd feel fulfilled with Jim if you didn't have your sons. Look me in the eye and tell me that."

She thought about it. "I can't even picture it."

"You and Jim, alone in the house every day till death do you part. Him refusing to have a child after you begged him. You'd be happy?"

"Bernie and I aren't going to have kids and I'm happy just being with him," Stacey said.

"Yeah but you already have a grown kid, Stace. And if you wanted another one, Bernie would do it in a heartbeat. He'd never refuse you."

"So this is your revenge on Scott, because he refused you."

"It's not revenge, it's rebellion," I said, relieved to the bone to have the kinds of friends who weren't afraid of straight talk, for even though I was arguing my case, the truth was that I didn't know exactly what I was doing or why. Their questions were helping me figure it out. "I'm not trying to hurt Scott, I swear. But I can't compromise anymore. I just can't. I'm going to get what I need."

"What do you need that Scott can't give you?" Maria asked.

I struggled to find the words. "Life," I said. "It's so quiet when it's just me and him. I need *life*."

They looked at each other. Stacey gave a slight shrug, Maria a slight shake of the head.

"Do you think I'm a bad person?" I asked.

"No," Maria said. "You're not a bad person. But you're definitely nuts." They both smiled, which made me smile, and we swigged our beer like we'd been doing since ninth grade and moved on to other topics.

I sat in the front pew of St. Mary's with Scott, Rocco, his wife, and the baby's godfather. Though he was only thirty-one, Rocco sported the elegant suits and receding hairline of an older man. The youngest of my brothers, he was the closest thing I had to a child of my own. His wife, five years his junior, was a long-limbed natural beauty with huge brown eyes and luminous dark hair twisted into a heavy ponytail. She held the baby, a peek-a-boo of pink face bundled in white satin.

Scott remained sitting and the rest of us, the parents and godparents, filed up to the marble baptismal font at the altar, where the priest waited in gold robes. He began his ablutions, casting out Satan and claiming the baby's soul for Christ. I took my turn making the sign of the cross on his forehead. I didn't feel like a hypocrite. Though I was no longer a practicing Catholic, I did believe in God—in the mysterious force that had shielded me as a child, the light that had filled me after my first panic attack. I believed in a darker, pagan aspect of the divine as well, the one personified by the painting of Pele in Delphyne's office, the goddess who creates new life by burning away the old. I believed without a doubt that the image of Demeter, the goddess of motherhood, inscribed on the candle Delphyne crafted for me had somehow helped bring about the pregnancy crisis that finally ended the dilemma Scott and I had clung to for years. And I was even starting to believe in Christ. The older I got, the further I ventured from the church, the more I saw in His eyes and words a quiet, all-pervading presence, a power untainted by dogma, scandal, patriarchy. I wanted to get to know Jesus not in the timid way of a well-behaved girl frightened of punishment, but in the way of a flesh-and-blood sinner, which is to say, intimately.

Rocco's wife handed the baby to me and I clutched all eight pounds of his squirming, precious mass to my center. The belly-deep urge to protect him emanated from the same channel through which orgasm had flourished on my honeymoon, traveled the same current that now carried me to the beds of lovers. I looked at Scott, sitting in the front pew wearing a salmon-colored shirt and tie beneath a crisp suit. Behind his quiet smile, his strength was unmistakable, strength he kept to himself. Part of me longed for him to grab my arm and say, "This open marriage nonsense is over. You're my wife. We're leaving San Francisco and we're going to . . ." Where? Take me somewhere, Scott. If you can't take me to motherhood, then take me somewhere else.

The baby squirmed in my arms, his tiny hands and feet punching at the air around him, little gusts of breath punctuating each effort. He snapped me out of it. My life was nearly half over, if I was lucky. There was simply no time left to wait for anyone else to take me anywhere.

14

The Writer

AS SOON AS I SAW THE MESSAGE in my Nerve.com inbox from a man named Alden, a writer in his late thirties living about an hour north of the city, I sensed I was in for something different. The first clue was when he said my profile jumped out at him because it listed *Middlemarch* as my favorite book. Any man who could appreciate the genius of George Eliot was worth at least one date.

He kept his emails short and focused. He suggested meeting in Dogpatch, an industrial neighborhood on the edge of town where a smattering of bars and restaurants had recently cropped up. He wrote, "Let me know what night you're available and I'll arrange the details." When the night arrived and I texted to tell him I was on the way, he responded, *You can't miss me. I'll be the tallest man in the room.*

Attention. Assertion. These were apparent the moment I saw him seated at a corner table near a window. He asked what kind of wine I liked, then chose a Viognier for me. He asked if I was hungry, and when I said yes, he called the waitress over and ordered a cheese plate. He was indeed the tallest man in the room, dressed in a crisp white shirt, cashmere pullover, jeans, and weathered black boots. His wide cheekbones and close-cropped hair evoked a secret agent. His countenance easily switched from a courtly sort of handsome to roguish.

After a glass of wine and the requisite recitation of our first-layer personas—jobs, schools, hometowns—I got up to use the restroom. As I rose, I was keenly aware of Alden's eyes on my backside, sheathed in a black jersey dress with white polka dots. At forty-four, I had never felt so comfortable in my skin. The loss of some youthful collagen was compensated for by a sensual ease in my walk. In a few years, the balance would tip, but right now I was at peak ripeness. Firmness had just started giving way to juice.

As I slid back into my seat and crossed one leg over the other, he glanced blatantly at my exposed knee, bit his lower lip, and said, "How about we leave here and go have dinner?"

We went to Slow Club, a small restaurant on a hidden corner in Potrero Hill. Inside, it was crowded and so dark we had to read the menu by candlelight. Throughout the course of burgers, fries, and more wine, we talked about literature, music, and a trip around the world he had recently taken alone.

"So, your ad said only three dates," he ventured.

"Yes."

Without missing a beat, as if only half-aware of doing so, he reached across the table to where my hand lay and lightly took the fingertips in his. His fingers were long and elegant as a pianist's but larger, more masculine. "Do you think we'll be able to do that, to limit it?"

His confidence buoyed me. "I guess we'll find out."

We decided he wouldn't come back to the studio just yet. We both had to get up early the next day. We walked to his car and he unlocked the passenger door, then turned to face me, pulling me gently toward him. "Can I have a kiss?" he asked.

"Maybe."

"Why maybe?" he said, leaning back and smiling.

"Because maybe's more interesting than yes." This amused him for half a second, then he kissed me. A confident kiss, soft yet urgent. Afterward he cupped my cheeks in his palms and said, "You're such a good kisser."

"I'm just following you."

On the drive home, the lights and sounds of the Mission receded outside the car window as I entered the liminal space between my world and his. I basked in the anticipation of those moments before the curtain rises: another human being, thirty-nine years in the making, all his joy and sorrow bound up in its one-of-a-kind tapestry. He parked at my curb and turned the car off, and we slipped into another dimension, a universe of two where we recognized each other like long-separated travelers. I know we spoke as we touched though I don't recall what we said. At some point I reached under my dress and leaned back in the passenger seat. There was a streetlight shining directly down onto the black gear shift. I don't know how long we were there or whether anyone walked by the car. I'd never touched myself in front of a man before.

My subsequent memories of Alden are sharp foreground against the rest. Him emailing the next day to say it was one of the most erotic experiences of his life. Chatting with him online and verging into chat-sex—another first—that proved more satisfying than most real sex. Meeting him in the darkened Presidio, halfway between our two places, at midnight, and climbing onto him in the backseat of his Mercedes. I was menstruating heavily and wearing my favorite white shirt. I couldn't get the stains out. Even today, reading the word "Presidio" or glimpsing the large green corner it occupies on a San Francisco map delivers the precise, jewel-like memory I had set out to gather from the project: My bloody animal body once roamed this earth, mingled with it.

Alden wanted to cook me dinner at his house. I drove over the Golden Gate Bridge on an August evening as the sun inched behind the headlands. He was on his deck grilling lamb. He handed me a bright red negroni with a twist of fresh orange, bitter and bracing. He flipped through his vinyl collection and put an album on the turntable, Nina Simone's *Pastel Blues*. His sparse furnishings were carefully selected, some geometric and modern, others built for comfort. While he cooked I scanned his bookshelves. He had so many books, beautiful hardcover editions of nearly every writer I loved and many I'd been meaning to read. Thick classics, coffee table tomes on architecture, fiction by James Salter and Italo Calvino. The latest bestsellers were absent from his nonfiction; instead there was Lao Tzu, Kierkegaard, and *Passionate Marriage*, which had caused a fight with Scott a few years prior when I'd asked him to read it with me.

My eyes landed on a handful of titles by David Deida, a teacher of—for lack of a better word—neo-tantra with a small but devoted following. I'd run across Deida a year ago while numbly perusing Barnes & Noble on my lunch break. The book was called *Finding God Through Sex*. Integral philosopher Ken Wilber had written the foreword, and Marianne Williamson and Gabriel Cousens penned introductory blurbs lauding Deida's ability to commingle the sexual and the spiritual. In short order, I'd scooped up seven of Deida's books, entranced by his descriptions of universal masculine and feminine energies and how to channel them. A few months ago, I'd nearly signed up for a weekend workshop in the Bay Area, but the thousand-dollar price tag gave me pause.

I went out to the deck and sat at the table where Alden was setting out dinner. He poured me a glass of dark Pinot Noir. The first stars peeked through a periwinkle sky.

"I love your books," I said. "I can't believe you've got David Deida. I've read everything he's written."

"I just discovered him last year when I was house-sitting for a friend. I went to one of his workshops this past spring."

"I almost signed up for that!"

"Weird. I would have met you. The group wasn't that big, and you change partners a lot, so you get to work with everyone. I'm actually going to another one of his workshops next month in L.A."

I dug into the lamb, which was as good as a restaurant meal. I tried to picture myself meeting Alden at a Deida workshop instead of on Nerve.com. "What kinds of exercises does he do?" I asked.

Alden described a row of women closely facing a row of men, looking into each other's eyes. "The woman would rate my presence on a one-to-ten scale. So when she felt I was really with her, she'd say eight or nine, and when she felt I lost focus or spaced out, the number would start descending: seven, five, four . . . It was a little disconcerting, to tell you the truth. Then we switched places and I rated her on radiance." He smiled wryly.

I shifted in my seat and took a sip of wine.

"Then you step down the line and do the same with the next woman. That's the basic setup. I remember one exercise where we repeated phrases Deida gave us. Let's see." He looked down at the napkin lying on his lap. "Okay, I had to tell the woman, 'You're beautiful.' Then we paused and she said, 'I'd follow you anywhere.'"

"Are you kidding?" I said, putting down my fork. "An affirmation of beauty in exchange for her turning her life over to you? That doesn't sound like a fair deal."

Alden laughed. "Well, you know the premise, right? Deida's more concerned with polarity than fairness."

I knew the premise. Deida defined three stages of relationship. Prefeminist stereotypes of masculine authority and feminine submission, adhered to from fear or dependency, were the first stage. Modern relationships that focused on autonomy, equality, and talking things out were the second stage, and the cost a couple paid for all that meticulous interchange was a lack of juice in the bedroom. Deida tried to usher couples to the third stage, in which the man consciously, temporarily relinquished his feminine side, allowing the woman to embody energy and emotion, while the woman temporarily gave up her masculine direction and focus, letting the man take on that role. What this model lacked in political correctness, claimed Deida, it more than made up for in physical and spiritual ecstasy, a result of the interplay of the divine polar energies: masculine consciousness and feminine light.

I stabbed at my lamb with a steak knife and sliced off a hefty bite. I routinely reacted this way to Deida, a spontaneous combination of righteous anger and painful longing that left me with an unscratchable itch. I didn't know whether to spread my legs or scream, and yet I kept buying his books, inexorably drawn to them.

"I have a love-hate relationship with Deida," I said. "I long for polarity, but if I'm all energy and you're all consciousness, then you're the only one who's fully human. I mean, plants and dirt have energy."

"A lot of women have that reaction," Alden said. "At the workshop, he was talking about how makeup and jewelry are necessary aspects of the feminine and some of the women were railing against it."

So, good. Alden wasn't necessarily buying the whole spiel. Anyway, my delight at the fact that he was drawn to Deida more than outweighed any fear that my feminist moorings might come undone.

In his bedroom, where a large platform bed sat flanked by two midcentury nightstands, a pile of fascinating books spilling from one of them, I let Alden push against my verbal and physical boundaries more than anyone ever had. Whatever he wanted to call me, I let him call me. Wherever he wanted to place his hand, however much pressure he wanted to use, however sharply he angled into me, I welcomed him.

He pushed energy outward, and I played with it. It didn't feel submissive or even receptive. It felt creative. Each word he uttered became my cue, considered for a moment and then embodied. In his sheets, I uncovered women who had lain dormant in me for years. Each time he exerted force, it caused me to grow larger—rather, it reminded me how large I was. He pressed against my edges until they expanded so far as to seem infinite. Then he looked into my eyes and told me I was a goddess, that he worshipped me.

After several hours, we went to the living room naked. I lay on his wide couch while he put another record on. He poured a glass of water and sat down, leaned over to kiss me, and within seconds mounted me again, this time with no condom. Before my mouth could form any words about safe sex or my marital agreement, my hips arched up to meet him and the moment he was inside me, I came. That had never happened to me before, to climax so immediately upon being entered.

We didn't stop at three dates. I rode across the Golden Gate Bridge five, six, seven times. I met Alden in the city. We texted daily and chatted online. On a Friday night at the end of August, when Joie had to suddenly move back into her studio full-time and I was left without an apartment, I packed all my things into my Volkswagen convertible, drove to a bar to have a drink with Alden, took him back to Joie's empty studio for an hour, then drove home. It was past 1:00 a.m. Nervous that Scott would smell sex on me but afraid to wake him with the noise of the shower, I slipped into bed as quietly as possible.

With Joie having moved back into her studio full-time and me now living back at home until I could find another apartment, the only way to see Alden was to schedule a few discreet hours here and there. And Alden was torn. He'd had his share of uncommitted relationships and was ready for monogamy. One month into seeing him, I could feel my lifelong tendency toward exclusive attachment rearing its head. I fantasized about living with him. I listened as he talked about his travels, previous relationships, and his writing. He had published in a few literary journals. He loaned me a copy of one and I read his work, a non-linear story about a stroke victim in love with his caregiver. The narrative twisted, circled back, made me work to keep up with it. It dove deep and stayed down, putting words to grief and longing that I believed only women and writers knew. I read it motionless in one sitting, and by the time I put the journal down, I thought, *I belong with a man like this.*

But I couldn't bring myself to leave Scott and I couldn't give up my sole attempt at adventure just to settle right back down with someone new. When I tried to imagine the reality of a daily relationship with Alden, I drew back. It looked, in equal parts, richly nourishing and impossibly treacherous. The trust and history I had with Scott, by contrast, loomed solid as the earth beneath me. This foundation gave me the strength to venture into the unknown to begin with, though with each step I strayed further afield of it.

The night before Alden left for the Deida workshop in Los Angeles, we arranged for me to spend the night at his house. He picked me up at work, drove us over the bridge, and for the first time, we awoke in the same bed. The next morning, he tossed an overnight bag in his trunk, drove me back into the city, and dropped me off in front of my empty house. "Wait here a second," I said spontaneously. "I want you to meet Cleo."

I carried the little calico out to Sanchez Street in my arms. "She's cute," he said. She yawned and looked out at him from drowsy lids. When he reached up to scratch her cheek, two little fireworks went off in my heart: one of terrible loss, one of distant hope.

I bent down and pecked him on the lips. "Drive safely," I said. Cleo purred as he pulled away. I went inside and dropped her onto her usual spot on the couch, then walked into the bathroom and stood gazing at the mirror. Rosy cheeks, bright eyes, hair that seemed to have quickly grown an inch, as if I'd swallowed a secret elixir. I got my phone out and took a picture. I needed to remember how this felt.

15

Sanchez Street

OVER THE YEARS, I hadn't just asked Scott to live with me, propose, move back east, have a baby, plan romantic weekends, and look at me during sex. I also asked him how he was feeling (fine), how I could help him (he'd let me know), how I could be a better partner (I was a good enough partner). I bought an introductory tantra video (which we watched once) and books on relationships (a few of which he eventually read). I tried to interest him in couples communication workshops (we attended one). I asked him to try out churches (we went to a Unitarian Universalist church for about six months) and whether he wanted to join me in meditation (no thanks). I asked what kind of lingerie he'd like me to wear (he preferred me naked) and whether he'd like to watch porn together (not really).

For many years I suspected Scott was consciously, or at least semiconsciously, trying to thwart my attempts at intimacy. I was beginning to understand—and it was pitiful to think it had taken me this long—that he was simply being himself. He wasn't a romantic by nature, Eastern spirituality didn't interest him, and he didn't spend time contemplating the state of our relationship.

He thought in broad terms about the world and his place in it. He loved nature. What he wanted from me was to go biking and hiking and edit the winemaking book he was writing. I did bike with him, in Philadelphia nearly every weekday morning and in San Francisco on weekends. I hiked maybe once a year, disliking every minute of it. As for his book, a gargantuan resistance I couldn't explain precluded me from sitting down to edit it.

As the project inserted its inevitable distance between us, the mist of my routine projections parted a little, leaving his actual outline more visible. Weren't our differences what had attracted us in the first place? Weren't many successful marriages composed of opposites? I even began to respect him for choosing the vasectomy. Although I remained convinced that parenthood would have been the best way to alchemize our differences into a harmonious whole, in the end it didn't matter what I believed. He had a right to his body and his fate. As I watched him stand strong in that, despite the terrible uncertainty both the vasectomy and the ensuing project brought, I found a new glint of appreciation for him.

And of course, the project was bringing out sides to Scott that no cajoling ever could—whether due to the influence of his own new lovers or simply due to the fear of losing me, I wasn't sure. He routinely woke up now in the wee hours and climbed on top of me without a word. Sometimes, in the middle of sex, he took my hand, led me to the kitchen, and hoisted me up on the butcher block, where things got a little more raw, him standing and my legs up around his waist.

If it had taken an open marriage to finally produce some change, then I reasoned that abandoning it too soon would only revert us to the status quo. And in its fifth month, the project had momentum. Lovers, by and large, weren't just dropping by the wayside after three dates. Instead, the connections we forged fanned out like contrails. Post-Denver and without the alcohol or faraway city to hide in, Paul and I were evolving instead into close friends. Though

Jude and I had stopped having sex after the first month, we saw each other every few weeks for hours of food, music, and conversation. After two dates, Andrew found a new girlfriend, though we continued to exchange texts and emails. Alden had returned from Los Angeles warning me that he'd eventually have to call things off, but I looked forward to however much time I had left with him. Considering the friends I continued to meet at OneTaste, there were a lot of new relationships to track. I just kept going with it, borne along, perhaps, by the backwash of freedom I'd denied myself until now. I continued my search for a new apartment.

I came home from work on a Tuesday night to find Scott practicing piano scales on an electronic keyboard I'd given him. "I saw a place on Craigslist that I need to go look at tonight," I told him. "It's out in the Sunset, so I might be a while." What I didn't tell him was that afterward, I was heading to Jude's.

Jude lived on the third floor of a stately old Victorian in the Outer Sunset, a foggy residential neighborhood south of Golden Gate Park. At one end of a long hallway stood his bedroom, which we'd used only once over the summer, and at the other end a big parlor held nothing but musical instruments and oversized floor cushions scattered over a gigantic Oriental rug. Jude and I mostly hung out in the outdated kitchen, where he sat on a flimsy couch playing guitar while I tried to cook a vegan meal with the two cheap pots he owned.

Why, I asked myself more than once, do I leave my insanely busy magazine job after ten straight hours of work and drive to the Outer Sunset to see an astrologer whom I'm not even screwing when I can go home to my clean, beautiful house with my comfortable furniture and handsome husband, who, though he didn't want a child or tantra instruction, nevertheless quietly adores me and just wants to make wine while I read in the living room? *Why can't I just read in the living room and be happy?*

Because. As I threw chopped garlic and soy sausage into the

skillet, behind me Jude strummed a song he'd just written. He pulled his salty baritone over quiet chords, the lyrics telling the story of a battle with doubt and darkness. I didn't care if he was a hippie or if he conducted fire ceremonies. What I cared about was the fact that I could see his beauty. I saw it in his music, in the filmmakers and dancers who comprised his friends, in the money he sent to his mother each month. I also cared about the fact that Jude gave me interaction. He asked me questions and pointed out aspects of my behavior that I was blind to and that my husband never commented on. "You get so pouty when you try to ask for something you need," Jude once said. Another time: "You could be a little more assertive in bed." Who was ever going to tell me these things?

I'd experienced the chemical rush of infatuation enough times by then to know its cycle was not entirely personal. It had something to do with humanity. Paul, Jude, Alden, all former strangers, approached and let me touch them. I basked in their proximity, captivated by every detail of their clothing, their tastes, their accents, their habits. Even after the sexual intensity wore off, a sheen remained. Everything bristled with light—the tourists in Union Square, the flowers sitting in buckets outside a shop, the train accelerating into a tunnel after dropping me off in the morning.

"Do you think you're manic?" Andrea had asked when trying to talk me out of the project. "Maybe you should see your doctor." I shot back angrily, "Andrea, you and I both know that I've never been manic."

Now I saw the sense in her question. I could quite possibly be manic, seeking one contact high after another in order to blunt the frustration of a marriage of opposites, the ennui of middle age, the longing of childlessness. Or it could be that my lovers shone a light on a more accurate reality underpinning the mundane one, that falling in love offered glimpses, however brief, into the grandeur at the center of things.

Jude and I sat down to eat, and I pulled my phone from my purse. I texted Scott, *I'm going to have dinner out here. I'll be home by 10*. Within seconds he responded: *I want a divorce*.

I froze. I typed *I'm on my way home* and threw the phone back in my purse. "I'm really sorry, I have to go," I told Jude. "Right this second."

"Seriously?" he said, standing up. "Are you okay?"

"Yes, but I have to go. I'll explain tomorrow. I'm sorry."

I got in the car and tried to keep my speed under control. I'd uttered the word "divorce" two or three times over the years, but had always taken it back within minutes. This was the first time Scott had spoken it. Tiny needles of panic jabbed the undersurface of my skin. I dialed Scott once, twice, three times. No answer. When I got home, his phone sat on the kitchen counter.

He didn't return that night or the next morning. I lay in bed all night staring into the dark thinking, *Okay, here it is, here is the collapse I've got coming to me*. At seven o'clock I dragged myself into work and dialed his office.

"This is Scott," he answered.

"Hi," I said, and started crying.

"Hi," he said.

"Were you going to come home after work?" was all I could get out.

"Yes."

"Okay. I'll see you then."

"Okay. Bye."

By lunchtime, lack of sleep overtook me. I went home, dropped my things at the door, and slid onto the bed. Cleo jumped up and settled herself in the crook of my arm and we lay there together, awaiting my fate.

———

Many years before, when I was thirty-one, Cleo and I had spent an entire summer, from May through August, on the bed in Scott's house in Sacramento. I'd lie on my back with her on my chest, staring at a stucco swirl in the white ceiling that looked exactly like a broad-shouldered man in a toga. Occasionally I'd turn to look out the screen of the bedroom window, where Scott's tomatoes bloomed on their vines. Birds chirped all day long in the Chinese elm in the backyard. The white cotton quilt below me, sewn by Scott's late mother, had a pattern of small blue flowers. Next to me lay Scott's old soft red kerchief, frayed on the ends and damp with tears.

That summer in Sacramento, I'd get up in the morning, brush my teeth, wash my face, change out of my pajamas into loose shorts and a T-shirt, then climb onto the quilt with the cat and the birds and the man in the toga, motionless. I couldn't concentrate enough to read a book. I couldn't bear to turn on the TV and watch simulations of normal people going about their noisy lives. Sometimes, in the afternoon, I'd shuffle to the galley kitchen and attempt to wash dishes, my unmoving stare aimed at the jade leaves in the planter window. But holding myself up vertically made me cry harder. I'd turn the water off, bend over, and sob, snot dripping into the sink, the dish towel hanging from my hand.

I'd been spiraling since a bike accident at age twenty-eight tore up my inner labia, sprawling me onto a vacant bike trail. By the time Scott had run for help, I'd soaked his T-shirt with blood. The gynecologist who patched me up refused to tell me how many stitches it took; he only said it was no worse than if I'd torn having a baby. He assured me I'd be back to normal in a month or two.

I did not get back to normal for four years. Most days my throat was sore. Some days my arms ached too much to brush my hair. Sharp pains shot through my chest and I had to hold on to walls to walk straight. Wavy vertical lines jerked in my vision

and my eyes burned. I lost twenty pounds and dreamed repeatedly of thick pus oozing from my body. An occasional pressure
around my neck made it feel as if someone were choking me.

I was tested for Lyme Disease, thyroid trouble, multiple scle-
rosis, leukemia, and a dozen other conditions; I added bodywork,
acupuncture, allergy testing, vitamin B12 shots, antidepressants,
and Klonopin to my ongoing therapy appointments. One doctor
called it depression, though I'd never heard of depression causing
such acute symptoms. One told me to stop eating wheat and sugar.
One said, "Sometimes people get sick and die without ever finding the cause." I learned a lot about the varying quality of bedside
manner in those four years. I became an expert.

Eventually they settled on chronic fatigue syndrome, which
added no information to the mix other than a label and a new
list of support groups I could choose to attend. By the time I was
thirty-one, three years into the illness, labels had ceased to matter anyway. The physical symptoms turned out to be mere land-
marks on a path leading down to a dark, bottomless well.

To attempt an explanation, I wrote Scott a letter, telling how
there was a terrible wound in me, something for which there
were no words, and how his gentle patience would first assuage
it, then open up an even deeper level of it. How I was falling
through the layers of a lethal despair, how every day it felt like I
would die and then I didn't. When Scott was little, his parents
nicknamed him Sunshine because of his sanguine disposition. I
explained how my gratitude for his strength alternated with shame
at my own wretchedness. Scott tucked the letter into his top
drawer next to his dad's World War II dog tags. When he got
home from his job at the software company at exactly 5:15 each
day, he came into the bedroom and lay down facing me.

"Hi, doll," he said. Sometimes he called me dovebar, or kitty,
or noodles. He told me about his day and I told him how I was
faring, each word willed out of me through a gauntlet of self-hate.

Then he turned onto his back and held me as I cried into his shoulder. This twenty-minute dose of simple contact gave me the strength to get out of bed, heat up some dinner, and maybe watch a movie with him on the couch before returning to the bedroom.

Looking back now, I can honor the mystery of it. I see it as my initial descent into the body, the bike accident a shock that yanked my awareness down below my neck for the first time, into my stomach, legs, arms, and sex. As I swirled in a cauldron of long-repressed feeling, little by little I was forced to confront the present moment head-on. I learned to breathe into pain, exhaustion, vertigo, grief. Three years in, after four full months of lying motionless on Scott's bed, I hit the nadir. I didn't have the constitution for suicide, so I decided that if this paralysis continued, I'd give up my dreams of journalism and travel and intimacy and go be a Buddhist nun somewhere.

I stared at the stucco man in the toga hour upon hour, asking where God was, why He hadn't made an unequivocal appearance since seventh grade. His silence must be due to my lack of sincerity, for however huge my need of God, my fear overtook it—a fear instilled by the Catholics, who'd taught me that coming face to face with Him was a task saints could barely muster without losing their sanity, and that mortals did well to shrink from. In lieu of God's mercy, I had to lean on my own. In my worst moments I would try to muster just a drop of compassion for what I was going through. A split second of simple kindness in a sea of chaos and resistance and despair.

One August afternoon, I managed to leave Scott's bed and drag myself to the movies. I watched Patricia Arquette playing a young widowed doctor who fights her way through the jungles of wartime Burma trying to get home. It was a small movie that registered on no one else's radar, but it contained one crucial scene in which Arquette's character suddenly decides to stay in the ravaged country to help its refugees, transmuting her grief into something useful. After the matinee, I walked outside to a little boardwalk that fronted the Sacramento River and looked down into its muddy water. As I traced the river upstream toward the bleached-out horizon of my asylum city, a tiny space opened inside me, a pinprick of light and air.

Within a few months I started working part-time again. The year after that I brushed up on some journalism courses so I could finally leave tech writing behind. As I ventured back into the world, I noticed a shift. When I entered Scott's house, I no longer sensed vague danger. When I walked down the street, the leaves on the trees no longer shimmered with all-permeating sadness. The desperate urge to control my environment loosened its stranglehold. At first I didn't know what to call this new feeling. It wasn't exactly happiness and it wasn't exactly peace, more like a hushed buoyancy, a feeling of space where something had previously been jammed. Eventually I learned its name: safety. Another human being had seen all of me, and he was still there. He was still kind.

The twelve-steppers and therapists and self-help books all said another person couldn't heal you. You had to do it yourself, or ask God to do it for you. They were wrong. What had healed me, or at least what had provided the foundation of my healing, was Scott's stoic, gentle love. The same love I struggled against now.

I awoke from a nap with Cleo still snuggled up beside me, the word "divorce" reverberating. I went out and sat at the kitchen table, trying to muster enough courage to look at this possibility squarely, at least for a minute or two. I saw a future composed not of endless affairs and sexual seminars and new friends, but of . . . nothing. A vacuum. Yet putting myself back into the box of our conventional, childless marriage right then felt just as impossible. For years, the safety that I'd found with Scott had been enough. Until it wasn't.

Scott walked in the door at 4:45, as usual. I braced myself. He came into the kitchen, sat down next to me, and said, "I'm sorry. I was angry. I didn't mean what I said."

"It's okay," I said, reaching for his hand. Tears of relief blurred my vision. "You don't have to apologize."

"I want our marriage back," he said. "We've been at this for almost five months. Haven't you gotten what you needed?"

I wanted to say yes, I've gotten more than I needed. You were bigger than could be expected of any man, and it's finished now and we're safe again. I'm the one who's sorry. I'm sorry I couldn't just get over the vasectomy and move on, that I couldn't grow up and honor the commitment I made to you on our wedding day, that I am out on some quasi-adolescent quest for god knows what. You don't deserve this.

"I need more time," I said.

He sat thinking. "How much time?"

"It's almost October. If I started another sublet on October first, we could revisit things at the beginning of the year."

"The new year isn't the time to make big decisions, right after the holidays and all that family stuff," he said. This was a maxim he oft repeated. "Let's just say February first."

"Okay, February first." Would four more months wash this storm out of my system?

We sat holding hands silently. His hands were on the smallish side for such a tall man. They weren't soft, though. You could tell by the rough-lined palms that they were used to fixing things.

"I'll make some dinner," I said. Cleo jumped languidly from my lap to the floor, and then effortlessly from the floor up to his. She settled in and he stroked her nape.

"Things can't be all that bad when there's a cat purring in your lap," he said. This was another of his favorite sayings.

And it was true. He was right.

16

South of Market

I FOUND A MONTH-TO-MONTH STUDIO in a loft building South of Market, though "studio" was too spacious a label. It was smaller than most hotel rooms, with a double bed, kitchenette, closet, and flat-screen television, and a bathroom off the entryway. The building was brand-new, eight stories of concrete and glass. It fronted Bluxome, one of SoMa's many narrow alleys. Each studio had a wall-sized window; mine, on the fifth floor, overlooked the fountained courtyard below. The roof had been made into a sprawling deck looking out toward downtown, mere blocks away.

I unpacked my clothes, bought only the most basic groceries for the mini-fridge, and hung a painting I'd made at Joie's, an oversized canvas of abstract blues, reds, and oranges reminiscent of an underwater plant. On the small corner table I placed the photo of my newborn nephew screaming in the delivery room.

I'd seen Alden just once since he returned from Los Angeles. He was house-sitting at his friends' place in the city for two nights before driving to Death Valley for a week, away from cell reception and Internet. He asked me to meet him at the Philosophers

Club, an old locals' hangout tucked away in a small neighborhood behind Twin Peaks. As we sat on stools at the bar, he said that our time together was coming to an end. He didn't want an ongoing relationship with an unavailable woman. He didn't want his heart broken.

"The holidays will be here before you know it," he said. "I can't imagine wanting to spend them with you and knowing I can't."

His elbow rested on the bar, a tattooed snake winding fully around the forearm muscle, consuming its own tail—shades of red and purple I'd never seen in a tattoo. For some reason, probably just my selfish need to keep seeing him, I had trouble believing he was as vulnerable as he claimed.

"Are you saying we have to stop right now?" I asked.

"No. But soon."

As he paid the tab, he looked at me with a mixture of desire and control. "So, are you coming home with me?" he asked.

I followed him to his friend's condo not far from the bar. Perched on the steep hillside of Twin Peaks, the wide living room windows looked down over the entire illuminated grid of the city, its piers, the water, and beyond, all the way to Oakland. Instead of taking me into the bedroom, Alden turned off the lights and sat on the couch. He placed a pillow on his lap and patted it. I lay down and he silently unzipped my jeans, removing them along with my panties. "Just relax," he said, letting his left hand rest on my pubic bone. "Just breathe."

Almost imperceptibly, he began nudging his finger, as if petting the tiniest, most fragile newborn animal. He kept it at the surface a good quarter inch from my clitoris, and only moved in closer as my legs gave way, stroking more slowly than seemed possible. He didn't say a word. Eventually my knees splayed and then my arms. My right hand fell to the floor. My eyes closed and my head rolled to the right as my jaw unhinged. The entire surface of my skin shimmered bright and awake, drenched in a pleasure devoid of urge or tension. I couldn't even call it arousal. It was more an oceanic tranquility, one I'd never been able to reach through drugs, meditation, or yoga.

The next night was Alden's last before leaving town. I showed up at the door fresh from dinner with my friends, tipsy and hoping for a repeat performance, with my iPod blasting Wolf Parade into my headphones. When he answered, I took one earbud out and handed it to him. He listened a few seconds, then put the iPod on the entryway table, kissed me, turned me against the wall and lifted up my skirt. He fucked me once like that in the hallway, then again a few feet away on the guest bed. As we lay in the dark afterward, our clothes scattered across the floor, he said, "Please remember how I feel about you."

I should have known then that I wouldn't see him again, but I had overestimated my effect on him, and completely underestimated his on me.

When Alden returned from Death Valley, I asked him to come see my new studio, but he declined. His texts became friendlier and less flirty. During the 2008 vice presidential debates, which I watched with my coworkers in a crowded hotel bar downtown, we exchanged jokes and rooted for my fellow Scrantonian Joe Biden. When it ended, I texted, *So can I come over now?*

I'm afraid not.

As Alden distanced himself, I became preoccupied by the fact that we'd had so much unsafe sex. When it had first happened, he'd told me not to worry, that his recent physical showed a clean STD panel. He even had a printout of it somewhere in his home office. "I'll show it to you if it makes you feel better," he'd said.

"Sorry to be such a stickler, but I need to see it, for my peace of mind."

Rationally, I didn't think Alden had HIV or anything else, but how could I be sure? I barely knew him. My underlying guilt over breaking the condom rule attached itself irretrievably onto the obsessive worry that I'd infect Scott with a disease. I found I couldn't rest until I knew for certain. I asked my doctor for a full STD workup, but she said I needed to wait eight weeks, since it took that long for certain markers to show up. Alden and I chatted online and he said he'd send me a copy of his test results to reassure me in the meantime. He also asked me to mail back the literary journal in which his story was published, as it was his only copy. That's when it dawned on me that I'd never see him again, and even though he'd warned me it was coming, I couldn't bear the reality of it. I called him and got his voice mail.

"Alden, hi, it's Robin. I know you don't owe me this, but do you think we could meet one last time, in public if you want, just to say goodbye? I don't know . . . I think I'm a few weeks behind you in this letting go process. I didn't realize that night in Twin Peaks would be the last time I saw you. I can give you your journal and you can show me the test and then we'll be done. Even if you can just spare fifteen minutes, it would help me a lot. Let me know, okay?" I hung up, shaking.

He didn't call back that day, or the next. Self-control left me by the minute. As I pulled up to my studio in the dark, I texted to ask if I could come by to drop his journal off, see his test, say goodbye, and leave.

No, Robin. Please just mail my journal back.

I stiffened. Was he trying to sucker punch me? I couldn't tell because the coldness of his words short-circuited my brain. A malevolent heat spiraled through my chest and up the back of my neck. The car interior twisted in around me, and the SoMa alley beyond the windshield suddenly looked like Pennsylvania:

a desolate street, night falling quickly, everyone and everything erased by the sweep of a blurry hand. The closest I could come to naming the feeling was abandonment, and that was a guess. It was too enormous and went too deep to fit behind any word. I'd been trying my entire adult life to master it, yet it remained unaltered, big enough to swallow me whole.

I started the car and headed down Bluxome and up Fifth Street. I'd drive to his house.

No, Robin. Pull the car over.

Turn around. Re-park. Go upstairs.

I closed the door of the studio behind me, sat on the bed, and took out my phone. I typed, *I will return it, as soon as I get a copy of your test.*

The phone rang.

"What are you doing, Robin?"

"I was asking to say goodbye in person, that's all." With these words, I shrunk to three feet tall.

"I told you I don't want to see you. I want the journal back."

My whole body went cold. Terrible danger hovered within inches.

"Fine, you don't have to see me. But you also said you'd show me your test, remember?"

"You can't hold that journal hostage . . ."

"I'm not holding anything hostage."

"You have no respect for my boundaries. Your need to tie this all up with a pretty bow is narcissistic."

"What are you talking about? Why are you suddenly treating me like some kind of stalker?"

"That's what you're acting like, a stalker!"

"And you're acting like a fucking lunatic!" I screamed, loud enough to hurt his ears. Rage helped. It pushed some of the suffocating pain from my chest out into the room.

He hung up. When he called back I didn't answer. The pain

was locking down now behind a steely reserve. I lay awake in the studio all night, listening to the fountain five stories below, facing down the gaping hole inside me. If I could just sit with it, stare into it without flinching, maybe I could finally grow large enough to contain it. I kept telling myself that, and then recoiling each time I imagined the scene minus my husband waiting for me at home. What kind of masochist creates abandonment outside her stable marriage after the marriage itself has stopped producing such drama?

The next morning I had an email from Alden saying he'd send me the test. "Thanks," I responded. "55 Bluxome. I'll send the journal today and you'll never hear from me again." I deleted the email, then his email address, then his texts and voice mails, and finally his phone number. I unfriended him on Facebook and blocked him on Nerve.com. I slipped his journal inside a manila envelope along with a note that said, "I'm trusting you to send that test. Goodbye." Each closure gave me back a modicum of control, sealing shut the vacant, silenced chambers of my heart.

Two days later, an envelope arrived at Bluxome. Inside was a handwritten note—"Sorry things got ugly, Robin. I hope you find what you're looking for"—along with a photocopy of his blood work. He had no diseases. I looked at his full name, birth date, address, height, and weight, tangible symbols attesting to the existence of at least one man on the planet who knew how to handle me. I ripped up the test and threw it away. I folded the note and put it into the small box where I stored prayers and worries. The only tethers I had now were this note and his street address. I bowed my head and said a silent prayer for the strength not to chase him.

I tucked the prayer box into its drawer. So this was the flip side of passion, the price for it. I understood why he had to leave, but I couldn't understand why so abruptly, and why, if he knew that night in Twin Peaks would be our last, he didn't just come out and say so. Or maybe that's exactly what he meant by "Please remember how I feel about you," and I just couldn't accept it. Maybe he imagined I held all the cards, being the married one, the dangerous one, and thus he couldn't afford another goodbye. That explanation made sense and soothed me. What hurt me most was the possibility that this intense diving in and pulling away was not even all that difficult for him, that it was something he'd perfected over time with lots of women.

I'd never know exactly why he couldn't give me fifteen more minutes of his time. But it didn't surprise me that the one man I'd chosen to surrender to was the same one who showed no mercy. Every banal self-help book I'd ever read had predicted that.

The Virgin America gates at SFO were a sparkling white oasis amid the usual dull airport gray, quieter and more upscale. Jude sat on a rounded white bench with bright red cushions, waiting for me. I was flying home for yet another godchild—my goddaughter's wedding this time—and stopping in New York City for a few nights beforehand. Jude happened to be leaving for New York on the same day, so we'd booked the same flight. When I saw him in his jean jacket and beanie, a small black canvas bag at his feet, my stomach dropped.

"Hi there," he smiled as I bent to kiss his cheek.

"Hi," I said. "Um, I'm going to run to the bathroom before we board."

I lingered in the stall as long as I could. At the sink, I ran warm water over my hands repeatedly. I noticed they were shaking. I glanced up into the mirror and immediately looked away. I stood at a touchless hand dryer for three long rounds of soothing hot air. I checked my phone; we'd start boarding in five minutes.

I walked as slowly as possible back to Jude. The bathroom ritual hadn't worked. The sight of him made me want to curl into a corner and cry.

"What's wrong?" he asked as I sat down. I was seized by the urge to run, straight out of the airport and home to my bed on Sanchez Street.

"I'm not sure," I said. "Flying always makes me nervous, but . . ." I searched for the words. He looked straight at me, calm, listening. "Traveling together feels weird."

Jude and I hadn't slept together for months. The dinners I'd cooked him, the songs he'd sung to me, our talks about childhood and religion all proved less intimate than sitting next to him on an airplane for five hours. Food, music, and hushed talks fell within the purview of sex. Traveling through airports together was real life, and I only wanted to do real life with Scott.

"I get it," he said. "We can just be quiet on the plane, or read or something. We don't have to talk much." Even that—sitting side by side reading together—was something I reserved for Scott. I found it impossible, as well, to hold any other man's hand or to sit on a lover's lap. At home, if I was cleaning up, I routinely went to sit in Scott's lap while he worked on the computer, swinging my legs over to one side, resting my head on his shoulder, and clasping my hands around his neck.

Other than making me quiet and sad, the flight turned out okay. When we landed, Jude and I gathered up our bags. He was heading to Brooklyn. He gave me a big hug.

"You going to be okay?" he said.

"Yeah, thanks, Jude. I'll see you back in San Francisco."

I boarded the train to Penn Station, then hailed a cab to take me to my hotel in Chelsea. The moment I told the driver the hotel name, a wave of nausea washed over me.

Nine times out of ten, my experience of nausea did not originate in or stay confined to the stomach. It was a direct effect of the vagus nerve going haywire. I knew this because I'd spent a lot of time researching the chicken-and-egg symptoms of panic in order to better manage it. The vagus is a maze of ganglia twisting from the brain stem down around the esophagus and into every organ in the body. Certain triggers, such as seeing blood or experiencing intense pain, can cause the vagus to overreact, which usually results in fainting. Blood, needles, and impact to bones had caused me to faint since I was a child. As an adult, it was usually a panic attack or emotional hit that sent me into vasovagal distress.

It starts with an intense burst of heat in my upper back, spreading up my neck like poison. Something in my chest collapses, making it hard to breathe, my stomach clenches, and my ears block. I begin sweating intensely, and, in order to compensate for the extreme blood pressure drop, my heart pounds about 150 beats a minute. I must lie flat to avoid passing out, and all functions vanish. I cannot sit up, speak, or move until it passes. I cannot dial the phone or call out for help. It's like one of those dreams where you're trying to scream and no sound comes out. No matter how often it happens, it's difficult to believe I will survive. I cannot rise to make it to a toilet, so I turn on my side in case I vomit, but I rarely do. I just lie there trying to slow my breathing until my system rebounds. It can last a minute or continue in waves for more than an hour.

This is what gripped me now in the cab on the way to Chelsea. I lay on the seat, which the driver didn't seem to mind or notice, and when I could sit up, rolled down the window for air. By the time we got to the hotel, the first wave had passed. I walked slowly to the front desk, hoping there wouldn't be a second.

"Hi. I'm checking in."

The woman took my name and typed it in. "Sorry, your room's not quite ready yet. I should have it for you in a half hour."

I took a breath.

"Are you okay?" she asked. "You look very green."

"I'm not well. Can you point me toward the restroom?"

Thankfully, it was far from the lobby and deserted. I sat in a stall hunched over with my head between my knees, quietly crying for a good long time. Gradually I became aware of a new sensation: a familiar pinch tugging at my lower abdomen near the pubic bone. Was my period due? I checked the calendar on my phone. My last period was . . . six weeks ago.

Alden. Could it be, at age forty-four? A forty-six-year-old friend had just had her first baby without the help of technology. In the past month I'd had at least a dozen instances of unprotected sex with him, more than in any previous month of my life.

I sat in the stall until I was sure I could get up without fainting, then walked unsteadily to a pharmacy down the street and bought a pregnancy test, avoiding the brand I'd used the last time that had possibly produced a false positive. Once I checked into my room, I went to the bathroom, opened the package, peed on it, set it down on the sink, and went to wait on the bed.

You around? I texted Ellen. *I'm in NYC, period is late, taking preg test right now. Kind of freaked out about everything.*

Absolutely, she wrote. *Standing by, LMK.*

I didn't even have Alden's phone number or email. I envisioned mailing him a note that said only "I'm pregnant. It's yours," and an illicit thrill shivered through me at the prospect of it. Like my secret wish to live in the path of an impending hurricane. Blow me over. Churn this shit up. Let's see what we're all really made of.

I walked into the bathroom too exhausted to rouse much hope or fear either way. The test shook in my hand as I lifted it. One blotty pink line pressed itself up through the wet oval viewing window. The second line, the one that signaled the ascension of nature over willpower, was nowhere in sight.

Negative, I wrote to Ellen.

☹. *It would have been kind of awesome if that's how this whole thing turned out.*

Would it? Was the project nothing more, at bottom, than a search for fresh, viable sperm? That could explain why I'd now let two men ditch the condom. I didn't even know anymore. All I knew was that, once again, Ruby had lucked out, remaining safe on the sidelines of infinity instead of descending into my chaotic womb to be fathered by a man who didn't know or want her.

17

Solitude in Motion

THE INTERNET BOOM of the late nineties changed SoMa from an industrial neighborhood of bland warehouses, furniture outlets, and bail bonds offices into a grid of soaring lofts dotted with the occasional trendy restaurant or brick-walled wine bar. A decade later, it was headquarters for the dot-com resurgence as well. Blanketed in concrete and devoid of trees, its wide intersections leading to various freeway ramps, it was a part of town I'd never want to live in permanently. But knowing I had just a few months to enjoy it, I quickly adapted to its rhythms.

On my way to work, I walked down Bluxome past the open garage doors of Station No. 8, where firefighters in navy blue pants and T-shirts washed their truck each morning. I grabbed a cheap coffee at a doughnut shop on the corner, then headed up Fourth Street. It took about fifteen minutes to get to Union Square, and at each corner, the crowd of black-clad thirtysomethings with messenger bags strapped across their bodies grew. As we waited for the Walk signal, everyone took a sip of coffee from one hand while checking an iPhone in the other. My phone held a continual stream of texts from recent and potential lovers—men I met at OneTaste, at work events, the last stray candidates from Nerve.com—so each glance at it induced me to either reverie or anticipation. I could pass much of my waking hours in one of those two states. While idly waiting in line at the supermarket or riding the train, I'd sink into a daydream, remembering the last sensual rush or looking forward to the next one.

Paul and I had slept together on only a few scattered occasions since the weekend in Denver. His knowing Scott and my having gotten to know his girlfriend kept us from taking it further. But we still met often for after-work drinks or late-night rendezvous at dive bars. To be truthful, ever since the first night at his house in Pacific Heights, I'd fallen a little bit in love with him, just as I'd predicted. Not head over heels. I loved Paul the way I'd loved the first boys I'd noticed in prepuberty, as part playmate, part specimen of simple masculinity: sturdily built, fun-loving, mischievous.

A boat engineer, Paul had access to several lightweight speedboats that were so fast and unsinkable they were sold mostly to the Coast Guard. Occasionally in the early afternoon, he'd text me.

Out on the bay. Ferry Building in 30 mins?

I'd gather my things and scoot from the office as if getting lunch. On Market Street I caught the F train or any bus heading westward toward the piers, and jumped off as close to the Ferry Building as I could. I rushed past the crowds standing in line for tacos and burgers to the small boat launch just north of the building, where Paul was waiting. Large twin black engines hummed at the boat's rear, their weight causing the bow to bob higher in the water. The entire craft beamed with the luster of horsepower. "Hello, love," he said as he helped me climb over the big inflatable rim onto the stern. "Hello, Paulie," I said, hugging him and pecking his cheek before taking my place in the thick padded seat just in front of the engines.

He climbed into the tall, middeck captain's seat, took the wheel, and slowly backed the boat into the bay, curving out of the pier and away from the crowds of the Ferry Building. This was my favorite part, leaving land, leaving everything else behind and heading into the waters around Alcatraz. The powerful engines quickly gained speed. The predictable chop bounced us like an amusement ride—boom, boom, boom, each landing swelling me with juvenile glee—until we reached the Golden Gate Bridge. In midday, the fog had cleared and the bright sun curtailed the penetrating chill. Cars looked like small, distant objects slowly traversing the span above. We passed under the ominous shadow of its towering orange beams. Emerging on the other side where the bay met the ocean, the boat suddenly took on bigger waves, went airborne. This was the place where ships arriving from Asia used to crash and sink in the fog. Paul calmly navigated the whitecaps with quick turns while I sat back near the engines, letting the spray hit my face. As he torqued right, I leaned over as far as possible, dipping my hand into the opaque water. It was bracing cold.

On our way back to the city, I took the passenger seat near him, watching the heart-shaped prow ply its way through the spray. The music blended with the noise of the engines and the satisfying plunk of fiberglass hitting water. He grabbed my hand, leaned closer so I could hear, and said, "I love you."

"I love you, too."

"As a friend."

"Me too. As a friend." We laughed out loud at how corny we sounded and I squeezed his hand, feeling a jolt of the passion we'd shared in Denver, happy to let it burn slow and long, fueling our friendship with its cellular memory.

The beauty of San Francisco's postcard skyline lies in its compact Mediterranean whiteness. It suggests that while the typical big-city sins will transpire here, the sea will wipe them clean as

sure as it has since the first weary urbanite fled to a beach town
to escape his past. This beckoning vision magnified before us as
we approached the pier. Paul slowed to no-wake speed and parked
where we'd started. I got up, hugged him goodbye, jumped out,
and rushed back down Market Street, skipping lunch and returning to my desk with the taste of salt on my lips.

When we weren't on boats, we were on bikes. Paul would call
around seven as the workday came to a close, asking if I wanted
to drive out to Ocean Beach. I'd shut down whatever story I was
working on and run downstairs. He'd pull up on his black Viper
wearing frayed jeans, thick-soled boots, and an expensive leather
motorcycle jacket zippered to the neck and loaded down with
secret compartments. "Robs!" he'd say as he flipped his visor back
and unlocked the extra helmet from the side of the bike. "Let's
do this." I'd stuff my hair into it, throw my bag across a shoulder,
and slide on.

Paul drove fast, up and over the steep slope of California
Street and out to Fulton, where there were fewer stoplights and
he could accelerate to highway speed. I'd need both hands to
keep from sliding off, my right gripped to the seat handle behind me and my left around his waist. He'd weave through traffic so tightly I could almost feel my knees brushing the sides of
the cars, could almost see the Viper's mirrors swiping theirs. We'd
pass mile upon mile of Golden Gate Park, a peripheral swath of
cool green darkening to black, and when we arrived at the beach,
he'd take a left down Great Highway and let the engine go, all
the way to eighty, eighty-five, ninety.

Waves broke to my right. Low pastel houses blurred to my
left. The dashed yellow line merged to solid below my boots.
One brake light, one rock, and we'd be killed. *So be it*, I'd think.
This is a fine moment to die. Me, the woman who once harbored a
body-wracking phobia of highways, and bridges, and tunnels,
and airplanes, and restaurants and grocery stores and even, in

my worst moments, of simply leaving the house. Paul and his Viper transported me back to the summery cusp of womanhood, when my unshackled mind and downy legs beckoned me toward the woods and the high rocks, when I roamed free, body and soul thrumming with the simple wonder of being alive.

This is why I loved Paul, why I called him my best friend: because he returned me to wind and water. As we sped down the seam of the Pacific, I let go of his waist, tempting fate, then grasped it, silently thanking him for helping resurrect a girl I thought I'd never meet again—the girl I'd been before the fear set in.

Once a month, Jude and I met at the city's best vegetarian restaurant for lavish meals. We sipped cocktails soaked through with fresh ginger and lemongrass while he successfully hit on one cute waitress after another.

"You're a real Casanova for such a sensitive vegan healer," I teased.

"You're just jealous."

"Not me. I've had you. Let the other girls take their turn." In truth, I did feel rejected by Jude's sexual nonchalance, though it also relieved me of worrying about breaking the serious-relationship rule I'd established with Scott.

Afterward, we rode a cab back to Bluxome and went up to the roof deck. We each took up a cushiony lounge chair and lay silent as the downtown skyscraper lights and a few distant stars twinkled awake.

"I often think we're perfect for each other," he said quietly. "I can talk to you about anything. But then I remember our age difference."

I turned to him. "And then there's also the fact that I'm married."

"It's so strange. I always forget that."

"Do you think maybe it's part of the reason why you're so comfortable with me? Because you can't have me?"

"Ouch," he winced. "Maybe."

"I mean, look at the women who swarm around you. You've got a certain something."

"The seduction cycle is so tiring, though. I'm tired."

"You'll figure it out," I reassured him. "You're only thirty-two. You have a lot of time." I'd have given anything to be thirty-two again, with ten years of healthy eggs left in my womb, for in my mind, regardless of child-bearing, that biological marker formed the dividing line between the first half of life, when every moment thrilled with potential, and the second half, when even the best moments harbored a seed of loss.

"What would you do if you were going to die in a month?" he asked.

I thought for a minute. "I'd go see my family. I'd probably go to Europe one more time with Scott. And I'd have to do something with my box of journals. Probably burn them. What about you?"

"I'd try to achieve enlightenment."

"Why? You're probably going to become enlightened the minute you die anyway."

"I want to transcend while I'm still in my body. I want to experience the in-between space when you're still incarnated but beyond the ego."

"I don't want to transcend anything," I said. "I feel like my spirituality goes in the opposite direction, down instead of up. The more I listen to my body, the closer I feel to God."

"That's the difference between you and me."

"That, and the eating animals thing."

We went downstairs and I made herbal tea while he cued up a new album on his iPod. "You have to hear these guys," he said.

"They're called Fleet Foxes." Jude had introduced me to Bon Iver over the summer, this being the year of haunting falsettos and wistful harmonies. Fleet Foxes sounded like they were singing from deep inside an ancient grotto, a jaunty meldody underlying a sad chorus that kept ending *shadows of the mess you made*. Once we crawled into bed, he quickly fell asleep, leaving me alone with the lyric resonating in my ears—shadows of the mess you made, shadows of the mess you made. I wondered why both Paul and Jude seemed eager to spend time with me when there was no sex. Perhaps being with me gave them a break from all those available women who expected a relationship to go somewhere. With me, they got acceptance, the very thing I couldn't bring myself to give Scott. Of course, it was so much easier to accept men who'd never seen me at my worst, and on whom I never let myself depend, than to accept the one who knew and loved me best. The irony of it turned my stomach, made me ashamed. I think I actually groaned, right there next to Jude in bed.

And yet, I couldn't usher myself to that level of acceptance. Among the cast of characters who roamed my mental landscape, one of the most vocal was a kindly old Asian man: round-faced, bald-headed, decked out in crimson robes. He looked a lot like the Dalai Lama, in fact. He said, *Your spiritual task at this juncture is to unconditionally love your husband. Ask nothing more of him. Expect nothing to change.* To do so, I'd have to surrender the thing I wanted most, which Scott had actually named. "You want a deep, psychosexual connection," he'd said. Exactly. Giving up that desire felt like dying. I had several personality traits I could stand to lose, but not this one. This one felt too close to my core.

Meanwhile, I continued to pine for Alden. In the two months since I'd last seen him, the project had stalled. Each day when I got home from work, I checked the mailbox, wishing for a message via the one avenue of communication I'd left open to him. All I ever found inside was junk mail.

The weeknights I didn't spend at OneTaste or with Paul, I spent with my coworkers at the various parties the magazine hosted— museum openings, mixology contests, concerts, formal galas. One week we'd sample tequila at the newest bar in the Mission and the next we'd don floor-length gowns for the opening of the San Francisco Ballet or Opera. The magazine's biggest party of the year coincided with the "Hot 20 Under 40," the annual issue dedicated to profiling the city's up-and-comers. We held that year's Hot 20 party at the new DeYoung Museum, an icon of modern architecture recently remodeled from the ground up and reopened in Golden Gate Park. I rushed home from the office to Bluxome, slipped on a silk turquoise dress and heels, pinned my hair up, and drove to the DeYoung, where I spent the night schmoozing with fashion designers, playwrights, and tech startup founders.

Several of us migrated to an after-party at a crowded new spot in the Financial District across from the Transamerica Pyramid. Our little group of editors was joined by men from San Francisco's top social tier: native sons, well-heeled investment bankers, Silicon Valley elite. One of the latter was a scruffy mid-thirties eBay early employee, synonymous with multimillion-aire. He was clearly smitten with my friend Ellen, but she was uninterested, and after she left to go meet the man she was dating, he asked if I wanted to get something to eat in Chinatown.

In the fluorescent 2:00 a.m. glare of Yuet Lee, where many of the city's chefs went to scarf down clams and squid after closing up their own kitchens, it quickly became apparent just how drunk Mr. eBay was. I wasn't sober either. Six hours of free vodka and fabulous chatter had my head spinning in that mildly delirious way that lends everything import. He had recently rented a house around the corner. In the course of our conversation, I learned that he'd likely bedded several women I knew.

"Come sleep over," he said.

"Not a good idea." I shook my head. "Ellen's one of my closest friends and you're kind of in love with her."

"I don't want to have sex with you," he said, motioning his hand back and forth as if wiping a window. "I'm totally into Ellen. But you're cool. Let's be friends! Seriously, let's just hang out and then go to sleep. My bed is really big. We won't even touch. Plus, you can meet my dog. He's the greatest dog in the world."

I laughed. "You're weird."

"I know. Whatever." He signed the check and put his jacket on. "So come on, just sleep over. Seriously. Wait till you see this dog."

"Okay."

"Cool!" He put his arm around me and we walked a few blocks, then turned into a dark residential alley. Beyond his security gate and up the front steps, his golden retriever was waiting at the front door, wagging his tail. He walked straight back to the bedroom and plopped onto the bed, picked up a guitar lying beside it, and started strumming it while his dog settled itself against his legs. The dog was indeed a beauty.

Before long, he was snoring as I lay on the other side of the king-sized bed in the dark, petting the retriever. What if he ended up dating Ellen? How weird would it be that I'd spent the night at his house? And also: Why did I keep finding myself reliving a perennial scene from my marriage, the man snoring soundly while I lay awake steeped in self-recrimination? All that had changed was the location of the bedroom.

The clock said 4:00 a.m. I slowly got out of bed, collected

my shoes, and tiptoed to the front door, where I petted the dog goodbye.

Fall is San Francisco's warmest time of year, and the air was caressing and tropical. I walked barefoot for a few blocks and emerged onto Columbus. The shuttered bakeries, shops, and cafés stood silent, the street deserted except for the occasional passing car. No distant sirens, no cabs, not a person in sight. When I started coming to San Francisco in my twenties, with my ex-boyfriend and later Scott or my friends, we always ended up in North Beach. I'd traversed Columbus a hundred times with the crowds. In my thirties, while living in Sacramento and then Philadelphia, I had a recurring dream: I was walking through a blacked-out San Francisco alone at night, up one hill and down another. I couldn't find a soul. All I could make out were the darkened windows of the buildings I passed and, as I crested each hill, the lights on the two behemoth bridges out in the vast expanse of water. I'd awaken from the dream frightened and lonely. Now that it had come true, I felt nothing but the intrepid joy of solitude.

Shoes in hand, I turned down Columbus and headed toward SoMa, wondering if I could walk two miles barefoot on asphalt.

18

Orgasmic Meditation

I WALKED INTO ONETASTE for the weekly Wednesday night In-Group and immediately sensed a difference. The downstairs room, where everyone gathered beforehand, went lopsided, its locus tilted to a corner where a tall, long-haired woman sat talking with a few others. I recognized her as Nicole, the founder, and even though people scattered about the room, all eyes aimed in her direction like compass needles leaning north.

Eventually we came within each other's orbit. It was hard not to stare. Her beauty was classic enough to surpass most women's yet unique enough to warrant inspection. She was of Sicilian stock, lithe, olive-skinned, and almost golden-haired, dressed in expensive jeans, high heels, and a silky blue top.

"Nicole, this is Robin," Noah said. They were friends from way back, before OneTaste.

She reached out a tapered hand, the ring finger adorned in a thin band of diamonds shaped like an X, and offered a hearty handshake. "Oh, I've heard a lot about *you*," she said, beaming. Her strong Roman features sat slightly off-kilter, and she spoke with the tiniest hint of a lisp. These imperfections only added charm.

"I've heard a lot about you, too," I said. The few articles published about OneTaste painted a somewhat murky portrait of her past: She had studied semantics and Buddhism, been married and divorced, and suffered a kind of breakdown in her late twenties after the death of her father. All this brought her to the hands of octogenarian Ray Vetterlein, a holdover from the seventies sex-commune scene in California, who took her under his wing and taught her about orgasm.

The remainder of what I knew I'd gathered piecemeal. I'd heard, for instance, she was currently on a macrobiotic diet, and noted that some others were trying it too. Several of the female instructors tended to dress like her. The group sessions she led were called darshans, the term traditionally used by Hindu gurus. Most strikingly, she had coined the highly specialized language used at OneTaste, which nearly everyone mimicked. Positive attention of any kind was an "upstroke," negative attention a "downstroke," and feelings of attachment were "limbic resonance." She preached the long-neglected virtues of the mammalian limbic brain as opposed to the rational cerebral cortex. Whatever she posted on Facebook, OneTaste members echoed word for word, thought ripples on a lake.

I barely recall the rest of that first brief meeting, perhaps because I tried to just stand my ground and not give in to the general swoon. The only swoon I craved happened in the bedroom, far from the realm of language and the power of naming.

After she left, I turned to Noah.

"She reminds me of someone historical," I said. "I know, Helen of Troy. The face that launched a thousand ships."

"I think of her more as Hector," he said. "The warrior."

Though I disliked the guru aura that surrounded Nicole, and the groupthink of OneTaste in general, neither worried me enough to quell my curiosity. My time in twelve-step groups had taught me to "take what you like and leave the rest." There was a lot to like. The more I learned about orgasmic meditation, the more I realized that it wasn't just some fifteen-minute endeavor in getting off. It was an actual meditation. Just as mindfulness meditation focused on the breath or transcendental meditation on a mantra, OM focused on the physical sensations of placing a finger on the clitoris. Nicole's aim was to make sexuality more attentive and thus nourishing. And while OneTaste also occasionally taught a male version of OM in which you stroked the penis, for the most part OMing focused on the clitoris for a definite reason: It was harder for women to consistently express their desire and act on it. If a woman's hunger could be tapped through OM, however, both partners would benefit. Nicole put forth OM as a counterweight to what she called the porn model of sex: penis-driven, full of verbal gymnastics and fantasy, high-speed and high-pressured. She claimed that women wanted as much sex as men did, just not the "sex that was on the menu." Porn sex.

Actually, I wanted both: the quiet, attentive, clitoris-oriented sex I routinely enjoyed with Scott and the fast, hard, dirty-talking sex I'd experienced with several lovers. The first pleasured me physically but lacked a certain penetrative force. The second left me ravished but its satisfactions proved more psychological than physical.

I wasn't in any rush to give up my fantasies, either. Every now and then, if I was close to coming and in just the right mood, I'd nudge myself over the edge by calling up a huge cock, often belonging to a beautiful black man, and a woman or two to share it with me. As I aged I noticed that the men in my fantasies aged with me but the women remained young and firm. They were physically ideal and ready to go, their abundant sexual energy nothing like my own ebbs and flows. They never looked like anyone I knew—it was all six-packs and spray tans—and

I could add players in as necessary. It made me feel shallow, even ashamed, to get off on such clichés but I kept them on call anyway like little imaginary friends, just in case. My orgasm fairies.

OMing aimed to remove all those extra layers and strip the experience down to mere sensation. I wondered what it could teach me about my moody little clitoris, some days ready to climax within minutes, other days shy and withdrawn, some days so sensitive I could barely tolerate first contact, even under my own fingers. Its relationship to my mind and heart intrigued me: how I'd climaxed so immediately with Alden but rarely with others, how I'd come the moment I'd mounted Andrew like a dominatrix, even while assuming it was ravishment I'd wanted. Was it hormones, emotional realities, or something altogether more mysterious that governed my orgasm? Soon, I found myself doing exactly what I'd told Noah I wouldn't do: taking my pants off in a room full of people.

I signed up for the Body workshop, the one that taught how to OM. My assigned partner was a pleasant-looking man in his forties. Noah showed the class, about thirty of us, how to set up what he called a nest for the OM: yoga mat underneath, pillow for the head, bolsters to support the legs, blanket, hand towel, rubber gloves, and a jar of OneTaste's homemade lube at the ready.

The nest complete, there was nothing to do but undress. Simultaneously, all the women's white thighs appeared, which made taking off my own jeans easier than I'd anticipated. I put them aside, lay down, quickly slid down my panties, and opened my knees onto the bolsters, hands resting on my abdomen. My partner sat to my right and put the white gloves on. Using his iPhone as a timer, Noah instructed us to start.

My partner dipped his finger into the lube and gently smeared it over my clitoris, then began nudging along the top edge of it. I closed my eyes and focused. It felt good the way a light breeze or warm sunshine feels good against the skin, nothing more. Every so often, a stroke ignited some tiny pathway of deeper pleasure, which gained intensity for a minute or so before plateauing. Noah walked about, coaching the strokers on touching as slowly and lightly as possible. The real luxury was mental: the absence of any goal or pressure. I needn't moan, grind, instruct, or reciprocate. I was free to lie back and simply feel. After fifteen minutes, Noah rang a meditation bell. I sat up, and my partner and I reported our sensations to each other, a post-OM exchange they called "frames."

"My finger and forearm filled with energy, almost like electricity," he said.

"This warm sensation kept building and spreading out in me, and then it would level off."

As I slipped back into my jeans, I thought of the second-to-last time I'd seen Alden. Lying on his lap in Twin Peaks, my legs open to his silent, barely perceptible touch—a touch nearly identical to what I'd just experienced. Yet Alden had produced in me what I could only call a spiritual experience, whereas OM had produced mere pleasantness.

According to Nicole, that type of neutral, friendly exchange was the whole point, a kind of clitoral laboratory in which to explore sensation free from entanglement and story. But the allure of physical pleasure without story, without a context or a narrative, escaped me.

Naturally, I asked Scott to try orgasmic meditation. Not that he needed more education in the workings of my clitoris. I just wanted to see what it would feel like to pay such close attention with someone I trusted.

I waited until Sunday afternoon, a day when we typically made love. I lay on the bed reading as he showered. When he came into the bedroom I put the book down, trying to maneuver my way past the historical futility I felt at asking him to try anything new.

"You know how you said you didn't really want to come with me to OneTaste, that I should go and let you know what I learn?"

"Yeah," he said, sliding out of a towel and into boxers.

"How about we try orgasmic meditation? They taught it to us in the last workshop. I could show you."

He scratched his nose. I could see him searching for a way out. I wanted to scream but I stayed silent.

"If you want," he said.

I lay down on the bed and propped pillows under my knees, showing him where to sit and which finger to use with the lube.

"This edge right here, one o'clock if you're facing it, is supposed to be the sweet spot," I said. It was amazing how embarrassed I could feel with my own husband. I couldn't tell if it was because I had a pathological aversion to intimacy or because his own inhibition had rubbed off on me. And, as always, because I might be the source of the problem, I had no choice but to keep trying.

He began stroking the spot, focusing his eyes not on my face nor on my pussy but a foot or two away on the bed. I closed mine.

"A little lighter," I said. OneTaste called this "asking for an adjustment." If I did it too many times during actual sex, Scott winced. "It ruins my mood when you do that," he'd said. But I figured this was different; this was an experiment.

He lightened up for a few seconds, then returned to his initial pressure.

"A little lighter," I said, scooching my hips a half inch away instinctively.

He repeated the cycle, lighter and then back to the pressure he wanted. Anger shot through me, followed by fear of expressing it, followed by sadness. In the end I simply checked out, waiting for the fifteen minutes to pass, trying to squelch my sense of failure. When it was done, I sat up and sighed. "You didn't seem all that into it," I said.

He shrugged. "I don't really feel like doing the same things you do with other guys at OneTaste."

"But you didn't want to come to OneTaste with me either. You told me to go alone."

"Oh, darling," he said. "Some days I feel like I could keep doing this, and other days I feel like I could just do something else."

"By this, you mean our marriage."

"Yes."

I could feel him willing me back into a place where my needs went unmet and I bore it mostly with a smile, blowing up every two years or so and asking for a divorce only to retract it immediately. Or was that actually some part of me advocating complaisance? I could never tell for sure.

It felt impossible to get what I wanted from one man. I had safety and love with Scott. Penetration and intensity with Alden. Childlike joy and adventure with Paul. All the goalless clitoral attention I could take from strangers at OneTaste. Maybe Nicole was right and monogamy was the problem. More likely, the Buddhists were right and desire itself was the problem: continually blooming, branching out, and curling into byzantine patterns to keep you fascinated and stuck.

I shrunk from that conclusion and from my own kneejerk reaction to get back in line and behave myself. Labyrinthine as my desire might be, I planned to follow it to its end.

———

Nicole apparently didn't have a problem reconciling the Buddhists to the desire-driven masses. At the Mind workshop, two dozen of us sat on the floor in a circle while she spoke for hours on end. Midday, she invited a saffron-robed monk to lead us in meditation. I gathered that she wanted to imbue orgasmic meditation with the same single-point focus the Buddhists used, but I hadn't come to a sexual education center in order to be lectured by one more celibate man. When Nicole made a point about inhabiting the body fully, I raised my hand and, gesturing to the silent monk, asked, "Is *he* fully inhabiting his body?"

She paused. "You," she said, pointing at me and narrowing her eyes. "You have a good mind. I like your mind." She often disarmed me with a much softer response than I expected. I don't recall her answer about the monk, just the afterglow of her compliment.

At another workshop, we lay on our backs and did holotropic breathwork, inhaling and exhaling fast and deep for several minutes while tribal drum music thumped through the speakers. Quite soon the hyperventilation made the room spin and my extremities go numb. People around me pounded the floor, danced wildly, and sobbed. I fell into a mildly psychedelic state that ended with me curled on my side, crying quietly because I missed my mother, an emotion I rarely let myself express.

One of the key beliefs at OneTaste was that all relationship, all communication was a game—an infinite game. The phrase came from the book *Finite and Infinite Games* by the religious scholar James Carse, which we once spent an entire Saturday exploring. Instead of viewing relationships as having beginnings and endings, winners and losers, OneTaste saw them as neverending, with continually evolving rules crafted solely for the purpose of play itself. One of their core mantras was "We remain connected no matter what." Relationships were like matter; they never disappeared, only changed form.

Some of their beliefs struck a chord of truth in me, while others rang completely random. The curious thing was that regardless of whether I agreed with the dogma, I almost always left OneTaste feeling light and alert, as if I'd been washed from the inside. Whatever else they were doing, the verbal and tactile intimacy rejuvenated me.

19

Yin and Yang

IN PACIFIC HEIGHTS, Ellen and I sat around a dinner table with a half dozen friends, all stylish designers and fashion editors in their late thirties. My favorite was a woman named Monica who was visiting from Brazil. She wrapped up a long story about the demise of her latest relationship by concluding, "I just want someone to pull my hair and slap my ass! Is that too much to ask?" Everyone laughed.

After dinner, I found myself alone with Monica at the kitchen sink. "I know how you feel about the hair pulling and ass slapping," I said.

"I call it the Club. The girls who like it a little rough." She winked at me.

"I think I'm a member."

"Of course you are. All the strong-willed chicks are."

"I mean, nothing too crazy. Just a little show of force. I want to know he has the *balls* to slap me. You know?"

"You want to know he's up for handling you."

"Right. And the dirty talk. I want to know he's not editing himself."

"Ugh, this last one was quiet as a mouse." She shook her head in disapproval.

"For some reason I'm attracting a lot of dirty talkers these days."

"Good for you! Send some my way."

Somewhere at a university or think tank, I imagined a feminist scholar, a woman smarter and less self-centered than Monica or me, tsk-tsking, theorizing about our regressive need to play out submission fantasies now that we'd achieved real emotional and financial power. She reminded me about the African teenagers still subjected to clitoral castration and the suspected adulteresses stoned to death in the squares of Afghanistan. And here we were, the luckiest women on earth, indulging our little power games instead of volunteering to help our sisters overseas.

Those Afghan women hidden under their burqas haunted me in deeper ways, too. Sometimes, in the midst of answering a Nerve.com ad or swooping into OneTaste for a sexy workshop, a hint of physical danger would sluice through me, barely perceptible unless I paused to pay attention. When I did, I felt a horrific truth running beneath the surface of my actions: a woman somewhere was being beaten or even killed right now for doing what I was so casually doing. A mere stroke of geographic and historical luck had placed me in one of the relatively few locations on the planet where I could safely explore the boundaries of an infidelity taboo running so deep it had resulted in women's exile, torture, and murder for centuries.

The only time I remember my dad following through on his threats to beat my mother, I was nine years old. I wasn't there when it happened, but a few hours later, when my grandfather's car pulled up to our house from the hospital, I sprinted down the front steps toward her and saw the line of thick black stitches holding the swollen skin above her eye closed. Two inches of black thread edged in dried blood. It sliced the world open and revealed the truth, the terrible power that underlay his rage—

the power of enforcement. They fought daily, about everything. What made this fight different was that he had accused her of cheating.

So I didn't take my predilection for ass-slapping or hair-pulling lightly. Sometimes upon entering our Sanchez Street house on a Friday night, I'd stand in the foyer very still, waiting for Scott to walk down the hallway, measuring his gait, his expression, to see if he was going to put up with me one more day or if today was the day he'd decide to put his foot down. When he invariably drew me into a hug, I'd grasp his waist—surprised, delighted, guilty, ashamed.

Soon after Alden cut off contact, I'd joined an online group called the Deida Connection that resembled a small, private Facebook with only two hundred or so members. On the home page, forums offered admission to topics such as nurturing feminine radiance, following masculine purpose, and progressing through Deida's three stages of relationship: dependence, independence, and polarity. Deida himself never appeared on the site, at least to my knowledge, though his books were oft quoted. "The feminine wants to be seen and adored," Deida wrote. "It longs to open."

Every time I logged on, I was jolted by the same one-two punch of attraction and aversion, starting with his breakdown of masculine consciousness and feminine light. When I sat still and searched for this feminine core of mine, to see if it was real, I found it easy to locate: a presence shimmering in the center of my body, not up my spine but farther forward, from vagina to belly through heart and throat. It didn't run up into my head, but pulsed with its own awareness, as if the functions of the brain had been pulled down into the gut. Reaching out in all directions, it sought pleasure, union, solace. Instinctual, but not indiscriminate. Exquisitely perceptive, its tenderness girded by an acute sense of justice.

That was the shape of my femaleness as I experienced it first-hand. And it could not be further from light. It was the essence of darkness: like soil, ocean depths, deep space. Where had Deida gotten his interpretation of the feminine as light, and how would he know, given the fact that he lived in a male body?

I also wondered about his downright Freudian orgasm theory. According to him, clitoral ones were nice but unevolved. Vaginal—that is, G-spot—climaxes were deeper and more satisfying. The holy grail was the cervical orgasm, a womb- and heart-opening explosion that could be achieved only after at least forty-five minutes of steady intercourse with a highly skilled partner. These were the kind of boundary-melting paroxysms that could "fuck you open to God," as Deida liked to put it. Whether the vaginal orgasms I'd experienced with Scott and Alden originated at the G-spot or cervix, I had no idea. But they were, in fact, more memorable and transformative, deepening my relationship to each man in a split second.

I trusted Deida only slightly more than I'd trust any man who graded women's orgasms, but he described something I longed for so fervently that I couldn't write him off. I kept coming back around to his quote about the feminine's calling *to love and to be seen*. I thought of the men with whom I'd relished the roles of nurturer and object of desire. Half the joy of the project was feeding their hungry need, as if I embodied the most cherished of resources. It made me feel appreciated in a way that went far beyond vanity or learned objectification; it felt primal and wholesome.

Deida's constructs might be nothing more than a tantric-clothed ruse to bolster men's egos post-feminism, men who found it difficult to deal with all the various aspects of a woman, not just the soft, wet parts. But like it or not, he was right about one thing: I wanted to open.

20

Golden Gate

I'D NOTICED LIAM on occasion in the halls of OneTaste—he had the kind of looks that drew the eye—but this same beauty kept me from paying much attention. The football captain, the beau of the class, the most eligible bachelor had never made it onto my radar. Their splendor intimidated me, so I simply ignored them.

When Liam friended me on Facebook—his profile photo all angled jaw and smoldering eyes—then made conversation at OneTaste, I thought little of it. Everyone flirted and OMed and made out interchangeably. Then there was the fact that he was twenty-five. People who knew little of OneTaste tended to imagine old, desperate men, or younger, timid ones, gathering round to touch the private parts of women who were only semiattractive. They were wrong. The place was teeming with handsome, well-employed men in their twenties and their feminine counterparts: long-haired beauties sitting on the hot seat talking about their world travels, tattoos peeking out from collars and sleeves. Several looked too young to even be there, diving headfirst into a sexuality still in its formative stages. Hell, *my* sexuality was still in its formative stages, and I was forty-four.

On Facebook, Liam and I talked music. We texted. He sent me several iTunes and I reciprocated. He was a newly minted chef, raised by liberal parents in Los Angeles, and had been meditating since puberty. Experimental communities were no big deal to him.

He flirted, pulled back, flirted, pulled back. By the time he asked me to dinner, it was nearly Christmas. I met him outside the Bluxome lobby door and we walked, hands in pockets, a few blocks away for Thai food. I ordered a glass of wine and he ordered tea. He didn't drink.

"I get panic attacks," he said casually, "and alcohol makes them worse." It had taken me until age thirty-nine to admit to my panic attacks without shame.

"I've had them since I was twelve," I said. "Bad. They wake me up at three a.m."

"Do you sweat and puke and all that?"

"Sweating, intense nausea, palpitations. If I try to sit or stand up, I faint. Then when it's over, horrible chills. When the chills come I know I'm home free."

"Oh, I puke. I do the whole routine. It can last for hours."

"They can be really isolating," I said. "If you're ever in the midst of one and you need help calming down, you can call me."

"Thanks. Sometimes I think it's just that I'm holding too much energy in my body. Too much sensation."

It was strange to hear that much vulnerability coming from an athletic-looking man. He embraced such contrasts. He was equally interested in Zen meditation and sensual pleasure. He alternated sensitivity with an edge of bravado; when I asked if he liked a song I'd sent him, he said, "Yes, but I like music more when I discover it myself."

Back at his car, I asked, "So where are you heading now?"

"Nowhere. I want to come up and see your place."

That was the moment when the mature forty-four-year-old

who acted maternally toward Liam began switching places with the fevered eighteen-year-old who couldn't believe what was happening.

He sat on the edge of my bed. I put Wilco's *A Ghost Is Born* on the CD player, forwarded a few tracks to "Muzzle of Bees," and settled into the small love seat about four feet away. We listened awhile in silence as the song slowly built from contemplative to rousing layers of guitarwork. "Listen to this," I said, holding a finger up just as Nels Cline launched into the climactic solo. Liam closed his eyes and didn't open them until the song was finished.

"If electricity could have sex, that's what it would sound like," he said.

I laughed. "That's one of the best descriptions of Wilco I've ever heard." But his sternum tensed and his forehead wrinkled.

"What's wrong?" I asked.

"I'm having a dilemma."

"What's the dilemma?"

"I'm very attracted to you, but I fear losing your approval."

He was very attracted. To me.

"How would you lose my approval?"

"By pulling back after we get physical. When it comes to women, I want to get what I want and then get out."

I couldn't help smiling.

"Me too, Liam. I wouldn't worry about it. I'm in an open marriage, but I'm still married." I held up my wedding ring finger.

His face relaxed and brightened.

"But I'm not going to initiate," I said. "I'm old enough to be your mother, and . . . I don't want to feel like a cougar."

"But I like older women."

"Still."

"We could talk it to death," he said.

"No, let's not do that."

"I've made a decision," he announced after a few more seconds of silence. "I'm coming over there."

He's coming over here. My mortality-stricken midlife self had somehow succeeded in snagging this gift to my inner teenager. I could feel myself getting younger by the second.

He sat down next to me and took my hands in his. He leaned in close and paused a full ten seconds near my lips, which drove me wild. His kisses probed in a tentative, youthful way. When I turned his chin in my hand and began nibbling his ear, he moaned.

"I have to run down to my car for condoms," he said.

"I have some here." I reached toward the bedside drawer.

"Those won't work. I've got extra large ones in my car."

"Oh." I tried not to clap.

He returned emboldened, tossing four black-packaged rubbers with gold lettering on the nightstand. "You smell so good," he said, sliding his hand under my blouse. "You're the softest thing I've ever touched." He took off his shirt, and I stopped to gaze at him: flawless, Platonic. What power flesh wielded, how easily it could incite worship.

"Touch me," he said, and after I had spent a while doing so, "Tell me what to do." I couldn't think how to answer him. If I were honest I would have said, "You don't have to do anything. Just lie back and approve of me. Retroactively reclassify me from the smart girl to the sexy one."

I sat him up on the edge of the bed and knelt in front of him. As I explored his cock from tip to base, he covered his face with his hands. "Everything you're doing is perfect," he said. Yes, that's what I was looking for. Before long, he opened the condom and put it on. I climbed onto him carefully, worried it would hurt, but it didn't. I moved slowly, worried he'd come too fast. For the first time ever during sex, I worried what my breasts looked like. He sat up and wrapped his arms around my waist. "You turn me on so much," he said. Bingo. Here I was, a full thirty years after a youth in which I'd never felt pretty or thin enough, in bed with the masculine ideal, and *I turned him on*. He got on top, held my hands down, and came. From start to finish it lasted all of ten minutes. He was the only lover with whom I practically remained silent.

Suddenly we were getting dressed. I immediately regretted not taking the lead and slowing it down.

I put another CD on. I could sense he was itching to leave. When he said he wanted to get in and get out, I didn't think he meant in the scope of twenty minutes. As he zipped his jacket, he motioned with his chin toward the condoms and said, "I'm going to leave the rest here. Save them for me, okay?"

When the door closed behind him, I was hungrier than when he first walked in. If there was any encounter during the project that should have made me feel used, it was this one. And yet I felt the opposite: like I'd used him, and not even very well.

On the Deida Connection, I started up friendships with women and men living in Scandinavia, Australia, Italy, India, and all over the United States. As I browsed through members' profile pages, I came across a face I recognized: Susan's former sister-in-law Val, now divorced and living in Los Angeles. I'd met Val a few times way back in Sacramento and reconnected with her now online. I also stumbled across a Virginia woman I knew from Mama Gena's. What a small world this Deida tribe was. Then, scanning through profile photos one day, my hand froze on the keyboard. A close-up of a male forearm emblazoned with a tattoo of a snake. I clicked on it and Alden's page came up. It was empty: no personal data, blog entries, or additional photos.

I took my hands off the mouse pad and sat motionless. Just

looking at the purple swirls of his tattoo caused my arms to go cold and my chest to constrict. I wondered if he'd gone browsing too and seen my photo, my blog posts about nonmonogamy and how I often felt as penetrated by good music as by sex.

I took Alden's note out of my prayer box and read it over. "I hope you find what you're looking for." I slipped it back into the envelope, turned it over, and stared at the small, tight curlicues of his return address and my name. I got a matchbook and a stainless steel bowl and set the corner of the envelope aflame, waiting until it had shriveled to black before dropping the charred remains into the bowl. I scooped the remains into a plastic baggie, drove across town to the Golden Gate Bridge, parked the car, and headed out onto the walkway with the Sunday tourists. Walkers used the eastbound side of the bridge, which faced the bay and city, and cyclists used the westbound lane, facing the Pacific. As I made my way to the bridge's midspan among kids and parents and grandparents, six lanes of fast traffic swishing by us all, a yellow emergency phone about a quarter mile out urged potential jumpers to push a large red button for help. "There Is Hope," it read. "Make the Call." About two dozen people a year ignored the sign and went over the edge, the epic skyline the last thing they saw.

A half mile in, I turned toward the city, leaned as far over the rail as I safely could, and emptied the ashes into a headwind that blew most of them straight back onto me. Only a small twirl of dust spiraled down away from the orange railing toward the water.

21

The Women's Circle

WHEN I WAS TWENTY-FIVE YEARS OLD, I stumbled across a slim book called *Circle of Stones* in the feminist bookstore in Midtown Sacramento. It contained nothing more than vignettes describing women gathering into circles to speak of their lives. In the primeval images the author drew, elders sat as witnesses and guides for women entering menarche or menopause, pregnant mothers, women suffering through loss. Interspersed between the impressionistic chapters were meditations that each began "How might your life have been different . . . ?"

> *HOW MIGHT YOUR LIFE HAVE BEEN DIFFERENT IF, AS A YOUNG WOMAN, THERE WAS A PLACE YOU COULD GO WHEN YOU HAD FEELINGS OF DARKNESS? AND IF THERE HAD BEEN ANOTHER WOMAN, SOMEWHAT OLDER, TO BE WITH YOU IN YOUR DARKNESS . . . SO THAT, OVER THE YEARS, CHAMPIONED BY THE WOMAN, YOU LEARNED TO NO LONGER FEAR YOUR DARKNESS, BUT TO TRUST IT . . . TO TRUST IT AS THE PLACE WHERE YOU COULD MEET*

YOUR OWN DEEPEST NATURE AND GIVE IT VOICE. HOW
MIGHT YOUR LIFE BE DIFFERENT IF YOU COULD TRUST
YOUR OWN DARKNESS?

The vision haunted me. It came to me during my lowest lows, when I was alone on a gurney awaiting surgery, praying for my dad in rehab, struggling not to be rendered housebound by anxiety. In my mind's eye I saw a group of women seated in a warm cave near its entrance, night gathering outside beyond distant mountains. In the circle sat teenage girls, women in their prime, and fat old ladies, their silver hair plaited into long braids. Among them sat my mother, grandmothers, and great-grandmothers—not the smiling faces in family photos, hair curled and lips painted en route to some special occasion, but their essential selves, stripped of finery and social mores, freed from all circumstances of history. The women in the cave could bear anything. No terror was too engulfing, no truth too painful, no rage too calamitous for them to hold. They carried a wisdom found nowhere else.

I looked for some semblance of this cave intermittently for decades—healing circles, women's group therapy, meetings of outcast neo-pagans looking like they'd just returned from a Renaissance Faire. By the time I hit my forties I gave up. Nowhere, it seemed, could I find what I needed: a place where the emotions that ran through me were not analyzed or transcended but simply expressed and contained. A place where I could contact an aspect of the divine that didn't come attached to a male visage. Yahweh, Buddha, Bill W., Carl Jung, even Jesus—each of them glorious in his own way, each of their systems invariably putting me at a certain remove.

My search wasn't polemical. I told no one. I just quietly ached for a spiritual practice guided by the feminine. I had a book of candle spells written by a half-crazy Hungarian witch, a figurine of the heavy-breasted Venus of Willendorf, and a vague but indelible knowledge that I was somehow connected to an ethos that predated every book of rules and myths ever written by a man. I had resigned myself to let these suffice.

Imagine my surprise when David Deida, of all people, led me—albeit indirectly—to just such a practice. I learned about one of Deida's assistants, a San Francisco woman named Sabrina, who held women's circles at her home. Because of her link to Deida I was half expecting instruction on relating to men, how to increase polarity, or some such. Instead, the moment I set foot in a large room inside her Castro flat, I felt the metaphorical cave close in around me.

A dozen women gathered on embroidered cushions arranged on the floor in a circle. Colorful silk depictions of Hindu goddesses hung from the orange walls. In the center of the circle, a small black statue of a fertility goddess stood enshrined in a golden veil. The women ranged in age from their twenties to their sixties, some dressed in jeans, some in yoga pants and florid tops. Soft instrumental music with an underlying world beat played in the background.

Sabrina, in her early fifties, was the most beautiful woman I'd ever seen of that age. Of Asian descent, petite as a dancer, she had flawless cocoa skin, lustrous black hair, dark eyes, and billowy lips that framed a wide smile. Her radiance was far from delicate, however. Small and soft as she appeared, her eyes and posture emanated quiet strength. She spoke in a low, melodious voice and allowed herself long pauses, during which she'd look slowly around the circle, gazing at each woman in turn. There was something of the jungle cat in her.

After we introduced ourselves, Sabrina had us stand. She turned the music up and told us to breathe, unwind, and move around however we wanted. "Make sounds," she said. "Let go of any energy stored up from your day." Some women gently stretched, others began to sway to the music. As I closed my eyes, I immediately felt where my body was tense. I shrugged my shoulders, rolled my neck in circles, bent forward to loosen my lower back, stretched my jaw wide.

Once we relaxed, Sabrina looked around the circle and paired us up. My partner was Natalie, a woman about my age with a thin, pretty face and square black glasses. She was dressed unassumingly in jeans and a long-sleeved T-shirt. Sabrina instructed us to gaze at each other—each looking into the other's left eye only, which made it easier to focus—and breathe.

After an initial wave of nervous laughter, Natalie and I settled in comfortably. Without the usual words, expressions, and gestures, my mind scrambled for something to occupy it. I had to keep returning to her eyes and my own breathing, like a shared meditation. After a few minutes, Sabrina instructed the woman with the curlier hair (me) to go first. I would "feel into" Natalie and tell her what I sensed residing in her heart.

This scared me. I knew nothing of Natalie except that she was from the East Bay and wasn't wearing a wedding ring. Sabrina said, "Instead of thinking, instead of assessing your partner or analyzing her, *feel* her. Use your own body and heart to feel into her body and heart. Speak from your body, not your mind. Don't worry about saying the wrong thing. If she's okay with it, you can also touch her. Go ahead and speak to her now."

It was like diving into a pool not knowing if the water was shallow or deep, warm or cold. Without a clue, I took a breath and dove into Natalie. The locus of my awareness switched from her eyes to her chest and belly. My first words came without thinking. "You've taken care of many people," I said. Then: "You're a mother to many." As soon as I uttered a sentence, the next one became clear. "Your wisdom is strong. Others seek you out for it." Her dark eyes moistened. Once I silenced my mind and homed

in on her with my senses, it wasn't at all difficult to see the stiffness in her jaw, the sadness in her smile, the thicket of frustration
tangled in her throat. "May I touch you?" I asked. She nodded
yes. I placed my palms on her hips and applied gentle pressure,
rolling them slightly right and left, then placed one hand on her
abdomen and another on her lower back. She closed her eyes.

"I feel like your energy wants to move here," I said. "It wants
to flow. You help others do this and now you want to help yourself." As I guided her hips slowly left and right, back and forth,
she bent her knees and let her chin drop to her chest, her long
hair falling over her face.

I can't recall what Natalie said about me when her turn came.
I do know that by the time we stopped, my nervous system had
softened to the point where every small ache, tension, or worry
had dissolved. Natalie and I hugged, not a social pat or an overly
empathic new-age squeeze but the long, relaxed embrace of old
friends. She told me she was a midwife. As we reassembled into
the original circle, I saw that all the women's faces had eased into
soft, authentic smiles. Their bodies swayed ever so slightly in a
buoyant warmth that suffused the room, a flock of mermaids
come home to a welcoming ocean.

For the next nine months, I spent every other Monday night at
Sabrina's doing some variation of that initial encounter with Natalie. We gave each woman two short minutes to speak her feelings, then gathered round to put our hands on her as she cried or
moaned or laughed. We danced, sang, rolled on the floor, pounded
our fists. We took ten-minute breaks to drink tea and eat fruit in
silence. When it was my turn, I usually went still, bowed my
head, and focused downward, wincing as I drilled for what lay
buried. Soon, I became familiar with the mundane layers through
which I had to plow for the truth: the weariness of work, the
burden of obligation, crankiness, resistance. As I squirmed my
way through these, I inevitably unearthed seething anger, and

below that grief, and below that a pure longing that quickly resolved itself into love. The energy could turn on a dime, carnivorous growls to innocent tears. Once I clawed at the collar of my shirt so violently that I popped five buttons off it. Another time I unintentionally knocked the black goddess statue to the ground, threatening to torch her ornamental scarf in a nearby candle.

Sabrina's circle showed me how to recognize my own intuition, a tug inside my solar plexus leaning left or right, yes or no, like a divining rod. While chronic fatigue had taught me to observe my emotions in stillness, the circle taught me how to move them through. "Emotional energy only becomes a problem when it gets stuck," Sabrina said. Instead of trying to lock down anger or sadness with lengthy explanations and judgments, I expressed them bodily, which took all of about thirty seconds.

The circle showed me what it looked like to trust women, not only to keep my secrets, listen to my problems, or chatter away happily over cocktails, but to nourish me and let me nourish them. In her circle I accessed the deepest part of myself directly, stripped of even the strongest archetypes—Wife, Lover, Mother. I learned I didn't need a man or a child in order to experience true womanhood.

That central lesson, though, hadn't yet registered when I first walked into Sabrina's in January. As February 1 approached, the deadline I'd set with Scott to reassess things, I wasn't ready to end the project. If I was going to return to monogamy, there were still a few things I needed to experience, like sleeping with a woman and having a threesome. I worried about telling Scott that I wanted to extend it a little longer. Over breakfast in our dining room one Sunday, I got up the courage and said, "February is right around the corner. What would you think about going to May first with the project, and making it a solid year?"

He looked up from his eggs and paper. "Yeah." He nodded. "I'm good with that. May first is good."

"Really?"

"Yeah. One year is a nice round number."

"And then it'll be over and done," I said, taken aback.

"Well, yes, but I'm imagining there'll be an adjustment period. It might take a while for things to get back to normal."

I nodded, and he went back to his paper.

We spent the following weekend in Yosemite, one of Scott's favorite places. He'd taken me there early in our relationship and we'd returned several times, always in winter because he hated the summer crowds. We hiked in the snow, read in the Ahwahnee Hotel's grand sitting room next to the roaring fireplace, and ate in the pitched-timber dining hall looking out at Half Dome. On the way home, as Scott was outside pumping gas, his BlackBerry beeped on the console. It was a text message from a South Bay area code. The phone was three inches from my hand. All I had to do was push one little button to see the content. A photo appeared of a pretty redhead in a black turtleneck, black miniskirt, and black stilettos sitting cross-legged and leaning suggestively so as to accentuate her curves. Her heart-shaped face, porcelain skin, and smiling apple red lips appeared to be a good several years younger than mine. Below the photo she had typed simply, *xo, Charly*.

I glanced back at Scott, his breath visible in the January air, the gas pump still running. I hit the End button on his phone, returning it to the home screen, and the little red text indicator shut off.

He replaced the pump and got back into the car, blowing on his hands before starting it. He pulled out through the slushy parking lot onto the small highway that connected Yosemite to I-5. Over the past eighteen years, we must have driven a hundred back roads like this one. We'd once spent the summer solstice weekend driving his antique Dart convertible from Sacramento through Nevada to Salt Lake City, down through Zion National Park to Vegas, and back up through California in a 1,600-mile loop. We'd driven a Winnebago across the country four times, through thirty-seven states, taking a different road each time.

As we made our way through the snowy foothills down into the flatlands of the Central Valley, I put my hand over Scott's on the console. He smiled.

"I'm looking forward to being home tonight," I said, leaning my head against the seat and closing my eyes.

He squeezed my hand. "Me too, kitty."

22

The Commune

MOST PEOPLE WHO CHOOSE TO LIVE at a commune probably do it for reasons more freewheeling than economics. For me, the cheap rent at OneTaste—only eight hundred dollars a month for a tiny room of my own, half of what I was paying for the Bluxome studio—is what cemented the deal. I reasoned that for the project's final phase, I could at least lessen the economic impact to our household if not the emotional one.

By this time, OneTaste had abandoned the open-style loft I'd read about in the newspaper and begun refurbishing a three-floor single-residency hotel next to the workshop center on Folsom Street. Beneath its new coat of paint, its elegant prewar bones were apparent in the hallway wainscoting and doorway moldings. The rooms varied in size, though most were like mine, big enough to fit a bed, small dresser, and not much else. Each floor had two old-fashioned water closets and one recently installed unisex bathroom where three people could shower at once across from a long mirrored vanity.

On a quiet Saturday afternoon, I packed up my single carload of clothes and books, said goodbye to the Bluxome studio, and drove with Scott to OneTaste to unload my things. It was strange to have him there. Lots of couples, monogamous and otherwise, attended OneTaste workshops together, but each time I'd asked him to come, he'd said no. His disinterest had frustrated me at first but by now actually caused me relief.

Few people were around. As Scott screwed together the rods of a clothing rack while I unpacked boxes, Roman walked by my open doorway and stopped. Only twenty-eight, he was Scott's height but beefier, and his ominous neck tattoo had failed to add an iota of menace to his cheerful face. He wore paint-splattered jeans and big suede work boots. I'd once seen Grace demonstrate the male version of orgasmic meditation on a supine Roman, slathering his penis in lube and kneading it gently with both hands until it hardened to its full impressive height and girth, his torso rising involuntarily off the table, jaw and biceps clenched. Afterward, when we took turns sharing our impressions of what we'd witnessed, I'd voiced the first image that came to me: "Primordial man rising from the ooze."

"Hi," Roman said, leaning against the doorjamb.

"Hey, Roman," I said, my heart suddenly thumping. Scott looked up from the clothes rack, screwdriver in hand.

"Roman, this is my husband, Scott. Roman lives here with his fiancée."

"Howdy." Scott nodded.

"Great to meet you, Scott," Roman said. "You guys let me know if you need anything, okay?"

"Will do," I said. "See you later." He made his way down the hall and I closed the door.

"Once that's up, honey, we can go," I said. "I'll unpack the rest on Monday."

My closest neighbors across the hall at OneTaste included soft-spoken Joaquin, who had just arrived in San Francisco after spending a few years in Mexico; Hugh, a barrel-chested, bearded mensch who wrote code; and Dara, a purple-haired creature with a sonorous voice and haunted eyes. Liam had a room upstairs where several of the instructors lived, including Noah, whose large corner room was the brightest in the building.

When I said Noah looked like a rabbi, I meant a rabbi just shy of forty who worked out daily and still had a thick head of black hair. In his previous life, Noah was a numbers man—accountant, stock broker, something like that—with a high-paying corporate job, which he'd chucked to follow Nicole's vision and keep OneTaste running in all practical aspects. Noah had been OMing daily for years, so if anyone knew the technique, it was him. By the time I moved in, I had already met with him for a private OM in his room. Now I knocked on his door for a second one, which we'd scheduled the night before.

Noah was a busy guy. He kept his laptop open and his iPhone in hand. He showed up a few minutes late, straight from another OM, and let us in. I dropped my bag on his floor and sat down on his thick beige duvet, afternoon light casting shadows on the white minimalist room, the swoosh of traffic echoing outside. I slipped my jeans and panties off, lay back on his fluffy pillows, and butterflied my legs. He sat to my right, took off his watch, set it down on the nightstand next to a jar of lube. He slipped on a new pair of white rubber gloves and dipped his left index finger into the lube. Only then did he look down at me. "Ready?" he asked.

I nodded yes. He started the timer.

As he began making small, light strokes, I had to let go of the habitual urge to help him along by shifting underneath his finger or by uttering sounds to encourage him. After a few minutes, the sensation began to build, though not in the usual way. The constant, mostly unvaried stroke failed to ignite my sexual yearning, the one that happened when that part of my body brushed against a hand or penis momentarily, then ached to return. Instead of this gradual reaching and subsiding, which allowed my sex to open of its own accord, Noah's insistent fingertip caused a purely physiological reaction. My breath quickened, my thigh muscles twitched. Every few minutes the pressure built to the point where I moaned and arched my back, my pelvic walls contracting for several seconds. My nose and lips tingled and my head swam. Noah's role felt more like a bodyworker's than a lover's. Yet I gripped his left forearm with both hands, feeling a familiar tug, a vulnerable nub of self that reached toward him tenderly.

Suddenly his cell phone rang, jerking me to awareness as if from a dream. Rage, distilled and irrational, surged through me and I glared at him. He kept his gaze on my crotch. I closed my eyes again, trying to focus on my breath, but I was having none of it. *If we have to turn our goddamn phones off during a stupid fucking InGroup, then maybe you should turn yours off while you're touching my clitoris.*

What the fuck was this place anyway? He and his gynecological gloves, running from one OM to another like a clockpuncher on a pussy assembly line. Fuck you, Noah.

It was common for strong feelings to arise during an OM, they said. Stay on your breath. Stick with the sensation.

When the fifteen-minute timer went off, Noah pressed gently on my pubic bone, looked down at me, and smiled.

"So how many times do we have to OM before we can fuck?" I said as I zipped my jeans.

"Twice," he said. Nice comeback.

"Tell me," he continued when I didn't respond, "what does your body want?"

I turned toward him. "I have no need to OM before we fuck."

"Well, you can have sex with anyone, but OMing is my specialty."

"I'll be the judge of that."

"You're sassy," he said, grinning as he tossed his rubber gloves into the wastebasket.

My childhood had trained me to absorb emotional chaos and plow forward with daily life, regardless of the broken glass, the hole punched in the bedroom door. Just keep going, each day a clean slate. And delayed reactions—by weeks, months, even years—were still my modus operandi. I could absorb a great deal of experience before needing to process it. Living at OneTaste broke that pattern, causing far more frequent ups and downs. Daily contact with so many other sexual experimenters flamed my desire as well as its flip side: rejection and competitiveness. My old defense mechanism, which consisted of casting myself as special for either my brains or my passion or some combination thereof, proved useless. Everyone here was passionate. Everyone had abandoned convention. And they were smart. They had MBAs or were working on PhDs in somatic psychology. A handful of them could diagnose and fix nearly any hardware or software problem. There was no drinking at OneTaste and no drugs. They ate healthy vegetarian meals and talked continually about their new workout regimens and yoga classes. It was nothing like the puppy pile of lost souls that many outsiders imagined when they heard "urban commune."

In this crowd, not only was my hardworking, hard-thinking personality common, but so was the little treasure between my legs, usually dependable for so much currency in the broader world. The men here differed from men elsewhere, whether single or attached, good-looking or not, in that they had twenty-four-seven access to a surplus of pussy. The power dynamic I'd taken for granted since I'd sprouted breasts at age thirteen dematerialized. Now I was just one of several dozen wet, available women of all ages, shapes, and temperaments in Nicole's orgasm army.

I didn't enjoy this healthy ego bashing one bit. I'd pass Liam in the halls and he'd flirt for a minute, touching my hip, his cheeks flushing, before vanishing into the crowd. He'd text to say let's make a date and never follow through. One night, when we finally did meet up in his room, we made out for several seconds before he stood up, unzipped his pants, and demanded with a smile, "Get on your knees." I couldn't help thinking he'd just learned that move in one of the men's classes.

"Later," I said, refusing to go that easy on him this time. But there was no later. He fucked me for five minutes, this time from behind, and then we went next door to the pizza place where everyone hung out. While we were eating, Amanda dropped in, another resident who was Liam's age and kept a detailed spreadsheet of everyone's chores. It soon became apparent that Liam was infatuated with her. After she left, he kept mentioning how seeing her threw him off balance and wondered aloud how to proceed. I offered a few lines of advice and hoped he'd shut up about it.

But as we headed back toward the residence, he said, "This is unbelievable. I'm literally shaking from seeing her."

I could forgive myself the first encounter with Liam, since I'd never slept with such a beautiful man in my life, but how could I let this happen again, a five-minute fuck, this time with the added insult of his openly obsessing over another woman?

"Hey," I interrupted, stopping short on the sidewalk to face him.

"What?"

"You just fucked me a half hour ago. I know we're all friends here but I don't want to hear about your crush on Amanda right now. I'm a woman, Liam, not a machine."

"You're right," he said. "Thanks for telling me that."

That's how everyone talked at OneTaste. When informed of another's perceptions or feelings, they habitually responded, "Thank you," as a way to acknowledge what they'd heard without reacting to it personally.

"And the next time we have sex?" I added. "I want it to last an hour." In retrospect I can't believe my ridiculousness, waiting around for a twenty-five-year-old to make his move, refusing to coach him through it, and then acting disappointed afterward.

"Okay." He smiled. "Thank you."

It wasn't only Liam who rattled me. The push and pull continued with Noah. His solid physicality—large-boned, dark, full-featured—both calmed me and fired me up. I went soft whenever he touched me in passing. One day, after our OM ended on his bed, he took his gloves off and lay down next to me, hugging me for a good ten minutes. When we finally pulled back to look at each other, he removed his glasses, put his mouth on mine and kissed me fervently. I reached up and pulled him closer, still dizzy from the OM and hungry for his weight. Our baroque kisses made me wetter than fifteen minutes of OMing had. After a long while he sat up and put his glasses back on. I sat up and put my pants back on. OneTasters touted this type of makeout session as a contained research experiment that went beyond the structure of an OM but didn't stir up as much "story" and potential enmeshment as actual sex.

Jude was still hanging around as well. He had several friends at the residence and often stayed overnight with me. Some weekends, he borrowed my room. He'd recently gotten back together with his ex-girlfriend Elise, a tiny, beautiful actress with a choppy shock of pink hair, whom, he reported, he could make come seven times in a row. He hadn't made me come even once. During an InGroup, Elise got on the hot seat, and when someone asked what was running through her head she said, "I was just thinking how awesome I am." My face went hot. Jude was next to me; I inched away so that my knee no longer touched his. When Elise sat back down on the other side of him, it was all I could do not to reach across and wrap my hand around her awesome, swan-like, multiorgasmic neck.

I'm no one special, I repeated silently, closing my eyes. Goals, competition, winning: the sturdy hooks I hung my fragile self-esteem on as a child. They were all that kept me from drowning in heartbreak. My father might rage but it wouldn't be because I was ill behaved or failing. He might consider women discardable but I'd never let him think of me that way. I'd forbid it by excelling. He could hurt me all he wanted—there was nothing I could do about that—but one thing he could never do was look down on me.

That's what made ordinariness so hard to swallow, and yet it was also a relief to let go of my little egocentric melodrama, which had long outworn its utility. "No one special" became my mantra. Rejection and anger, sadness and yearning were my medicine. I chewed on them slowly.

Nicole would say that this new stew of emotion wasn't just a result of communal living. It was also because I had begun OMing on a regular basis, and stroking the most sensitive part of a woman's body opens up her entire, interconnected limbic system. Three days a week, I'd set my alarm to 6:00 a.m., brush my teeth and wash my face, then pad over to the workshop center in my yoga pants to OM with the group. My partner changed each time. Noah's strokes were solid and rhythmic; Hugh's fluctuated according to my mood; Joaquin's I could barely feel yet they could unleash me to tears; Liam's finger annoyed me. And now that the focus was all on me, whatever I was experiencing—pleasure or numbness, intensity or boredom—I secretly questioned. Two or three of the women predictably climaxed about ten minutes into the OM, their breathy moans rising steadily before dying down. This pissed me off mightily.

When I asked myself why them and not me, the answer was that the light, insistent stroke used in OM put too much direct pressure on my clitoris without a break, and not even the whole clitoris but just one small edge of it. My sexual being went almost claustrophobic when reduced to a single point swollen with nerve endings; turn-on happened when I entered a full-body, intimate force field with a lover—kisses, looks, neck, nipples—a field that, contrary to OneTaste dogma, encompassed our hearts and words and the story between us.

Trusting my sexual response was not something that came easily, even at midlife. When I heard those few women coming at the drop of a hat, the eternal female mantra rose up to proclaim: *Maybe there's something wrong with me.* With time I began to see that my orgasm had a mind of its own, a discerning I could barely predict but always understood in hindsight. It had surfaced with Andrew because of a certain self-sustaining presence he offered that freed me; with Alden because of his fearless penetration; with Paul only once, right after we confessed how much we cared for each other. Inwardly, I was glad my surrender didn't happen easily, that it lay buried and tethered to the realities of each relationship. My clitoris was an astute barometer. It knew things before I did, and unlike me, it neither sought approval nor performed on command. It dealt solely in truth.

Climax or not, OMing had a tangible upside. I began to notice that on the days I OMed I ran a steady supply of long-lasting energy, similar to how limber and clearheaded I felt after a good yoga class or massage. After the OM, several of us would order breakfast at a homey diner next door. Then I'd shower, put on my editor's outfit, and walk briskly to the office down Sixth Street, through the ugliest part of the city, humming along to my headphones. On those days, my energy rarely lagged even in the late afternoon and I often went until 11:00 p.m. feeling alert. It was as if OneTaste was stirring up all my shit and, in return, handing me the physiological fuel to process it. Not such a bad deal.

My regular friends disagreed. When I told Paul I had moved into the residence, he winced and said, "I'm worried, Robs." He called and texted less often after that, which saddened me more than any disappointments taking place at OneTaste.

"What do the men get out of it?" Ellen asked.

"Let's see." I paused for dramatic effect. "A nonstop selection of hot women who are amped up and wanting sex all the time? Starting out each day gazing at a constant rotation of naked young pussy? Sanctioned nonmonogamy?"

"But isn't it all about the clitoris?"

"Yeah, for fifteen minutes in the morning and fifteen minutes at night. That leaves twenty-three and a half hours for anything else. OneTaste is a male dream."

My friends' main concern was that OneTaste was a cult. People were certainly free to come and go as they pleased and no one was discouraged from contact with their family or outside friends. Nevertheless, it was cult*ish*, with its charismatic leader, esoteric language, guided rituals, and the dopamine highs generated by all that physical contact. The gap between the way people operated at OneTaste—showering together, touching one another daily, taking an eccentric woman's word as gospel—and the way they operated in the larger world was huge. Sometimes it troubled me. I knew exactly whom to seek for perspective.

"Are you afraid I'll get sucked too far into OneTaste?" I asked Scott one Saturday at home. "A lot of people think they're a cult."

"I don't worry about you, button. I've seen you dive into all kinds of things, but you don't drown in them."

I went and sat on his lap sideways, clasped my arms around his neck, and lay my forehead on his shoulder.

"I'm only staying three months anyway," I said into his collarbone.

23

Infinite Games

NICOLE DIDN'T LIVE AT ONETASTE. She lived with her boyfriend, Reese, splitting her time between his house in Russian Hill, one of San Francisco's oldest and grandest neighborhoods, and his place out in Stinson Beach, about an hour north of the city. It seemed that only the inner circle got invited to the beach house—OneTaste teachers routinely disappeared from the residence and stayed out at the beach for days at a stretch.

One Monday afternoon a few weeks after our makeout session, I got a text from Noah while I was at work.

When are you coming up to the Stinson house? it said.

As soon as I'm invited.

How soon is now?

We had just shipped the magazine and it was one of our two slow days of the month.

Give me the address and I'll see you in a few hours.

I left work, packed a change of clothes, and headed across the Golden Gate Bridge into the Marin Headlands. The winter sun was low in the orange sky and I had to drive slowly in its glare around Highway 1's single-lane switchbacks. It was dusk when I finally descended into the windblown little town of Stinson Beach. Reese's house was a large, shingled beauty just steps from the sand. Noah let me in and I set about helping him with dinner. He said Reese had just gotten home and was in the bedroom with Nicole.

We cut up bell peppers, mushrooms, and zucchini and Noah prepared them with tofu, no butter, salt, or spice. Nicole and Reese joined us and we sat down in the dining room, drinking water and eating our vegetables. From what I'd gathered, Reese was some sort of Silicon Valley entrepreneurial genius; he'd been there at the birth of the Internet and was currently involved in a handful of futuristic think tanks. But you'd never know it. Reserved and self-effacing, he ate silently, as did Noah, while Nicole and I did most of the talking.

She casually delved into her past, which had included a long bout of celibacy. She described living with Ray Vetterlein, by then in his seventies, for three years and him stroking her clitoris daily.

"You need to write a memoir," I said.

"Oh, I already have. I've had two different men try to edit it, but it didn't work out."

"I should edit it." In fact, Noah had already hired me to edit some of Nicole's writings—her thoughts on relationship, the limbic system—and I found that I could barely keep up. She was no mere touchy-feely hedonist. There was a multilayered abstraction to her writing that reminded me of when I'd tried to read geniuses like Ken Wilber.

"Maybe you should," she said. "It probably needs a female editor."

"When is your interview with *The New York Times*?" I asked. They were sending out a reporter to do a feature on OneTaste.

"Supposedly in a few weeks."

"Be careful," I found myself saying. "It's an easy target, a bunch of California new-age types taking their clothes off. I'm sure the *Times* is going to be even-handed, but if I were you, I'd focus on the aspects of OM that appeal to the average woman, you know? The housewife in Kansas, the busy working mom. What can those women get from it? How it might help their marriages, for example. Just think how it could affect their energy levels and well-being." I had to stop myself from the sudden urge to ramble on.

"Exactly," she said. "I don't want it to be a fringe thing. One day OMing will be as routine and accepted as yoga is now. When women finally access their turn-on and take responsibility for it, the whole world will change." She smiled wide at this thought.

I felt strangely split. I was all too aware of OneTaste's shortcomings, its complicated terminology and guru worship. For me, orgasmic meditation wasn't anything close to the sexual or emotional grail others claimed. So far I actually found it to resemble all other kinds of meditation—physiologically healthy and a little boring. At the same time, I couldn't help cheerleading its female focus and even Nicole herself. Sitting with her now, I realized that her appeal wasn't that of a guru. It was something much more uncommon: the sensual power of the courtesan combined with the intellectual power of the scholar. Nicole was a fully formed woman, equally comfortable operating from her body as from her searing intellect. That, I believed, is what pulled people to her, so rare was the sight of a woman truly at ease with these dual aspects of her power.

After dinner we went into the great room, a library-like central space laid out in Oriental carpets and faded, elegant sofas. Bryan, a former OneTaste teacher, arrived from San Francisco with his girlfriend, who sat eating a salad while he and Nicole exchanged elusive communiqués I couldn't follow. I got the impression that there'd been some kind of falling-out between

Nicole and Bryan, and that he'd perhaps been connected to Werner Erhard, the founder of Est, which had gone on to become Landmark Forum. Lots of OneTasters were fans and alumni of Landmark, a hardcore self-improvement program that stressed self-responsibility and aggressively stripped away participants' defenses over the course of a weekend. Whenever anyone mentioned Landmark, I glazed over, uninterested. Bryan must have sensed this. He turned to me at one point and impatiently asked, "Why are you here?"

Good question. I was tempted to say, "Believe it or not, because my husband didn't want to have a baby!"

"Noah invited me," I said.

Nicole motioned to Noah with her eyes and he came over to me and reached out his hand. "Let's go take a walk on the beach," he said.

We bundled up and walked down a narrow footpath to the sand. It was soft underfoot and lit by an almost-full moon. He touched the small of my back as we climbed over a thick stump of driftwood and sat down. The inky plain of the Pacific was broken only by a lace trim of whitecap on the small waves that rolled in. Noah had approached and retreated so often that I had no idea whether he'd take advantage of the obvious ripeness of the moment. A few weeks prior, he'd said he was waiting for me. Then, a week ago, he'd told me that he saw himself more as a producer of my experiences than a participant. That statement had landed like a punch. I didn't need a producer.

"You just don't want me badly enough," I'd responded.

"You mean I'm not desperate?"

"I don't want desperation. Okay, maybe a little bit of desperation, an edge of it. Controlled desperation." We'd laughed.

"I am attracted to you. I want to make out with you. But I feel like our friendship is on a different level than sex. I'm past the point where I have to sleep with every woman I'm attracted to."

Fair enough. Now we sat on the log making small talk. The dense buzz his touch had generated was already beginning to fade. When we got cold, we headed back. I walked through the living room, bid everyone a quick goodnight, and Noah showed me to one of the guest bedrooms, a farmhouse-chic little accommodation made up in cozy, thick white bedding. I stood beside the bed while Noah went and got a stack of towels.

"Here you go," he said, handing them to me. I put them on the bed and faced him.

"Okay, thanks," I said.

"You've got everything you need?"

"Yep." I hugged him, achy but resigned to his standoffishness. "Thanks again."

"I'll be in the bedroom right next door." A smile lit his eyes.

"Okey-dokey."

"Just knock if you need me."

My chin angled itself in query. "Okay . . . goodnight."

I climbed into bed and pulled up the covers, listening to the dimmed voices in the living room, mostly Nicole's and Bryan's. Through the opposite wall, I heard Reese on the phone with what sounded like a colleague. It was 11:41 p.m. I heard him say "shareholder" and "dollars."

What *was* I doing here, anyway? Witnessing the birth of the next sexual revolution? San Francisco was full of risk-taking, independent thinkers who founded companies and nonprofits instead of climbing corporate ladders built by others. Even so, what kind of woman would have the guts to found a nonmonogamous commune based on female orgasm, sign herself up for the suspicion that would inevitably comprise most people's first reactions to such a concept? Whether I agreed with her or not, I couldn't help admiring Nicole's brio.

Now Noah joined in the conversation. I could hear his low voice a few feet from my bedroom door.

And then I realized what was going on. Noah was probably playing one of his "infinite games." That's why all the back-and-forth, the approach-and-withdraw. He'd sized me up, possibly with Nicole's input, and decided that I needed to take charge. Just as Jude had said: *You could be more assertive in bed.* Just as I'd failed to do with Liam. Instead of hanging back and waiting for the man to make the move, I needed to initiate.

It was true. I wasn't very assertive in bed. Did I want to work on changing that? Did I want to work on anything anymore, other than my actual job? Suddenly I remembered George, our therapist back in Sacramento, sitting in his leather chair wearing his shiny oxford shoes, listening as I debated whether to fly home to Pennsylvania for my tenth class reunion. "Let your body decide," he'd told me.

"What does that look like?" I'd asked. I was twenty-seven at the time and hadn't yet fallen off my bike. I couldn't tell you at that point what I felt in my little toe; the entity called Robin existed only from the neck up—unless I was in the midst of a breakdown, at which point every repressed bodily sensation would ambush me at once.

"You'll either walk over to the phone and call the airline to make a reservation, or you won't. You don't have to think about it. Your body will do it for you."

I'd sat staring at the wall above George's head, trying to comprehend what on earth he was talking about, how my body could walk to the phone without my brain's direction, and how my brain could direct anything without agonizing over all the possible outcomes first. It had taken eighteen years to understand what George was trying to teach me.

I flashed forward to texting Paul from the Castro bar that rainy night, chasing him to Denver, plowing ahead with the open marriage regardless of my fear of losing Scott. I thought of Susan driving to a fertility center, filling out form after form, going alone to appointments to be injected with donor sperm. She had recently emailed me about some letdown or other. The last line of the email said: "Let's get everything we want, Rob, and if we don't get it, then let's decide we didn't really want it."

That struck me as the smartest thing I'd ever heard anyone say, Nicole Daedone included. She and Noah were speaking now, probably turning in for the night, because I heard footsteps walk toward the bedroom adjacent to mine and its door close.

My arm reached up to switch off the light, my torso snuggled under the covers, and my eyes closed. That's how I decided to stop waiting for Noah.

24

Girl on Girl on Boy

I SAT STARING DOWN at Dara's inner labia, layers of dark flesh pierced with a silver hoop. I had never seen another vagina up close. I'd only begun looking at my own a few years ago, during Mama Gena's pleasure course. Dara's looked exotic and vaguely dangerous. Grace sat nearby, coaching me on where to place my fingers and how to gauge Dara's reaction. I'd decided it was time to learn what it felt like to be the stroker.

I followed Grace's instructions, keeping my index finger on the outer edge of Dara's clitoris and stroking lightly upward. I was afraid to move too roughly and hurt her and simultaneously afraid of touching too lightly and boring her. Her breathing grew fast and she began to emit loud, sharp "Ah" sounds, jerking a little with each one. I felt like a first-timer given a bucking bronco to steer instead of a pony. Alarmed, I looked to Grace. She quietly said Dara was just releasing stored-up emotion. If I wanted to calm her I should switch to a downstroke, from the apex of the clitoris toward the vagina. When I did, Dara's "ahs" mellowed into a smoother rhythm and her breathing lengthened again.

Thank god the fifteen-minute timer went off. The complexity of the clitoris, the responsibility for awakening it or failing to, the knowledge of what depths it lay connected to, was all so much more intimidating than the resilient, straightforward penis.

In my teens, I never gave same-sex attraction a second thought. In my twenties and thirties, on the rare occasions when the topic came up, I didn't have the emotional bandwidth to explore it and bear the brunt of the lesbian taboo. Now that I had a second chance at sexual experiments, I finally gave myself permission to ponder it.

But there was a hitch. Though I found the female body sublime in the abstract, I'd never met a woman I felt personally attracted to. In a room, my eyes gravitated to men, continually if discreetly scanning the field between myself and any of their species, a psycho-spiritual urge toward completion that bloomed into sexual attraction when a number of key signals lined up. Women's beauty far outweighed men's—the olive smoothness of skin, the bountiful sphere of ass, the long hair falling over geometric collarbone. And Sabrina's circle was proving that women were actually better than men at helping access the femine energy that made me feel happy and fulfilled. Still, the thought of an intimate one-on-one relationship with a woman scared the hell out of me. I could only imagine it as myself times two, exhausting and potentially treacherous.

A few weeks after my OM with Dara, Grace stroked me. Just like taking my pants off for the first time in a room full of people or stripping down and entering a communal shower with two strangers, it proved surprisingly simple. After a few seconds of initial awkwardness, a comfortable sense of instinct took over.

As Grace began stroking, I noticed the absence of a subtle layer of tension, which always accompanied a new man's touch. I didn't ponder her reaction to seeing me naked, whether it turned her on, how my pussy might rank in comparison to others'. I didn't worry about making too much or too little noise. I didn't give a thought to whether or not I climaxed. The result of all this lack of thinking was that I could feel more.

Eventually, Grace and I decided she would come to my room one night around ten and we would cuddle and see where it led. No plans, no pressure. I showered and changed into warm pajamas—it was early March and the residence was chilly. When she knocked lightly on my door, she was in PJs too. Grace and I both had strong builds and snappy tempers. But she was strawberry blond, a decade younger, and more visibly vulnerable than me. Her freckled face hid no emotion at all. Sadness, mirth, anger, and joy passed over it like weather systems over a tropical island. In an effort to manage it all, she instituted very clear boundaries, which she articulated slowly and with purpose.

"I'd like to get under the covers, face each other, and chat," she said after we hugged hello.

We got into bed and turned to face each other. I left the bedside lamp on. "It's like a slumber party," I said as we pulled the blankets up to our faces. We talked like any two women would when catching up: one at a time, excavating the feelings that lay below the surface of events, while the other nodded her understanding and asked occasional questions designed to encourage further revelation. She told me about her ex-boyfriend, the man she was currently involved with, her confusion over the next step in her career. I told her where things stood with Scott, how I missed him and my home but was also nervous to move back in full-time, how I still secretly pined for Alden.

As we talked, we encircled each other's waists. Gradually, I turned onto my other side, away from her, and she spooned me.

"Have you been with many women?" I asked as she burrowed her face into my neck.

"Six of them," she said. Her voice was soft but she spoke with authority. "What about you?"

"None. You're the first." I had French-kissed a friend once in a bar, a stunt enacted for the sake of the male bystanders. This was different.

"I like going down on women," she said. "Would you want that?"

"Yes." I giggled from embarrassment. On the nightstand was a small packet of Valentine candy hearts, which I'd been passing around to my friends. I picked up a white heart that read "Kiss me" and handed it to her over my shoulder. She popped it into her mouth as I turned to face her.

"I can lead the way," she said after she'd swallowed it.

I felt like one part hormonal seventh grader experimenting with a best friend and one part anonymous porn actress, that serving as my only mental image of two women having sex. I also pictured myself bigger and stronger than Grace, even though I wasn't, even though she was the one now hovering above me, exploring my mouth with her tongue.

The female body. The core of my fascination revolved around the breasts. I ran my hand over hers, firm in appearance but soft beyond belief, thumbing her nipple to stiffness before sliding it into my mouth. She moaned, grinding her hips against me. As I sucked, my hands moved down. We slid off each other's pajama bottoms. I grabbed her by the hair as I bit her nipple, and she dug into my shoulder and kissed me more hungrily. She was more layered than solid, a hydra of pale ivory arms and legs encircling me.

"Push against me," she said. I pushed her up by the shoulders, causing our hips to hinge tighter. I could feel her strip of short pubic hair against mine, the sliver of wet insides exposed and then hidden again as we moved. I lost track of time as we alternated between making out and my kissing and sucking her breasts. It could have been five minutes or a half hour. I gathered her ass in my hands, then reached into its crevice as far as I could, sliding her pussy open, dipping my finger in and then trailing it back upward. When I was on top of a man, this was one of my favorite ways to be touched, perched on his teasing finger, my tits in his mouth. As I tilted her ass up, she threw her head back and groaned. I inhabited both her body and my own, felt her excitement and the intoxicating power of producing it. I was subject and object. A quiet, pronounced orgasm ripped through me without a shred of warning.

She sensed it. She looked at me and smiled.

"Oh my god," I said. "I came!"

"I know. It felt amazing." She rolled to the side and snuggled against me. "I can go down on you next time."

"Don't you want me to go down on you?" I asked.

"No. I feel completely satiated."

I wasn't sure I believed that, but Grace was known for her honesty, and I wasn't sure how to proceed.

After a few minutes she asked, "Want to have another date next Thursday?"

"Yes."

"Okay. I'm going to go back to my room to sleep now." We put our pajamas back on and hugged.

"I love you," she said, looking me in the eye. She meant it in the usual way, friend to friend, though a little shock zinged through me.

"I love you, too," I said automatically, my throat tightening around the words.

When she left, I closed the door and lay down, staring into space, trying to trace the ripple of anxiety. Was it the lesbian taboo reaching out its prongs across the years? I couldn't remember ever climaxing with a man so quickly, other than Alden. Was it the combination of the physical intimacy and the "I love you," something that never happened on the first instance of sex with a man? No. It was the simple fact that I couldn't bullshit her, and that I had to be as careful with her feelings as I was with my own. That's what scared me: her female combination of perception and vulnerability.

A week later, Grace knocked on my door in her pajamas again. We repeated the ritual of snuggling, talking quietly, and slowly kissing for what seemed like a luxurious hour. When a new man went down on me, I tended to brace for the possibility that he'd start off too fast, with frantic flicks and switch-ups that killed my mood before I could even get started. But I opened my legs for Grace with complete trust. She made small, slow circles, her tongue flattened and soothing. She pulled away every minute or so to let me rest, and by the time she returned I was more swollen than before. In five minutes she made me come with no effort, tension, or hoping on my part.

Okay, maybe I was a lesbian after all.

I switched places with her and attempted the style she'd used on me. She seemed to enjoy it, but after about fifteen minutes she said, "Okay, that's all the sensation I can handle tonight." I felt inept. If Liam had turned me into a teenage girl again, Grace turned me into a teenage boy, all raw lust and incompetence.

"I want to use a strap-on," I said as we cuddled.

"Yes! Let's do that next." But a week later, Grace told me she was putting all connection on hold for several weeks while she worked through some emotional issues that had come up.

Her prioritizing of emotions conflicted with my prioritizing of sexual goals. I was drawn to her body but shrunk back when she expressed unfettered feeling. I got off, she didn't. It only took sleeping with one woman to help me understand the behavior of nearly every man I'd ever known.

As if to allay any misgivings I harbored about my heterosexuality after sleeping with Grace, along came Roman, the six-foot-four man-god whom I'd witnessed rising from the ooze during the male OM demonstration. Size was just one aspect of Roman's overall sense of physical ease. He was always smiling, and his flirting was devoid of hungry sneers or sideways glances. He displayed no fear of women, no need for either conquest or approval. Whenever our eyes met or even when I sat within three feet of him, something rich and steady vibrated between us.

Roman was engaged to Annie, the fieriest little soul in the commune, only twenty-three and smart as a whip. The first time I met her, during my second OneTaste workshop, she materialized in front of us wearing a pink pinafore, her hair pulled into tight pigtails, and sang an a cappella tune I'd never heard that sounded part Broadway lament, part Grimm's nursery rhyme. She looked like Dorothy of Oz gone astray. In groups, she had a habit of contradicting the approved-of responses, blithely stating how much she hated intimacy. She did so not with the reactionary rebelliousness of youth but with a weary air of self-deprecation usually reserved for the mature.

Roman and Annie had an open relationship, even though they planned on leaving OneTaste later that year to move into their own apartment before getting married. They were both free to do as they wished, as long as they got preapproval from the other.

I looked forward to the morning OM session when Roman was my scheduled stroker. His long legs and body shielded me from the rest of the room. He had a knack for intuiting the right amount of pressure. My breathing tended to match his, audible, building in intensity. Holding on to his arm was like holding on to a grounding pole; he never dropped me by shifting attention or losing focus. Our OMs filled my being—more than just my body—with a liquid gratification, like a plant that had been watered.

Afterward, Roman said, "I feel this amazing chemistry with you. It turns my whole body on."

"I feel it, too."

"We should make out."

"Yes, I want to! When?" There was no time to play it cool. I had little more than a month of the project left.

"Let me clear it with Annie and we'll shoot for next week."

"Okay, let me know." He squeezed my hands, then pulled me into a long embrace.

A week later, he showed up at my door around 7:00 p.m., wearing jeans and a T-shirt and smelling of soap. He lay down on the bed, propped a few pillows behind his head, stretched out his right arm, and gestured for me to come lie against his shoulder.

"So how are you doing?" he asked. "Tell me what's going on with you."

I paused, mentally reviewing how much of my life he knew about.

"Well, I'm overworked, as usual. I go from this job with constant deadlines to living here with all the OMing and making out to being married on the weekends. It's a lot."

"I don't know how you pull it off."

"I feel like my body's leading me on this intense journey, and then it takes a while for my heart and mind to catch up."

He nodded, pulling lightly at a corner of my shirt as if grooming me.

"I don't know if I told you, but I started this whole open marriage thing after my husband got a vasectomy. I wanted to have a baby with him."

"I remember. Do you still want to have a kid?"

"I don't know. Maybe it sounds stupid, but I can't seem to imagine having one with anyone else. Maybe that just means I don't want one badly enough."

"It doesn't sound stupid," he said.

"I have no idea what's going to happen. I feel like I'm at the halfway point of my life and I can't see beyond it. I can't envision a future."

"That's good. It means you're living in the present." Roman was still at an age where those kinds of platitudes sounded believable.

"Are you and Annie going to have kids?"

"Yeah, we're pretty sure," he said. A jolt of envy flashed through me regarding Annie, her youth, her devil-may-care assertiveness, her unabashedly masculine fiancé with excellent communication skills, and as many children as she wanted.

"I'm jealous of Annie," I said apologetically.

"She's jealous of you, too. She's a little nervous about me being here. She's been less open to me having intercourse with other women since we got engaged."

"Are you allowed to have intercourse today?" My hand rested on his sternum. I could feel the hair on his chest through his thin T-shirt.

"Yes," he said, smiling.

"Good. So what about you? How are you doing?"

He said he liked OneTaste well enough, and was happy he had met Annie there, but he was eager to get off the farm, return to running his own moving company, get married, and start his life.

"Have you slept with a lot of women here?"

He ran down a short list and summarized the problems that inevitably arose when they wanted more than he could give. It reassured me to hear that regardless of the antiromance dictate, the urge to not layer story over sensuality, the women at OneTaste were still acting on their own feelings. Personally, I didn't buy Nicole's theory that our monogamous urges were mere social conditioning.

"There's something different about you," I said. "The fact that you can handle Annie speaks volumes."

"She is a handful, isn't she?" he said with affection. "She's so fucking smart, too. I've never met anyone like her."

"You seem so comfortable with women."

"A great mom and lots of aunts who adored me," he said, stretching wide and yawning with one arm still around me.

We must have talked for an hour. His patient, focused attention readied me more than a finger ever could. I was hovering, eager to pounce by the time he pulled me toward him. We made out for ages, his hands on my face. Every so often he gathered my hair from underneath and tilted my neck back to kiss it. After a long time, he slipped my shirt off and unhooked my bra with one hand.

"Mmmm," he said, running the rough stubble of his face and shaved head down over my breasts. "That's a good girl," he said as he tossed my pants aside. He still had one hand on my nape. I was a feline caught by a larger animal. Its penis unfurled from the foreskin. I climbed up and guided it into me, leaning forward to fit it all inside.

"It hurts."

"I'll go slow," he said, his hands holding fast to my waist. "How's that?"

"Oh my god."

"Fuck," he whispered. He growled but didn't speed up. Inch by inch, over the course of a minute or so, he entered me fully.

It lasted two hours, which I only realized when I looked at the clock later. He used dirty talk as highlight, not narration, alternating tenderness with force. His cock inspired fellatio to new heights. He was the first man to voluntarily go down on me the first time we were together. When we were done, we lay naked in our initial position, completely at ease. His capacity to talk and listen was breathtaking.

"I really loved this," he said. "I hope we can do it again."

"It was perfect."

Well, almost perfect: I hadn't come. But I was beginning to trust my body's wisdom on this. The only other lover who'd held this much promise, Alden, had hurt me terribly. I'd no doubt hurt him, too. Roman was too good to be true, combining Scott's capacity for patience with more force and presence. He was also taken, and so was I.

Roman and I made out again the following week, though Annie told him she didn't want us to have sex for the time being. His boundaries were impeccable. He didn't even let us come close to intercourse. Whenever I ran into him, he smiled wide, scooped me into a hug, kissed the crown of my head, and said, "Hello, love, how are you?" If he was with Annie, we said hello while staying a few feet away. I began to notice the other women whose eyes traced Roman through the room.

He updated me on their negotiations. "She knows I want to have sex with you again. I think she's working up to it."

"I don't know how you guys do this with so much honesty," I said. "Isn't she hurt that you're so attracted to someone else?"

"A little threatened maybe, but not hurt. My sex drive is a lot higher than hers. We've known it from the beginning."

A few weeks later, perhaps with the knowledge that I was on my way out, Annie gave him permission to have sex with me again, three-hour sex that couldn't have been better if I had scripted it. When it was over and he was enfolding me in one of his signature embraces, I pulled back and said, without a hint of sarcasm, "Tell Annie I said thank you."

It was noteworthy that of all the men at OneTaste, the one I found most virile was engaged to be married, planning to have children, and on the brink of moving to the suburbs. "Some men are good at containing," Sabrina had once said in casual conversation. "Others are good at penetration. It's rare for a man to be naturally good at both." Roman seemed to be that rare man, but how could I tell—after a mere ten hours total—whether that was his true nature or just his best behavior magnified by my own projections? That, for me, was the inherent flaw in nonmonogamy. It sufficed beautifully as a tool of exploration, but I couldn't imagine bonding with a lover to the depth I craved if we were constantly allowed to seek out shiny new objects on which to cast our fantasies. Of all the women who lingered around Roman asking for more, I was sure there was only one who actually knew him.

25

The Other Woman

THE MAGAZINE was owned by the same company that published *Spin*. Early one spring morning, the arts editor said out loud, "Is anyone free to drive to San Jose tonight? Spin.com needs some-one to write up the Bruce Springsteen concert." That's how I ended up in the fourth row of a Boss concert by myself, jotting down the playlist in a reporter's notebook, singing along to my favorite East Coast anthems and feeling lonely.

It was 1:00 a.m. by the time I got back into the city. Most of the SoMa parking spaces were taken at that hour. I found one near an underpass where the homeless tended to congregate and walked several blocks to OneTaste. When I got there, I couldn't locate my front door key. I dug through my purse and pockets. I backed up and scanned the second- and third-floor windows of the residence, looking for a light that signaled someone was still awake. They were all dark. The 6:00 a.m. alarm meant most people fell asleep long before midnight, and made me loathe to rouse anyone. I decided my best bet was to just drive home to the Castro.

I hadn't been home on a Wednesday night in nearly a year,

and though I was pretty sure Scott wouldn't have anyone at the house during the week, I texted him just in case.

I need to come home, I'm locked out. Is that a problem?

He didn't answer. Scott usually fell fast asleep at 10:00 p.m. sharp.

I made a lot of noise letting myself into the house: the front door, the door to the flat, my keys, my shoes. "Hello?" I called out. "It's me, I locked myself out."

I waited in the living room in my socks, at the far end of the hallway from the bedroom. Cleo emerged out of the dark and snuggled up to my shin. I scooped her up and padded back to the bedroom. It was empty. I turned on the light and sat on the bed, surprised at my surprise. I hardly ever let a man spend the night with me, other than Jude, platonically. I'd slept at Alden's only once.

I undressed and got under the soft blue comforter Scott and I had recently bought. To my right was the locked antique trunk holding our photos and my journals; to my left, Scott's latest batch of wine, bubbling away in the tiny en suite bathroom; and in front of me, William Blake's illustrated "Proverbs of Hell," framed in black and hanging in four installments from the picture molding.

The road of excess leads to the palace of wisdom.
He who desires but acts not, breeds pestilence.
You never know what is enough unless you know what is more than enough.
The tigers of wrath are wiser than the horses of instruction.

I fell asleep trying to envision the room Scott found himself in. Was it cramped or spacious? What was the view outside the window? Was he sleeping on his usual side of the bed? And who on earth was this new person here under our covers, the one who used to shriek with envy if Scott happened to brush by another woman too closely or let his eyes linger too long? Had I really matured to some level of sanguinity or was my jealousy just one more little demon lying in wait, ready to circle back around when the time was ripe?

The woman was Charly, the redhead I'd seen on Scott's phone. She was a thirty-five-year-old software programmer whom Scott had met in a bar six months prior. He'd been seeing her once or twice a week since then. She knew about the project and our plans to reunite in a month. He told me all this the next day when I mentioned that I'd come home the night before.

"Once or twice a week for six months, and you spend the night. What happened to the no-relationship rule that you wanted so badly?" I had no right to ask this after the rules I'd broken. But the words tumbled out of my mouth like a train pulling out of the station too early.

"After we decided to continue past New Year's, things changed," he said. "I'm too old to be out in bars picking up a new woman every week. I'm not interested. I'd rather see one person over a long period of time."

"So you're saying Charly is the *only* woman you're seeing? For the past six months?"

"Yes."

"And are you the only person she's sleeping with?"

"Yes."

I threw up my hands. "And you think she's just going to let you go without any drama when May first comes around? A single, thirty-five-year-old woman you've been fucking for half a year!"

"Yes. It won't be easy for her, but she knows the deal."

It won't be easy for her. The words stuck in my gut like six little arrows.

Scott found with Charly what I'd secretly wanted with Alden: a love affair. In a bar, by chance, without joining a dating site or an urban commune or putting up with the jerks on Craigslist, he found a woman twenty years his junior who quietly accepted his marriage and the temporary nature of their relationship. He was better at this than I was.

I counted three distinct reactions to Charly. Intellectually, I told myself I had created the situation, Scott had done nothing (or at most, very little) wrong, and I had to cease and desist from further questions. I prayed for self-control. Over and over I whispered, "Please stop me from asking Scott any more questions."

Emotionally, the knowledge of his exclusive relationship with Charly threw me into what I considered my underlying reality, the dark pit of abandonment above which my life had hovered well before the project, and which I secretly feared had even helped initiate it, all so that I could wreck my marriage and fall reliably into its gaping mouth. I lost sleep, endured heart palpitations, imagined myself old and alone with no one but me to blame.

Most interestingly, a third part of me began to look at Scott with new eyes, admiring his ability to seduce, respecting the fact that I had thrown him such a huge challenge and he had risen to it. My awareness of young Charly caused Scott to grow larger somehow, almost as large as he looked all those years ago when I was unsure and he was strong, long before he had collapsed in despair at the thought of impregnating me. And so while my less mature self resented Charly for entering my marriage more deeply than any of my own lovers had, the woman in me silently thanked her for giving back a reflection of the Scott I'd fallen in love with.

Oh, how I swung back and forth between the self-contained woman and the wounded girl. One day I was a liberated hedonist, planning out my last few weeks of freedom, the next a shivering urchin locking myself in the office restroom to sweat out a wave of panic, the next a righteous harpy tearing into a cell phone bill for clues to the scope of his involvement with Charly. I had no idea how to manage my lurching emotions other than to ride them out, like I was riding out everything I'd set in motion—riding a tidal wave begun a year ago far out at sea. There was nothing to do now but let it crash us both into the beachhead and hope to survive.

On the morning of my forty-fifth birthday party, Ellen and Caresse, another officemate of ours, picked me up and took me to Foreign Cinema for brunch. Once we had settled in on the crowded patio and ordered, Caresse wrapped her hands around her cup of coffee, leaned forward, tilted her chin down, and shot me an interventive look.

"How is it going with Scott?" she asked.

"Great, other than the fact that he has a thirty-five-year-old girlfriend and I'm living at a sex commune."

Ellen laughed. Caresse didn't. I was sure they could see through my blitheness for the defense it was. It rattled me when my friends expressed concern.

Nevertheless, I continued in the same vein. "Thank god he had that vasectomy. If he ever mistakenly got this girl pregnant, I'd murder both of them."

"I think what happened is that after the vasectomy, you lost all respect for him," Caresse said. I could tell she'd been rehearsing. "But now that you're moving back in, you have to find a way to regain it. Your marriage will never work unless you forgive him and start to respect him again."

"Actually, knowing about his girlfriend increases my respect for him," I said more earnestly. "Don't underestimate Scott, Caresse. He's stronger than you think."

"All I know is that if I told Martin I wanted an open relationship, he'd dump me."

"And you think that makes Martin stronger than Scott?"

"That's not the point. The point is I'd never ask because I respect Martin too much. I think between the vasectomy and Scott's agreeing to go along with this, you've lost all regard for him."

"That's partly true," I said. "There were times I wished he would have stopped me. Just said 'no fucking way.' But I'm not sure what would have happened if he had."

When approached with words, truth was as multifaceted as a crystal. Everyone's opinions fell on it at varying angles, illuminating so many versions of truth as to render them all moot. For as many friends who counseled me against the project for reasons of fidelity, there were others who counseled prolonged infidelity instead of open marriage. By now I was long past the observational approach: Is A true or is B? Which is best? Which is right? It took too much energy and produced little change. Working from instinct, feeling my way through the situation half-blind was a savage method, amoral if not worse, but I trusted it would yield a more foundational truth than the myriad versions at the surface.

That night, fifty people crowded into our house for my birthday. I'd invited only a handful of OneTaste friends, none of whom I'd slept with. Among them were Margit, a raven-haired Austrian, and her Swedish boyfriend, Oden. They both owned their own companies, Margit's based in Vienna, Oden's in Stockholm. They didn't live at OneTaste. Oden had a flat in Nob Hill, where they met when not working in Europe. I'd been through many workshops with them in the past year. Though they planned to marry and have a family, they considered themselves primary partners with no need to prohibit sex with others, even after marriage. Margit spent many evenings with both male and female lovers while Oden had a long-term liaison back in Stockholm. They took tango lessons, sailed the Caribbean, and vacationed in Lake Como. Margit spoke five languages.

Margit saw all my dilemmas—about children, nonmonogamy, my marriage—through the opposite lens than did Caresse. I wasn't struggling because I'd demanded too much of Scott but because I'd expected so little. As soon as I owned my desires without drama or apology, without waiting for the other shoe to drop, it would be smooth sailing. Whenever Margit framed things this way, I let her talk, not wanting to say what I believed: that she was an extraordinary woman—gifted and fearless, not to mention lucky—who should refrain from touting her embarrassment of riches as easily attainable.

Margit had made it clear that she was attracted to me. When I told her I wanted to try a threesome, she suggested we share a man.

"How about Roman?" I asked her at my birthday party. I'd already mentioned the idea to Roman and he'd lunged at the prospect.

"Ooooooo, yesssss!" she purred. She'd given me a long string of pearls as a gift and was now holding on to them as we danced. Oden had just done a comic turn around the stripper's pole.

"You'd like him. He's a little aggressive."

"Can we do it next week?" she shouted into my ear over the music, her strong Austrian accent flipping her *w*'s almost into *v*'s.

"Yes, I'll set it up." I had only three weeks left.

It was a good thing, too. I could feel the marriage sputtering toward the project's finish line like a marathoner about to collapse. The emotional swings and attendant discussions around Charly opened a more forthright channel of communication. Scott no longer verbally evaded me every time we talked; crisis mode rendered him more present. But after an initial surge of sexual exploration—a playful slap here, one abandoned attempt with a blindfold there—the damage now showed itself in bed. In the month following my discovery of Charly, he stopped going down on me. He no longer climaxed when I went down on him. Foreplay practically disappeared. One Saturday night, he suggested we go out to dinner and treat it like a first date. Over seafood just doors away from the bar where I first texted Paul, we sat across from each other asking probing questions about our worldviews, our likes and dislikes, things we already knew. But Scott and I had long ago explored every last nook and cranny of our significant intellectual connection. The new territory didn't lie in that direction.

The day after this failed date, both the AmEx and cell phone bills arrived. As I brought the mail back to the kitchen table, Scott quickly tried to scoop them away from me. I pinned them to my chest.

"Don't," he said. I kept my eyes on his as I split open the AmEx. Two charges leapt off the list: a florist and an expensive dinner at A16, one of the city's best restaurants. On the phone bill, a dozen calls to a South Bay number that had to be Charly's. Calls at 6:30 a.m. and on weekends.

Quite unlike myself, I put the bills down, changed clothes, and went to the gym.

When I got home an hour later, he came into the bedroom as I was undressing. "Yell at me if you want. Go ahead. But please don't go silent."

"I wish I'd learned to go silent years ago. It gets more of a response from you."

"I really don't think I'm in the wrong."

I sighed and sat on the bed. "You're not in the wrong. I've broken the rules too. But flowers, A16, calling her on weekends? I don't call guys on the weekend, Scott, when I'm here with you. I begged you for years to romance me, and it kills me to think it comes so easily with someone else!" Even as I spoke I couldn't help remembering his belated attempt to woo me at Michael Mina, and how I had checked my text messages in the restroom. The daily love notes he used to leave for me on the dining room table in Philadelphia.

"Of course it comes easily with someone new. I can't help that. You're the one who wanted the open marriage."

"And you're the one who wanted to make sure neither of us got into a relationship."

"I'm too old for casual sex, Robin," he said.

"Do you love her?"

"No. I love you."

"You don't call a woman at six-thirty in the morning unless you're in love."

"She needed to talk that morning."

I closed my eyes and took a breath, trying to digest the idea of some redheaded programmer *needing* to talk to my husband at 6:30 in the morning. Did I blow this marriage open because it had given me too little or did I feel compelled to go and ruin it precisely because it had offered me so much?

"Well, okay, she needs to talk to you the minute she wakes up, so she must love you." Women had always loved Scott. When they left, it was only because they wanted more of him than he could give.

"I don't know. Maybe."

After we'd sat in silence awhile I asked, "What have we done here, Scott? This is all my fault, right? I should have just quietly given in to having no children and no passion?"

"New women seem to think I have plenty of passion. They don't seem to have trouble feeling fulfilled around me."

"That's because they're new," I said wearily. "It's all so easy when it's new. Just like it's easy for me to get what I want from new men."

Stating the plain truth out loud drew us toward each other

somehow. Eventually he leaned over to kiss me. We lay back on the bed. When I reached down to feel him, he wasn't hard—a first. I stroked him slowly as we kissed, but nothing. I pulled away and looked at him.

"Are you not attracted to me anymore?"

"That's not it," he said. "It's not you."

"Of course it's me." I was a bitch and a castrator who had finally destroyed the last vestige of my marriage.

"It felt like you were really open to me while we were talking," he said, "but you just shut down." Rarely in eighteen years had Scott voiced an emotional observation like that.

"Can I tell you what I appreciate about you?" I asked. I had no idea where this was coming from. I hadn't read it in a book or heard it on a Deida CD.

"Okay."

"Most men would never have the strength for this whole thing, but you do. You take care of the house and Cleo all week. You're fair. You treat me like an equal. You suggested the first-date idea last night. You took me to Michael Mina. You're kind. No matter what happens you don't give up on us."

I paused. "It's weird but I even respect you for getting the vasectomy. You stood your ground."

I bent over and kissed his cheek, running my fingers through his thick hair. He pulled me into a kiss, then pressed me against the mattress. After several minutes of kissing, I felt him get hard. He entered me carefully, as if afraid of disturbing the fragile thread of connection we'd spun from the conflict. But I pulled at his neck desperately and arched my hips to meet his. I felt his cock rooting a poison from my system, cleaning up debris that words could only scatter. In no time an orgasm burst from me in sobs.

His orgasm, however, was small and quiet. Afterward, when he returned from washing up, he lay down next to me.

"I think things will get better in bed once we're back together full-time," he said. "It might take a while."

Would it ever be enough, though, given my new breadth of experience? Even in the midst of my afterglow I thought: *probably not*. I recalled the other steps Scott had taken—the vibrator he bought, the lingerie set, the weekend at a romantic inn—and how my reaction to each had been *too little, too late*. For the first time, I found the guts to admit that this cycle of need and lack actually brought me a strange kind of comfort.

I was so used to wanting more than Scott delivered, to living in a state of frustrated compromise, that the thought of him—of us—changing for good scared me. If the marriage headed to more fertile ground, I'd have to commit to it, mentally close all other options. That was something I'd never done. I'd been physically faithful to him for seventeen years prior to the project but I'd never fully committed. Part of me knew, without wanting to, that I'd chosen Scott precisely because he wasn't terribly interested in, as he put it, deep psychosexual connection. That way, I'd never have to endure its rigors, and yet I wouldn't need to blame myself for missing out. Just like with motherhood, I could point to Scott as the reason I didn't have it.

26

The End of the Bucket List

I CHANGED into the flowery cotton pajamas I'd bought especially for OneTaste, a long-sleeved thermal top, and big, floppy slippers shaped like monkeys. The sun had just gone down and dinner was over. I turned on the lone lamp in my little room, ripped out a blank page from a notebook, and made a sign in thick marker that said: "Tonight I'm yours. Knock on the door, tell me what you need, and I'll try to give it." I taped the sign to the door and got back in bed to read and wait.

Joaquin knocked first. I let him in and we sat on the bed cross-legged, facing each other. He'd spent two years living in Mexico and moved into the residence about the same time as me. He had the look of a wanderer, a man who'd seen things: thin and dark haired, with intense, knowing eyes and a soft voice. He moved and spoke slowly.

"I just want to talk," he said. He told me how he'd reconnected with his ex-girlfriend, how he couldn't stop thinking about her, but each time they made a date for coffee or a drink she canceled. He took out his phone and showed me all her text messages.

"What do you think?" he asked.

"The more you chase the more she's going to back away."

"I know. But how do I not chase?"

"She's the one who contacted you, so if you give her a little space, she'll probably approach in her own time. Look where you are, look at all these beautiful women. Why not focus on them for now?"

"Why is that so hard?" He said it more to himself than to me. "I always want the one who runs away instead of the one right in front of me."

"I think we're all like that. It's not just you, it's human nature."

As he got up to leave I pointed to the canvas I'd painted at Joie's, which had followed me from Mission Dolores to Bluxome to OneTaste, and said, "I'm moving back home in a few weeks. When I go, I want you to have that."

"Really? Thanks." He hugged me and smiled, lamplight reflecting in his brown-black irises. Someone knocked.

Hugh entered as Joaquin exited. "Was it good?" Hugh asked him, laughing.

"Hef, my man," I said. "What can I do for you?" I called him Hef to counter his chubby, nerdy persona with a reminder to let out his inner playboy. He was actually sturdily handsome and had killer rhythm. Whenever one of the workshops called for dancing, people cleared the floor around him.

"I'm just here for a good long hug." I walked up to him, got on my tippy toes, and sank my head onto his shoulder, letting his big arms engulf me. We took several breaths like that. I pulled back and kept my hands on his biceps.

"And I want to OM with you tomorrow morning," he said.

"You got it." I kissed him on the cheek and he left.

Later that night, Jude came by. He often did so after attending a workshop next door or hanging out with various women in the residence. We were both hungry, so I got dressed and we walked to a twenty-four-hour diner in Union Square, where we ordered a huge plate of French fries. When we got back, we crawled into bed, him spooning me. "Goodnight, Jujube," I said, squeezing his hand. He nestled in closer and I felt his erection against my sacrum.

"My god," he whispered. "I'm suddenly so turned on by you." We cuddled often but hadn't had sex in nine months. Surprised, I turned to look at him and without thinking pulled him to me. Memories of our first kiss at Joie's apartment flooded in: his thick lips, long hands, the tattoos on his forearms. I barely remember the details of the sex, just the initial rush toward each other, how warm his arms and legs felt around mine, and the fact that we ended in missionary position like an old, established couple. In the morning I awoke to find him seated on my floor meditating. "What the hell happened last night?" he said.

"You're gonna miss me when I'm gone, that's what happened." I grabbed a towel, rubbed the crown of his shaved head, and stepped over him to go take a shower.

Andrew circled back around that same week. He emailed to tell me that he and his girlfriend had broken up. Was I free for a drink? We met downtown and ordered manhattans. She didn't appreciate the work he was trying to do with his dissertation. She didn't allow him time for it. She was jealous and controlling yet she couldn't commit. She'd already started seeing another guy. As the waitress took the bill from him he exhaled loudly and said, "It's so good to just get all this out."

He walked me back to the residence. At the door I simply unlocked it and went upstairs, letting him follow me. In my room, we grasped at each other. I recall loud grunting, flinging our clothes off with gusto, his legs in the air as I fingered his asshole. I got on top and came easily, just as I had the first time with him. The next morning while I dozed he tucked his shirt into his jeans and sat on the edge of the bed.

"Thank you," he said. "I mean it. Something happens when I'm with you. I feel healed."

I was brimming with goodwill: for him, for Jude, for Joaquin and Hugh and anyone else who needed me for a minute or a night. That week was my best at OneTaste, possibly—with the exception of Alden—the best week of the entire project.

Though I wasn't officially related to Amelia, the child Susan had six years earlier, she called me Auntie. I'd been privy to so much of Susan's decision-making before she went to the sperm bank that I felt I'd known Amelia since she was nothing more than an idea. The two times a year when Susan and Amelia came to visit from Los Angeles were typically some of my happiest, a chance to cook for more than two, gather on the couch for *The Sound of Music* or *The Wizard of Oz*, and watch Scott read to Amelia or show her how he bottled wine.

Susan and I had never lived in the same city during our twenty-year friendship but each always kept keys to the other's house. She arrived with Amelia on a Friday. On previous visits I'd leave work early and meet them at home, but this time I couldn't. I had an afternoon date with Roman and Margit for a threesome. Margit was leaving the country on Monday, Roman had secured permission from Annie, and I was moving back home in two weeks. The timing was terrible, but no more so than the timing of the entire project. I should have sown my oats during my short stint as a single woman in my twenties. My threesome should have happened spontaneously, in the wee hours after the rave I never went to, and I should have met my one-night stands on European trains I never rode, instead of on Nerve.com and at OneTaste.

I scheduled it so that I'd have Roman to myself for the first hour. He was waiting for me in my room. I straddled him, both of us clothed, and began kissing his ears and neck. He slipped his hands under my dress and grabbed my ass, then flipped me over and kissed his way down my belly. Roman was the rare man who gave as much head as he got. After he was done going down on me, he propped my head up on several pillows and planted his knees astride my shoulders, fucking my mouth in slow motion. On every stroke he pulled out completely, letting it hover above me until I reached for it again. I could have sucked his cock like that for hours, except the doorbell rang.

Margit entered, flushed and smiling, unable to contain her giddiness. She dropped her coat and purse to the floor and without aplomb climbed onto Roman, making out with him. I lay next to them on my side, watching. Fevered, panting, she sat up to unbutton her black shirt and black lace bra, revealing perfectly formed breasts. She impatiently pushed her jeans off. Roman and I both sat up. He slid his finger into her from behind while she and I kissed. Then I moved down to her nipples while Roman kissed her, and so on, until she and I fell onto the bed and he burrowed his mouth between her legs, never taking his eyes off mine.

There were things I would have wanted to initiate—having her go down on me with him in my mouth, for instance—that didn't occur to me until later. In the moment, my senses surrendered to overload. Several times I stopped to merely watch them, overtaken by the thrill of seeing two people up close having sex. Margit moaned and laughed and gasped, much louder and faster than me. I deferred to her, since I was, in a way, the hostess.

It ended with us going down on Roman together, a scenario over which I'd long fantasized. He gathered my wavy hair in one hand and her thick, straight hair in the other. We made out like that, then sucked at each other's breasts while one of us took his cock, and finally we shared him, her above and me near his balls, until he came with a violent groan.

I looked at the clock; I was late. As Margit and Roman joked and thanked me for setting up the date, I quickly slipped on my dress and gathered up my bag. "Stay in my room as long as you want," I said, kissing each of them on the cheek before heading out to catch the train.

When I got home, everyone was at the kitchen table playing Uno. Scott and Susan were drinking glasses of homemade strawberry wine. Amelia, a darling child with brown tendrils and intelligent eyes set in an imp's face, was drinking a sippy cup of water.

"Hiiiiiii!" I sang, dropping my things, hugging Susan, kissing Scott, and gathering Amelia up in a cuddle. "I'm so glad to see you guys."

"Was work busy?" Susan asked.

"Yeah," I said, avoiding her eyes. "As usual." She was the closest thing I had to a sister, the one friend who knew all of the project's details, and she supported me unconditionally—listening, asking questions, empathizing, which was amazing, given the fact that she had long graduated from sensual adventures into the maturity of single motherhood. I desperately wanted to tell her what I'd just done, but even when I got her alone later that weekend, I didn't.

Scott poured me a glass of wine and I joined the game. After a few rounds, I got up and said, "You guys keep going, I'll start dinner."

"Rob!" Susan said, pointing. "Your dress is unzipped!" Amelia looked up and erupted into six-year-old giggles. "Auntie Robin!" she squealed, hiccupping with laughter.

"What?" I said, reaching back to the zipper. It was open to the waist, my bra strap showing. Scott looked up from his cards momentarily, then back down. "Oh shoot, I must not have zipped it back up when I went to the bathroom." I felt my throat and face go scarlet with a shame that was more sorrow than embarrassment.

It was obvious the dress didn't need unzipping to go to the bathroom.

"She must have stopped at OneTaste," Scott said, louder than necessary, still looking at his hand. He sighed and flipped his next card onto the table. Later that night, when Amelia asked Uncle Scottie for a bedtime story, he told her the tale of Pandora's Box.

When Margit returned from her business trip, she was more than willing to step into Grace's shoes where the strap-on was concerned. Scott went camping for the weekend, leaving the house to me, and okayed the idea of my bringing Margit there. In preparation, I went to Good Vibrations and bought a white, medium-sized silicone dildo with a bulbous head, and a black velvet strap-on harness.

I met Margit for dinner at my favorite restaurant near the house. We sat at a table in the bar and ordered martinis and finger food. As usual, she was in high spirits, alternating her own excitement with rapt attention whenever I talked. In conversation Margit was spontaneous and unedited, completely unafraid to speak her mind. Everything I said she playfully challenged.

When the bill came, she swiped it from the center of the table and pronounced, "You're my date."

"No, Margit," I protested.

"Plus, you bought the dildo!" she said, inserting her credit card with a smile.

Back at my house, Margit put her hand on the pole. "Will you dance for me?" she asked.

"Really?"

"Yes," she declared with a sharp nod. "I'll sit right here." She walked to the nearby chair, plopped herself down, and crossed one leg decidedly over the other. "I just hired you. Now show me what you can do."

"I'll be right back."

I went into the bedroom and changed into the G-string, stripper's shorts, push-up bra, and tank top I'd used for Scott's lap dances. I squeezed into the six-inch Lucite platforms, mussed my hair, applied a quick coat of dark lipstick, and clicked on down the hallway to the living room, the heels forcing me into a snaky burlesque gait.

I had a playlist on my iPod called "Pole." I lowered the lights, cued up Massive Attack, and did the same routine I'd devised for Scott. When I backed my ass up against the pole, she shaped her mouth into a silent "ah." When I crawled up onto the chair, she took in a sharp inhale. When I peeled off my tank top and ran my fingers under my bra, she said, "Oh my god. You're amazing."

In the bedroom, I slid into the strap-on harness first, naked now except for the platform heels and the white dildo hanging from my hips. I felt neither sexy nor awkward, just curious. I entered her slowly and soon she wanted more. Unlike the exhilaration of penetrating Grace with my own finger or mouth, the dildo put me at a remove. While Margit panted and moaned below me, I watched as if from a slight distance.

I was eager to switch places. When we did, the hardness of the dildo surprised me, much harder and more unyielding than even the most erect penis or any vibrator I could recall. It didn't hurt exactly; it just felt dead somehow. Visually, I kept registering the thrilling scene taking place. Sexually, I had plateaued, the artificiality of it all neutralizing whatever excitement the novelty had generated.

After Margit left, I couldn't wait to put on my warm robe and monkey slippers. I pulled my hair into a ponytail, brushed my teeth, poured a big glass of water, and crawled into bed. Cleo jumped up on my chest and I lay with her a long time, reading. Out front, the Castro weekend was just revving up, but here in the back of the house, facing the yard and garden, it was as quiet as evening in any small town. It didn't occur to me until much later that Margit was the only person I'd slept with in our bedroom.

And the last. I made a mental count: twelve new lovers in the past year. Some had become close friends. Most had helped me befriend parts of myself that had been lying in wait: little girls both wounded and free, teenagers both adventurous and insecure, grown women both fierce and unsteady. There was a loving mother inside me, a sacred whore, a wise healer, a selfish bitch, and an observer of them all.

From what I gathered, sex wasn't the only route to this kind of self-discovery. I probably could have taken up painting or traveled the world or sat in silent contemplation and ultimately discovered the same lost facets of myself. But I will say one thing about self-knowledge gained through sex. When you're pressed for time, it's efficient and sure. It lands in the body, and the body remembers.

PART THREE

House of Shadow and Desire

Do I contradict myself?
Very well then I contradict myself,
(I am large, I contain multitudes.)
—WALT WHITMAN, "Song of Myself"

27

The Crash

THE WILD OATS PROJECT ended one year to the day after it began. As April came to a close I had begun spending weeknights at the house. I thought we might just end things a few days early, but Scott told me he wanted to spend the night of April 30 with Charly—she was expecting it—so I decided to stay at OneTaste.

"You're going right up to the line," I said, worried about how emotional their parting might prove after such a long affair, and about Charly's ability to let go in the long run.

He shrugged. "It'll probably be the last time I ever sleep with anyone else."

When I awoke on May 1 at OneTaste, it was cold and raining. I had all my things packed into one suitcase. I'd promised Grace a ride to Berkeley before heading to work, so at 6:30, we went downstairs and I propped my suitcase outside the front door of the residence. The others were inside the workshop center doing their morning OMs.

"Wait here, I'll go get the car," I told her. Just then a blue pickup rolled toward us down Folsom Street, silently, as if stalled. Without a screech or a brake light it careened straight into the parked cars along the curb. I heard the sickening sound of metal on metal and saw the driver's head collide with the steering wheel, causing the horn to start blaring. Instead of bouncing back, whiplash-like, it remained there.

I was shocked immobile for a second or two, then ran up to the driver's open window. He was conscious but seemed paralyzed. His right cheek lay on the steering wheel, drool hanging from his chin, and his eyes rolled lazily in their sockets. He kept trying to lift his head up but it kept bobbing back down onto the horn.

Grace ran over and called 911. I opened the driver's door, leaned him back in the seat, and held his arm. His face wasn't cut. "You're going to be okay," I said. "The ambulance is coming." He focused his uncontrolled eyes on me for a second, then dropped his chin to his chest. He didn't seem drunk. There was no smell of alcohol, no redness. A stream of saliva ran over his bottom lip into his lap.

Grace got off the phone with 911 and stepped closer to him, touching his shoulder. She looked at me silently. I saw her visibly inhale and exhale.

"You're okay," I kept repeating, holding his arm while Grace held his shoulder. "They'll be here any minute." He took ragged breaths, looking about the cab with confused eyes, his free hand grappling with the air in front of him. He made little nonsensical sounds as if deep within a dream.

The ambulance finally arrived and the paramedics took over. They said he was having a seizure, maybe a stroke. The police arrived and Grace and I had to answer two pages of questions about the accident. By that time, she'd decided to skip Berkeley. I got in my car to go to work and found myself driving toward Scott's office instead, down Folsom and up Spear Street. It was a little after 7:00 a.m. and he'd probably just arrived, straight from Charly's. I called him as I approached.

"Hi," he said.

"Hi. Can you come downstairs for a minute? I was just leaving OneTaste and a man had a seizure and crashed his truck into the curb."

"Shit. Are you okay?"

"Yeah, I just want to see you for a second."

"I'll be right down."

I pulled up to his office building and saw him standing outside in black chinos. I got out of the car and walked straight into his body, wrapping my arms around his waist. He put his hands around my shoulders. "It was really upsetting," I said into his chest, smelling his familiar earthy scent, hoping I wouldn't detect anything feminine. Luckily, Charly hadn't left her trace behind.

"I'm sure he'll be okay, dumpling," he said as I pulled back, looking at the wet spot my tears had left on his purple shirt. "The paramedics are taking care of him."

"I'm just . . . I don't know . . . I'm glad you're here," I said, wiping my eyes with the back of my hand.

"I'll see you at home tonight," he said. "We'll have a quiet weekend."

"Okay," I said, nodding. "I'll see you tonight. I love you."

"I love you too, doll." He kissed my forehead and turned back toward Spear Tower. I got in the car but didn't start it, watching him walk through the glass-enclosed lobby, waiting until his long body rounded the corner of the elevator bank, out of sight.

After months spent in one-room studios, I took to my kitchen with renewed vigor. I cooked Persian rice and lasagna. On weekends Scott lounged in the sunny dining room reading the paper and drinking coffee while I made pancakes. I took baths in my large tub and we lit nightly fires in the fireplace. Upon waking, or turning a corner into a room, I would momentarily be struck by the beauty of our home. I'd pause and stare out the window or at the sepia photos of Scott's parents and my grandparents lining the hallway, and breathe a sigh of relief.

Our emotional and sexual connection was slower to rebound than our resilient domesticity. We were careful with each other, as if tiptoeing away from a minefield. The once-a-week sexual frequency that had satisfied me for years now left me wanting two or three times that. I'd assumed that a year of talking dirty to nearly every lover would free up my inhibitions with Scott, but sure enough, when I tried to utter even the most mildly raw sentiment—a simple "Fuck me" or "You're so hard"—I found that the words still stuck in my throat. I'd wince below him, mystified at the strength of the force keeping them locked in. Afterward, as we lay side by side, I confessed, "It's so weird. I want to talk dirty to you but I literally can't."

"You can say anything you like."

"I know. You always say that. But I can't. It won't come out."

"Why? Are you embarrassed?"

"Maybe. It's not quite embarrassment. It's more like, dirty talk just isn't us."

"I don't want to be the guy you have the boring sex with."

I wondered if he felt freer with others, too. If Charly liked dirty talk.

"Do you ever want to talk dirty?" I asked.

"Not really. But you should say anything you want."

The ruptures to our intimacy showed most in oral sex. Scott lost interest in my going down on him, and he rarely did so for me.

"Why don't you go down on me anymore?" I asked one night in May.

He looked pained. After many moments of silence he said, "I don't know."

More silence. "Oral sex is more intimate than intercourse," he finally said.

"And you don't want to be that intimate with me?"

He didn't answer.

"Did you go down on Charly?"

"Robin . . ."

"So you can be intimate with a woman you've known for six months but not with me."

"I've done bad things," he said, suddenly looking up at me.

"Like what," I mouthed, keeping my eyes on his.

Half a minute passed. No one spoke.

"Like what," I repeated.

"One Tuesday a few months ago, you were sick and you wanted to come home. I told you I had a writing group that night, but I didn't. I had a date with Charly."

I surprised myself by saying, "I've done worse than that." I saw myself flying off to Denver before the project even began, Paul entering me without a condom, Alden doing the same. I shivered, recalling the emotional attachment that ensued once the condom came off, immediate and irrevocable. And then it hit me.

"Oh my god," I said, almost laughing at myself. "You took the condom off with her. Of course you did."

"Yes."

A black wind began to spiral inside my skull like a twister gathering speed on a barren plain.

"You've been having sex with Charly for half a year with no condom."

He nodded, avoiding my eyes.

"Please tell me she's been tested."

"She's clean," he said. "She doesn't have anything."

"How do you know that?" The doctor's appointment, the angst I suffered over just a few condomless weeks, the terrible fight with Alden, the test he finally mailed, my own follow-up blood test all tumbled through my mind chaotically.

"She told me so."

"She told you so. And you believe her enough to risk my health on it."

"Yes," he said, looking up at me defiantly. "I trust her."

My brain went dark. Suddenly I was punching his arms. I could feel my fists land on thick muscle with each thrust, and though I pushed with everything in me, I couldn't make them land hard enough. I heard myself grunting with the effort. I flailed at his head. When he grabbed my shoulders and held them fast, I bit down on his hand. I wanted to crack the bones under my teeth, but something stopped me.

This was the bare reality between us. A frightened girl working to break out of a cage. A bad man working to cage himself. Remove the constraints and see what happened. How easily he could do what it killed me to do. How free he was at his core compared with me. Free to snip his own balls just to keep them from me.

So as not to crush his hand, I turned from him and toward the dresser. My feet and legs ground firm to the floor while my upper body fanned out to everything within reach, an unstoppable engine of wrath. I wiped the framed photos and trinkets and a bowl of coins from the bureau with one sweep of my arms. I pulled racks of clothes down from the closet and tossed shoes into the middle of the room. When there was nothing left to smash in the bedroom, I picked up my heavy wooden jewelry box, barreled into the bathroom, and tossed it through the shower door, shattering it into hundreds of jagged pieces. It was only when I felt glass under my bare feet that I began to regain something like regular consciousness. I stood amid the rubble, panting like a dog, and looked around. Scott was gone.

I pulled on shoes, bolted out the front door, and ran to the corner of Market Street. It was past midnight and few people were out. I could see his large frame about three blocks away, walking quickly toward downtown. I ran after him on weak legs. By the time I caught up he was half a mile from the house, standing at a red light just across the street from a cheap motel. Breathless, I grabbed the tail of his coat and he whipped around.

"Please come home," I said. "Please." I wanted to die.

He exhaled deeply and we began walking back toward the house in silence. When we got there, we went to the ruined bedroom. The sight of it shocked me nearly to terror. I hadn't seen a room in that condition since I was a teenager.

Still in his coat, Scott walked over broken glass and sat down on the edge of the bed, elbows on knees and head in hands.

"Are you going to leave me?" I asked.

He looked up from the floor briefly, then back down. "I think so," he said.

The next day I got home before Scott so I could clean everything up. I cried as I shoveled pile after pile of broken glass into a dustbin, pulled shards of glass from every corner, lifted scratched family photos from the rubble, recovered the pieces of a statuette I'd bought him in New Orleans. The fact that I had caused so much destruction dumbfounded me.

By the time Scott got home, the room was restored, though the bureau was empty of decoration and the shower door was gone. He asked me to come sit down at the kitchen table.

"If you ever hit me again, I'm leaving you. No discussion. What happened last night can never happen again. Do you understand?"

I couldn't believe it. My spouse was threatening to divorce me for hitting him. If that happened, I'd not only lose him and the marriage, I'd have absolutely no idea who I was. I'd be left to live out the rest of my days as a person I didn't recognize and couldn't accept.

"I'm so sorry, Scott. I swear it won't happen again." I heard those words and thought, *That's what all perpetrators say.* "I've already made an appointment with Delphyne." There. Real perpetrators didn't make their own therapy appointments hours after the incident, did they? The master manipulators probably did.

In the days following, I entered a dark space much like depression except less powerless and more appalling, brought on as it was by my own volition. My arms and legs dragged the way they do in bad dreams. My thoughts walked a tightrope, alternating between wincing remorse toward Scott and ghostly images of my father: not the usual ones of him screaming or threatening, but silent ones in which he appeared alone at the kitchen table after chasing us out, crashed in the darkened bedroom, hungover on the couch with the TV blaring. I'd spent most of my life ensuring I didn't end up an abused woman. It had never occurred to me that I might become the abuser instead.

28

The Aftermath

THE PAINTING OF PELE the fire goddess above Delphyne's door was still there. Her blazing eyes had witnessed me parsing out my maternal longing, Scott announcing his decision to get a vasectomy, me concluding that I couldn't carry on with the status quo. Pele might be revered for her transformative powers of destruction, but here on earth I had to abide by the laws of human decency. I related the details of the bedroom blackout to Delphyne and told her Scott would divorce me if it happened again.

"What was so infuriating about knowing he didn't use condoms?" she asked. "Because he broke a rule?"

"No. I broke it, too. But when I did, I agonized. He was almost proud of it. The way he said, 'I trust her,' it floored me."

"I think you two are going to have to deal with Scott's anger about the project."

"Scott's anger? I'm the one who just destroyed our bedroom."

"You're over-expressing it. He's doing it passively."

The following week, Scott and I went to see the San Francisco Opera and ran into Tara and Jackie, two friends we hadn't seen in months. Afterward, we went for drinks. "I'm so glad you two are back together," Tara said, leaning in to sip her margarita. "You're my favorite couple." Jackie was unaware of the project, so Tara briefly explained it.

"Are you kidding?" Jackie said. "And you're still married?"

"You're amazing," Tara said. "Half the married people I know want to do this, but they're too afraid. And you made it through! That's love."

Scott and I glanced at each other cautiously. Jackie launched into a disclosure about her boyfriend, who had left his marriage for her two years back. She'd recently found on his laptop a batch of Craigslist emails between him and several other women. When confronted, he admitted to flirting with the women as a distraction, but insisted he hadn't even met any of them in person. Scott and Tara analyzed the merits of Jackie forgiving versus leaving him. It was a toss-up.

"Jackie, how's the sex?" I interrupted.

She sat back and put both palms on the table. "Incredible," she said. "It's the best sex of my life."

"Then let it ride. If and when you need to leave him, you'll know."

"Let it ride," she repeated. "That's exactly what I'm gonna do."

As Scott and I walked home, he said, "You really think she should stay with that guy?"

"It doesn't matter. She's not going to leave him if they're having great sex. She might as well accept it and just move forward."

"Sex isn't everything," he said.

"Oh, come on. We just went through the wringer for a whole year over sex. Sex and kids. Or maybe it wasn't even kids, maybe it was just . . ."

Suddenly I was up against the brick wall of a building to my right, Scott's hands pinned around the collar of my coat, lifting me to my toes. He was baring the pointy tips of his bicuspids, screaming, "Do you know how many nights I cried myself to sleep when you moved out!? Do you care about anyone's feelings but your own!?"

I was too stunned to reply. I could feel my hair bunched up against the cold brick. A car pulled over to the curb. The passenger rolled down his window. "You okay, ma'am?" he asked.

"Yes," I said as Scott took his hands from me. "Really, it's okay, thanks." We watched the car slowly pull away.

"I had no idea you cried yourself to sleep," I said. "My god, Scott, why didn't you ever call me?"

He looked at me and shook his head. "Call my wife crying after she moves out to sleep with other guys," he said flatly. "I grew up in the Midwest. You think I don't know what masculine means?" He had me there.

I wanted to encourage him to say more if he needed to. "Delphyne said it's good for you to get your anger out."

"Delphyne's a new-age gong-banger who made a buck fifty an hour watching us drive our marriage into a ditch."

I didn't even mind him throwing me against a wall. It actually felt like progress.

Delphyne did in fact have gongs in her office, though she didn't bang them. I was relieved to tell her about Scott's outburst. She told me Scott was right; it was going to take time to readjust, and we both needed to be patient as we integrated what we'd experienced over the past year. By the end of the session, she somehow wound the conversation around to a discussion of what I'd learned during the project.

"Think back to the day you took the positive pregnancy test," she said. "Do you remember how it felt?"

I easily called up the winter skirt I'd been wearing, the December chill as I walked toward the train, the mauve tint of the morning sky.

"Why were you so happy that day? What did you imagine it would bring you?"

"A lot. A second chance at family life. A new connection to Scott. A life path that everyone respects and celebrates. Something to commit to."

"Yes, but go a little deeper. Sum it up in one word."

"Purpose."

"And now sum up the project the same way. What did it bring you?"

"Feminine energy," I said. "It taught me how to act from my body."

"Purpose, and your essential feminine energy," she repeated. "You know that a child and lovers aren't the only means of getting those things, right?"

"Now I do, yes. I can access my feminine energy in Sabrina's circle like that." I snapped my fingers. "It's like I've learned how to recognize it. I feel it in yoga. At the ocean. When I listen to music."

I waited. She leveled her eyes at me.

"What is your purpose, Robin?"

"Writing. Even if I'd had kids, they would have come second to writing. No, actually, that's not true. I would have probably put the writing aside for eighteen more years, and that would have been a huge mistake."

She nodded.

"But writing is so agonizing. I wanted to create something with my body. Something I didn't have to think about."

"Creation is never easy, whatever form it takes."

I suddenly felt dizzy, as if I were being led blindfolded into a bramble.

"So write, and do yoga and go to the ocean and listen to music. And surround yourself with women who are doing the same."

"Wait. Is that why you were always asking me about my female friendships?"

She smiled and raised her eyebrows as if to say, *finally*.

My voice mail showed my father's number. He called maybe twice a year.

"Hi, honey, it's Daddy. I just wanted to give you a call because I was thinking about you. I hope everything's okay there. I don't know . . . I got a feeling. I'm here if you need anything. All right? You let me know. I could be out there in five hours. I love you, honey, and I think about you every day. Okay, just give me a call when you have time. I love you, 'bye."

Since the day I moved out, whenever we talked either in person or on the phone, he spent half the time asking if I was okay and if I needed anything. As a teenager, I'd pass through the kitchen quickly, trying to ignore him sitting there in his underwear, leg bouncing involuntarily, a Lucky Strike between his fingers hovering above an ashtray piled with butts. Next to the ashtray sat a cup of black coffee laced with vodka.

"Is everything okay?" he'd ask as I ate my cereal.

"Yeah." You're a maniacal bookie and my mother hates you and her life, but we're all alive, and I'm headed out to see my friends.

"You know I'm always here for you. You can always talk to me."

I'd look at him in disbelief. There was nothing to say except "I know." Life in this house was a cruel joke, but luckily, this wasn't my real life. It was just the starting line. Once that gun went off and that gate opened, just wait. Just watch how far and fast I run. That's what I'd be thinking as I tossed my cereal bowl into the sink.

The old wisdom says that time heals and the new wisdom says it takes time plus awareness. All told, I'd spent at least fifteen of the twenty-five years since I left home in therapy, so if anyone could heal her childhood, it should be me. I went to therapy not knowing what combination of trauma, genetics, and collective realities was at play. Fifteen years later I felt a lot better, but still not knowing exactly why. Because I'd learned how to identify emotions and make boundaries? I mostly failed when I tried to tie any present-day pain to a singular long-past event. After the first few years, the way my parents treated me in the past became much less important than the way I treated myself in the present. Enumerating their faults began to feel naïve and useless, as did the hope that someday I'd get over my childhood and be made new, never to feel the old abandonment or panic or despair again.

Therapy gave me skills; only time and living began to yield answers. My difficult childhood no longer felt like a mistake or a failing. If I imagined all the childhoods taking place around the world—in war zones, in places of dire poverty, in repressed families who never showed affection, in happy homes where a parent simply died too soon—I felt like mine fell somewhere in the middle.

Likewise, the accumulating years helped me gradually come to understand my father. The compromises, deferred dreams, wrenching decisions, and inexorable ticking clock of adulthood proved much more harrowing than I could have imagined when I tossed my cereal bowl into the sink and left him to his morning vodka, certain that when I had my chance, I would do it all so differently. I wasn't sure when it had happened, but even the angst I'd long felt about him being a bookie had evolved into a sense of pride. When I was small, all I wanted was for him to join the other dads at the offices and factories Monday to Friday instead of poring over odds, threatening deadbeats on the phone, hiding wads of cash in drawers. But after sitting in twelve-step meetings listening to the children of insurance salesmen and house painters describe the same alcoholic rage, and after spending twenty-five years in cubicles myself, I came to admire his refusal to go the quiet, numbing way of the masses.

Now that I'd explored my own appetites, indulged my own selfishness, and even slipped over the edge into violence, my dad seemed to have shrunk a size and I seemed to have grown until at last we looked something like equals. The voice on the answering machine sounded less like a patriarch's and more like that of one more struggling human being.

It was the timing of his call, the fact that he got a feeling about something being wrong, that jarred me. I especially wondered how such a sharp intuition could reach him if—as I suspected after listening more closely to his voice mail—he was drinking again. He'd had long bouts of sobriety punctuated every four or five years by a relapse, and sober he was a completely different person, the father I remembered from my preschool days who took me out for egg sandwiches every morning and sang along to *The Music Man* whenever it was on TV. His longest stretch lasted about a decade and coincided with my own twelve-step years, so he was sober when he read my angry letters outlining all his misdeeds and when I started going home again for Christmas after a five-year absence. He was sober when he met Scott and immediately asked, "What are your intentions with my daughter?" He was sober when he walked me down the aisle and for all that, I was grateful.

I made a mental note to call him back in a few days. I needed a little distance on more recent memories—Scott's arm bruises, the broken shower door, the scene after the opera—before I could handle talking to him.

29

The Broken Heart

I WAS DOING SIT-UPS at the gym when my brother Rocco called at 7:00 a.m. Our dad had gone to the hospital the day before to detox, and last night he'd had a heart attack. Besides the fact that his body had been through so many instances of withdrawal over the years, complicating the situation was his tracheostomy, the result of a bout of throat cancer many years ago. They were keeping him sedated in intensive care while they awaited test results.

"How serious is it?" I asked.

"The doctor said if he makes it through the next twenty-four hours, he'll probably be okay."

"I'll get the first flight out and call you from the airport."

I landed in Scranton at 11:00 p.m. and Rocco drove me to the hospital. We pushed the intercom at the door to the ICU and the nurses let us in. Between two thin pink curtains my father lay surrounded by machines and LED printouts, face gray, mouth agape. A thick, ridged tube connected the trach at the base of his throat to a ventilator, and white plastic cuffs pinned his swollen hands to the gurney.

Rocco had been there all day. "Every now and then he opens his eyes for a few seconds," Rocco said. "But he's totally out of it. The nurse said he's probably not really aware of anything even when his eyes are open." He went downstairs to get coffee.

I sat there watching the ventilator expand and contract his barrel chest. Its movement, so decided and dependable, made it appear sentient, possessed of its own will. We liked to joke about how tough my dad was, how he had nine lives, even though we knew the truth. All those rehabs and withdrawals. With the throat cancer he'd been hospitalized for weeks after having his larynx removed. He'd also done two stints in federal prison for bookmaking, once for eight months and once for four. I hadn't seen any of it. My brothers had gone to the Sunday rehab meetings, the cancer hospital, the prison visiting room while I stayed far away in California, unable to face it.

Time and awareness, and now there was perhaps less than twenty-four hours remaining in the story of my father and me. How did I want the story to end?

I stood up, put my hand over his, and leaned down close to his ear. "Daddy," I whispered almost inaudibly, "it's Robin. You're going to be okay. We'll take care of everything." I took a breath. "I forgive you, Daddy. I love you. I'll see you tomorrow."

I looked down at his placid, sunken face, asking God or Goddess to carry the message to him somehow. Then I gathered up my purse and, for the first time in twenty-five years, went to my mother's house to sleep.

I woke up in my old bedroom and headed to the hospital with my dad's wife. My brothers were there already. We waited all day and night for the cardiologist to give us a prognosis, but time and again he was called into surgery. Finally, the following morning, he gathered us around a small conference table off the ICU waiting room. He was a tall, tanned, handsome sixty-year-old with cropped white hair and an efficient Nordic name, the picture of health.

"Your father's heart is this big," he said, spreading his palms about eight inches apart in front of his face. "It might be the biggest one I've ever seen. It's the size of Wyoming."

"Is that good?" Rocco asked.

"No, it's very bad," Dr. K said. "His heart muscle has been stressed beyond the maximum. He hasn't taken care of himself." He met our eyes and for a brief moment I felt ashamed that he was called away from patients with genetic heart disorders in order to save a man who had most likely smoked, drunk, and eaten his way to heart disease. Then again, guys like my dad probably kept him in business.

Dr. K said three of Dad's five main arteries were almost fully blocked; he was a five-alarm heart attack waiting to happen and needed a triple bypass immediately. But his body also needed another two days to recover from acute alcohol withdrawal before it could endure more stress.

"We're gambling with the timing here," Dr. K said somberly. "Hopefully he doesn't have a major heart attack before we get him into surgery. Your father's blood oxygen level is sixty-two. Normal blood oxygen is near one hundred. I'm not sure how he's still alive."

"What's the survival rate with a triple bypass?" I asked, looking up from the notes I'd been scribbling.

"Normally, when the patient doesn't have other problems, ninety-nine percent."

"What about a patient with all his other problems?"

"About ninety percent."

We all looked at one another, then started laughing. Two of my brothers had inherited my father's gambling gene. The oldest one leaned over and swiped Dr. K on the arm affectionately.

"Ninety percent! I thought you were gonna say thirty! We'll take it."

Our moment of levity was soon overshadowed as we sat alongside my father's bed watching his blood pressure surge, then plummet, his blood oxygen level creep toward the 50s, and his heart rate hover at 120 over the next two days. Every so often, he emerged briefly from sedation, opening his eyes in abject fear, turning his chin to pull away from the tubes, and arching his back in a struggle against the wrist cuffs. As he twisted, the ventilator began beeping its loud alarm, and the nurse came in to put him under again and readjust the lines.

My dad's closest brother gave me a medal to put around his wrist. The small saint engraved on it was called Padre Pio. "When I was in the ICU that time with kidney failure, remember? I was there for seven weeks. No one thought I'd make it, but Padre Pio saved my life. I believe that. You put this on him and he'll be okay."

My father was unconscious for five days. His sister drove in from Philadelphia with her husband. His oldest brother flew in from Florida with his wife. My cousins came. My stepbrother came. My sisters-in-law came with my nephews. Each morning I picked up my dad's wife on the way to the hospital and each night I drove her home. My mom accompanied us several days in a row. She and Dad's wife hadn't always gotten along; now they went for lunch together and sneaked outside for a smoke. When I got back to my mom's house late at night, I'd change into my pajamas, have dinner with her at the kitchen table, then go lie down in my childhood bedroom. All the vicious 3:00 a.m. fights I'd heard from that room receded back into its walls, neutralized by the more pressing life-and-death concerns of the present.

After the surgery, an aortic pump kept my dad's heart going while the respirator worked his lungs. Days later, when he finally began to wake up, we gathered round the bed. His wife went to his side. He looked at us slowly, then up at his wife, and began mouthing words. His mouth was free of tubes because the ventilator attached to his trach, but since he needed to cover the trach with his finger in order to talk, and his hands were still restrained to the bed, he was rendered mute. We had to read his lips.

"Rak-ton," he seemed to say, slowly and with great force.

We looked at one another. "Traction?" Rocco asked.

He shook his head no.

"Dad, are you in pain?" I asked.

He nodded no. Then again, "Rak-ton."

We stood there helpless. "Crand," he mouthed.

"Cramps?" his wife asked.

He looked down at his cuffed hands. This went on for several minutes until he was exhausted.

"Scranton," my mother suddenly said from the foot of the bed. "He's saying Scranton."

My dad opened his eyes wide and nodded, mouthing, "I want. To go. To Scranton."

"He wants to go to Scranton," my mother repeated.

"You're in Scranton, Dad," I said. "You're at Mercy Hospital."

Relief flooded his face. He closed his eyes. Later on, when he could talk, he told us that he dreamed he'd been transferred by train to a hospital in upstate New York, where he kept telling all the nurses to please take him home to Scranton.

I stayed home for two weeks, until he left ICU for a regular room, spending most of every day at the hospital and each night in my mother's kitchen. As the nurse changed my father's medication bag one night, I asked her, "Doesn't that man next door have any family?" Every day I passed by his room and no one was ever in there. He lay alone amid tubes and machines.

"I don't think so, honey." She unhooked the empty plastic bag and tucked it under her arm on her way out. "Your dad's lucky."

I looked at my father, asleep in the dim light of the Turner

Classic Movies channel, at his wife's purse on the nightstand, at Rocco out in the hallway, at the cell phone in my hand, with which I'd just texted an update to ten people. My uncle's Padre Pio medal dangled from his wrist, glinting silver in the glare of the television.

"We'll always have each other," my dad used to say from his cigarette-strewn corner of the kitchen table while I seethed silently. "Your mother and me, your brothers, those are the people who will be there come thick or thin. You don't understand this now, but you will when you're older."

Now I was older.

30

The Message

WHEN I RETURNED TO SAN FRANCISCO, a sense of calm settled over the house. While in Scranton, I'd bought a small figurine of a rabbit sculpted out of anthracite coal. I'd intended it for my makeshift altar, to represent roots and family. I placed it amid a laughing Buddha, a crucifix, the Venus of Willendorf, and a red-stone carving of Pele.

In bed, Scott and I began to go down on each other again. I gave up on trying to say the nasty things I'd so easily uttered to my lovers. I was no longer a little slut, a sexy bitch, a fuck-toy, or a goddess. I was kitty, noodles, doll. I used the blindfold we'd bought as a sleep mask on the mornings when I slept in. Now that I was through with the project, I tried to have faith that I might finally adapt to the dispassionate kind of love my marriage required, a strong love that ran like a vein of gold in bedrock. Even if it rarely surfaced in enthusiastic expression, I knew it was there.

I focused on my job, where I had recently been promoted to managing editor. I spent nights and weekends working on the newest editions of two dance books I'd previously written. I finally got around to editing Scott's wine manuscript. I took a peek into a book proposal I'd started back in Philadelphia, which I'd titled *Preconceptions: Letters to an Unborn Child*. The rough chapter outline described about twenty letters I had planned to write as meditations on the question of motherhood, their titles clearly conveying both my hope and ambivalence: "All the Right Reasons," "All the Wrong Reasons," "What I Can Teach You," "What I Cannot Teach You." When I got tired of staring at computer screens, I changed into my workout clothes and headed to the gym.

About once a month, Scott had dinner with Charly. He told me he wanted to remain friends with her and encouraged me to remain friends with my ex-lovers as well. I knew she was having trouble adjusting to his absence: I knew because I looked at his phone and saw her email apologizing for crying at dinner. There were other emails too, flirty midafternoon notes reminding him how close her office was to his, calling him babe.

I saw Jude every so often for lunch, Paul now and then for coffee or a drink. I still attended the occasional workshop at One-Taste. Scott said he was fine with me continuing to OM with others, since he wasn't interested in it. So I tried it. I scheduled an OM with Roman, who was in the same boat as me; he and Annie had returned to monogamy. We met in one of the empty rooms of the residence. We hugged, chatted a little, and got into position. His touch set off a slow, thick whirlpool in my middle, descending and stirring up sediment. I groaned and arched under his hand. As he inserted his finger into me at the end of fifteen minutes, I opened my eyes and exhaled slowly.

"Are you getting enough sex?" he asked.

"I think so. Why?"

"You seem . . . I don't know, ready to erupt." He laughed.

I sat up and pulled my pants back on. "It's probably just the sexual energy between you and me. I feel good, actually."

I didn't schedule another OM with Roman, or anyone else, again.

I sat staring at my Gmail. It wasn't my main email and I only checked it once or twice a week. Alden's name cemented me to the seat. I had forgotten he had this address, given that we'd done almost all our communicating by phone. The date stamp showed he'd sent it two days ago. I'd been home from Scranton a little more than a month.

Head: Delete it. It will ruin your life.

Heart: Open it.

The email was formal and friendly. He was just saying hello after seeing my profile on the Deida Connection, hoping I was well, noting it was a year to the day that we first exchanged messages on Nerve.com. True, we ended on a rough note, but he often thought back to those weeks with affection and gratitude. Hope you're not upset that I wrote. Please don't feel obligated to write back.

I sat still a long time before daring to type. I'm not upset that you wrote. Between the harsh ending and complete severing of ties, we made things more dramatic than they needed to be. I'd welcome the chance to be friends. Feel free to be in touch.

The next week we agreed to meet for a drink downtown. I told Scott exactly where I was going and what time I'd be home, giving myself an hour and a half. Alden was sitting on a low banquette in the back of the bar, one long leg bent atop the other, ankle resting on thigh, arms spread wide on the seat. We said hello and I sat down. We didn't touch.

He signaled to the waitress and ordered me what he was having, a gimlet. When it arrived, we lifted our glasses and sipped.

"So, are you still married?" he asked, putting his glass down.

"Yes."

"Are you still separated?"

"No. We're together full-time and monogamous."

He nodded, unperturbed. Since I'd last seen him, he'd spent several months in a relationship with a woman in Seattle. The distance had proven untenable and they'd broken up two months ago. He was dating again. He'd started the novel he'd had in his head for years.

The air around us bristled. I took shallow breaths. I was still hurt by our final phone call but I couldn't shake the feeling that something big was bound to happen between us. Of course I knew the theory about love interests who glowed with an aura of fate, that in actuality their physiognomy, gestures, words simply evoked those of our earliest caretakers, and in my case the way Alden broke things off was a powerful reminder of how quickly my father's affection could turn to rage. Before the project, I would have reacted to such a possibility by completely avoiding Alden. Now I only noticed a curious mix of mistrust and admiration. *Finally*, I heard myself say. Finally I've met my equally vulnerable, equally ruthless match.

"What are you thinking?" he asked as he signed the bill. He had a quick, linear, illegible signature, like a doctor's.

"I'm wondering what it would be like to be your girlfriend," I said, staring past him. He paused at that, and I looked at him and shrugged. "That's what I was thinking."

Outside the bar, I reached up to hug him goodbye. "Thanks for the drink," I said.

"You're welcome. It was good seeing you." If he was surprised that I wasn't going home with him, he didn't show it.

I turned and walked toward the train. The lights in Union Square had just blinked to life. Throngs of tourists hauled shopping bags along the wide sidewalks while natives weaved their way faster, with purpose. Crowds gathered at stoplights and a thick line of people snaked down half a block waiting to board the Powell Street cable car. I stepped onto the subway escalator and it carried me underground, a current delivering me to an unnamed destination. From this moment on my choice would be binary: I could stay in the current or jump out. But I wouldn't be able to stop it from moving.

I held out for a month. I don't mean that I steered clear of him. I put myself in front of him, just out of reach, without giving what he wanted. It was as much a power play as a necessary delay tactic, so that I could observe him before losing my wits to sensation. Every minute we spent together, every molecule of my being performed a preverbal scan: of his home, his clothing, his body language, his smell, the amount of papers piled on his desk, which photos he'd chosen to arrange on his shelf, the angle of towels hung in his bathroom. How often he used credit cards, how full he kept his gas tank, which TV shows he watched.

Why try to fudge the truth at this point? In my forty-fifth year, I became a cheater. Actually, it happened in my forty-third year, that very first night at Paul's door, though I subsequently dressed it up with the notion of open marriage. I harbor no shame about the open marriage but I'm deeply ashamed of the cheating. The right thing to do would have been to avoid Alden, or, barring that, to leave Scott.

I didn't do the right thing. One fall morning after Scott left for work at 6:30 a.m., I showed up at Alden's door and followed him to the bedroom. The sun was still low on the eastern horizon. My legs spread, our eyes locked, and it quickly became apparent we were playing for keeps. No half measures or rationalizations. It was wrong and it was most definitely temporary. Within weeks Alden told me I needed to make a decision. "I'll wait a little while because I don't have a choice," he said. "But I won't wait long."

The sex was as passionate as I remembered, mostly fiery and forceful, sometimes whispered and meditative. If I closed my eyes or looked away too long he said, "Look at me." At the end, when he pushed in and held it there, I could actually hear the liquid burst from his body into mine, the way you can sometimes hear your own heartbeat.

When we fought, we fought hard and bitter. Not like my parents—we were both too old and therapized for that—but our anger had the power to cleave each other's heart. One sharp word, one look, and we'd spiral into attack mode, hanging up the phone, slamming the car door. Alden didn't let me get away with much. He fought back and wasn't afraid to initiate conflict. Afterward, he was quick to apologize and forgive. He challenged me on points no one ever had, like my habit of talking over people and my condescending tone. I learned things during our fights. They changed me and brought us closer.

All of it transported me to a fertile ground that my soul recognized. A long-lost, familiar voice said this overgrown landscape was where I belonged. I had no good reason to trust such a voice, to throw out twenty years' worth of hard work and love in order to fall away into a wilderness of hunger and occasional fury. And so I didn't trust it. I struggled.

Three important things happened during the following two months. The first occurred the night I sneaked off to Alden's after ducking into a work event for a half hour. I sped over the Golden Gate Bridge. He waited for me at his door as usual, ready to devour me without preamble. He led me into the living room and put Led Zeppelin on the turntable. I pushed him into a chair and began dancing for him. When it was over—him slumped in the chair, me collapsed in his lap, the turntable needle hiccupping on the album's inner edge—we took long breaths to recover. He lifted his head and looked down at me.

"Where did you come from?" he said.

I knew what he meant. Once in bed I had asked, "Who are you? What do you want from me?" Now I opened my mouth to say something poignant.

"Please don't say Scranton," he interrupted.

I have no idea if that's actually funny, but I started laughing, and then he started laughing, and we laughed so long and deep—rolling on the floor, stomachs cramped, tears and snot flying for what seemed like five or ten minutes straight—that afterward I felt reborn. It dwarfed all other memories of laughter.

The second thing: Saturday morning at Alden's house. Scott was out of town. We drank coffee from a French press at his dining room table while he shuffled a deck of tarot cards. Alden and I were cut from the same cloth, part old-school, part new-age. He'd learned how to read tarot and meditate but he didn't attend drum circles or believe in *The Secret*. He read Dostoyevsky and ate red meat and listened to jazz.

I shuffled and cut the deck, and he laid the cards out in a Celtic cross. It began with the High Priestess, symbol of the divine feminine, progressed through the King of Swords (intellect and judgment), the Magician laid upside down (manipulation, confusion), and the Ace of Wands (new beginnings, breakthrough). In the middle of the spread, Alden turned over the Two of Swords, a blindfolded woman in a white gown sitting on the shore of a lake holding up two crossed sabers. The image represented the process of making a decision based on intuition instead of external stimuli. The final spot in the spread, the conclusion card, was the Sun: radiance, joy, victory.

I didn't retain much of what Alden said as he laid the cards down. I was lost in the medieval renderings and muted colors of the deck. It was the first time I'd seen tarot cards up close. I took a picture of the ten-card spread and later spent hours looking up the detailed meaning and position of each card. Even so, I couldn't explain its narrative. Rather, I felt the gist of it pulsing below the surface of my life: the feminine, the intellect, confusion, intuition, breakthrough, victory. At the office the following week, I opened a package addressed to me. Inside was an advance copy of a new novel along with a press packet. Tucked into its pages, the publisher had included a tarot card as a bookmark: the Sun.

There are seventy-eight cards in the Rider-Waite tarot deck, and the Sun is certainly one of the more well-known. It was like getting an ace of spades in the mail as a bookmark days after winning your first poker game with the same ace. It might have been nothing more than coincidence, but when I saw it, I gasped.

The third thing happened one night after Scott and I had some friends over to dinner. They were heading to Cafe du Nord, a club virtually across the street from our house, to see a local band. Scott was tired and told me to go along, seemingly at ease with the new distance I'd inserted between us. For the past several weeks he'd spent his time making wine and building a website for his buddy's fiftieth birthday. About once a week he'd tell me to plan a vacation and I'd say okay, then put it off.

At the club, I checked email on my phone. Alden had written a long love letter completely out of place in the electronic realm. It said, I suppose, all the usual things a man says to his married lover on nights he can't see her, but no one had ever said them to me. My eyes settled on one sentence in particular.

We are at the beginning of something profound.

Maybe it was my age, or the life-changing decision I faced, but I often found myself thinking forward to the grave. So much of life was repetition that immediately faded into background. So few words and experiences would matter at the end. Against this tide of mundanity, of half starts and crossed purposes, I'd been grasping for an anchor for so long.

I went into the bathroom of Cafe du Nord and sat in the small stall, the bass thumping, muted, through the walls. I read the letter over, held the phone to my chest, and closed my eyes, resting in one small moment of eternity. They didn't come often; this might even be my last.

With my hands crossed over my chest this way, I touched the other small pillar of timelessness within my grasp, my wedding ring, worrying it back and forth around my finger. I didn't yet know whether I could bring myself to leave Scott for Alden, but I was sure of one thing. I needed this letter inscribed onto parchment and sealed with wax. I needed to be buried or burned with it.

31

The Master of Polarity

A LARGE DENIM SHIRT hung on Deida's tall, thin frame as he paced the stage of a conference room in a Miami beachfront hotel. He looked about fifty, balding with a trim beard and mustache, like any regular guy. He wore loose jeans and practical walking shoes.

"This isn't therapy," he said. "Therapy is about creating safety, making boundaries, healing wounds. There's nothing wrong with that, but this is more like yoga. Or art. You can be broken and still practice beautiful yoga. You can be broken and still make great art. This is about opening your body to let more love and light shine through."

As he spoke, his hands moved gracefully—rolling an imaginary ball in front of his chest, extending outward like wings—and he roamed the stage on bent knees like a dancer. Every so often he'd stop, face us head on with feet planted and arms relaxed at his sides, and slowly scan the crowd. During these pauses I could see him breathing evenly and feel his mind working.

"Therapy and boundary-making are the work of the second

stage," he said. "That's when you learn to take care of yourself, balance your own internal masculine and feminine. The third stage is about letting go of that balance, surrendering your boundaries, dancing with your partner in a way that opens you more than you could open yourself."

I was just now learning to create a kind of cooperation between my own masculine and feminine energies, my need for structure and goal-oriented achievement versus sensuality and emotion. I looked around the room and wondered if I was spiritually behind the others. Had they already matriculated to the third stage? Couples and singles of varying ages, they were all white and well dressed, ranging from what looked like vibrant middle-aged entrepreneurs who golfed a lot to young West Coast and European progressives. Next to me sat Val, Susan's former sister-in-law, whom I'd contacted after noticing her profile on the Deida Connection. I'd last seen her fifteen years ago when we were both living in the Sacramento suburbs, me with Scott and she with Susan's brother, a hardworking, pragmatic guy who reminded me of Scott. Now she lived alone in Los Angeles doing special effects for film and television. A mane of long, straight blond hair framed her blue eyes and tiny diamond nose ring.

I didn't have much truck with Deida's three developmental stages. I'd lived through the therapy culture of the nineties and saw how experts tried to encapsulate the fluidity of emotional states into blueprints that were only temporarily helpful at best. Psycho-spiritual dogma changed every few years. I was there for a more practical reason: to see for myself what kind of alchemy resulted when men fully inhabited their masculine energy and women their feminine. Deida was one of the few people on the planet who made polarity his full-time job. Here I am, David. Show me how this works.

———

In the first set of exercises, the women formed a circle facing the walls of the room and the men formed an outer circle facing the women. The workshop comprised an equal number of males and females. Couples who had come together stood facing their partners, though they would soon migrate to others. Deida instructed us to simply say hello, and then give each other feedback on our voices and body language before moving to the next partner.

To a man, every partner who exchanged hellos with me asked me to smile more. They noted how intense my gaze could be. One man said, "When you smile, you're the most beautiful woman in the room." The command to "Smile!" shouted from construction workers and homeless men alike usually annoyed me, but the exercise made me wonder if an unsmiling woman actually scared a man.

Instant feedback was the method of choice. Men went up to the front of the room and stood facing us. Deida asked how many of us could feel the man's presence. Did he have integrity? Could he penetrate with love? Then Deida would whisper into the man's ear and his posture would subtly but visibly shift to something less timid, or less cocky, more quietly forceful.

Women volunteered to do the same. A pretty, meek-looking woman in a floor-length skirt stood before us with Deida behind her. He told her to take her hands from behind her back and lay the palms outward. "Let your hands be open to receive love," he said. Then he had her lift her arms to the side and arch her chest slightly while looking directly at us. "Open the front of your body, your breasts, your throat, your belly," he instructed. It sounded simple but looked difficult to do.

Deida took questions. A tall woman sitting in the front row raised her hand. She had on a flowing white sheath that showed off her ample breasts and small waistline. Her wheat-blond hair wound into a casual French twist, her skin was flawless and her lips swelled with injected collagen. Though she spoke for several minutes, alluding to an older husband at home, a nonexistent sex life, she was unable to finish a sentence, to the extent that Val and I looked at each other worriedly as she tried. Later, after standing in a circle watching the women dance, the men had to choose two women: the one whose dancing most inspired them, and the one whom they most wanted to sleep with. They chose the woman in the long skirt for inspiration, and the inarticulate blonde with the French twist for sex. As Deida invited her into the center of the circle and the room applauded, Val walked up behind me.

"Dude," she whispered, shaking her head in disapproval. I looked at her and sighed. Neither of us clapped.

That was the rub, the double-edged sword of woman as energy: not that boobs and blond hair were a turn-on—of course they were—but that intelligence counted for nothing. To see the majority of men lust after the sole woman who couldn't form a single thought astounded me. "The song is called 'Something in the Way She Moves,'" Deida joked, "not 'Something in the Way She Talks.'" All these so-called third-stage men wanted the same thing any frat boy did: the easiest chick possible, so that they didn't have to do any work.

But how could I blame them, when I wanted the same thing? My ideal man didn't take a lot of work, either. He was handsome, brilliant, wealthy, stable, but also passionate, artistic, spiritual. He could contain my emotions with steadfast calm but fuck me to smithereens when necessary. He treated me as an equal but also—every so often, only when I felt like it—as a princess in need of protection and special handling. I could throw up defenses and he could tear them down. The woman in me wanted, quite literally, *everything*. I'd been subconsciously asking myself a question for months now: What was the difference between this ceaseless font of "feminine longing" and mere narcissism?

As for surrender, I wanted it only in the bedroom. Outside of it, I had no intention of letting anyone direct my life, tell me how to speak or think, what city to live in, what to do with my time, when to smile. The perfect man served my desires—cue Mama Gena and the whole modern goddess movement; cue the popular wisdom "If Mama ain't happy, ain't nobody happy." In short, I wanted to totally dominate while playing at surrender.

We formed two circles again, the women on the inside. "Men, you're about to experience the thing you most fear," Deida said from the center of the circle. "I want you to stand up straight, breathe through your nose, keep your eyes focused on hers, and don't move. You're about to see that you don't need to hide from her rage. And ladies, you're about to see what it feels like when a man consciously contains even your biggest, wildest emotions."

Some of the men laughed nervously. I looked over at Val a few feet away and we exchanged gleeful smiles. We were about to get permission to do something we'd never again be allowed outside this room. My heart pounded with anticipation.

The man across from me, in his thirties with a thick build and short-cropped hair, wore a polo shirt and had the wholesome look of a high school football coach.

"Women, I want you to breathe slowly and start to get in touch with any anger you can feel in your body. The anger might be from something that happened today or twenty years ago. Let it come up from your belly. When I say go, you are going to use sounds and express it with your body: Scream, moan, stamp your feet, pull your hair. The only rules are that you don't strike anyone, you don't use any words, and you stop when I say stop. Okay? Everyone ready? Go."

Vague thoughts of Scott refusing to impregnate me and of my dad's old cruelties flitted through my head, but within seconds

I simply bent my knees, crouched over, opened my mouth wide, and let out an ear-splitting roar that trailed from my perineum to my throat. I curled my fingers into claws and wailed as if someone were stabbing me with a cleaver until Deida said "Stop," at which point I stood dizzy and gasping, tears filling my eyes.

Deida told the men to take one step toward us with outstretched arms. My partner did so, looking at me with soft, fearless eyes, which made my tears come faster. Then we repeated the process: ten more seconds of rage followed by the men taking one step closer until they were standing inches from us, their arms almost encircling but not touching us.

I had never felt so alive and present in front of a man. Tears trailed down my face but I wasn't sad. A clean, grounded current zigzagged through me, linking my most embedded self to my skin, like a swimmer who had surfaced. My partner's face flushed and his breathing quickened.

Deida said, "You'll notice the level of sensual possibility that exists in the moments right after rage. This could easily transition into a very powerful sexual encounter between a couple, even though we won't be doing that now."

Everyone laughed. Other than a scratchy throat, I was restored. I couldn't imagine how happy and healthy I—and every woman I knew—would feel if we could do this on any kind of regular basis.

By the time the rage exercise ended it was going on 11:00 p.m. Val and I changed into our bathing suits and walked out the hotel's back door, past the pool to the beach. It was a clear early-October night, about seventy-five degrees, and the sea was lukewarm. The full moon cast so much light that we could see our feet on the ocean floor. We waded up to our waists, then gently lay back, spread our arms, and floated for about a half hour, silent. The small waves were as calm as a lake's. Every so often, I lightly paddled my arms, swinging myself back around to face the moon. Through my peripheral vision I could see Val's white-blond hair splayed on the surface of the water.

Deida devoted many of the workshop's final hours to questions and working with individuals. From the center of the room, I raised my hand. He pointed to me. I told him my dilemma: Should I stay with my husband, whom I loved but who had less interest than I did in developing polarity, or should I leave him for a man with whom I had much more natural polarity?

"Does your husband love you?"

I said yes.

"Is he a good man?"

I said yes, definitely.

"Well, your husband's not here, so I can't speak to his part in all this. But I can give you feedback because you're here. I wonder if you invite his presence. To me, you seem depressed. Look at how you're sitting." I had my shoes off and my legs crossed Indian-style on the chair with palms resting on my thighs. I'd intentionally turned the palms up and open as he'd told the woman in the long skirt to do.

"I think if your husband is a good man and you love each other, you should stay with him. Work on opening. You can always open no matter what the other partner is doing. Focus on the ways he is trustworthy. Work on inviting more of his penetration with your body. You've been together a long time and you have to give him a chance."

Openness. Not verbal demands, not sex, not even flirtation or seduction. Despite the pole lessons, the womanly arts courses, had I been open in my marriage? And would changing my gaze and smile and the position of my palms do the trick now? It felt too subtle for Scott to even notice at this point, a homeopathic remedy applied after chemo had failed—not to mention after I'd delivered the additional blow of infidelity.

"Okay, thanks," I said, and Deida moved on to the next question. I wasn't done, however. When he brought his male assistant up onstage and asked who wanted to work with him, I shot my hand up again. Deida called on me and I went and stood next to them.

The assistant sat facing me in a hard-backed chair, feet planted on the ground, hands resting on knees, staring at me—or rather, through me. He was demonstrating the energy of a man burdened by work and by his own thoughts.

Deida stood between us. "How are you going to lure James out of his head and into his body?" he asked. All eyes were on me. I stepped closer to him, took some slow breaths, and looked into his eyes, trying to slowly call forth my inner seductress. I smiled but his harsh stare didn't soften.

"Use your voice and your body," Deida said. "Try to draw his energy down toward his legs." I knelt down and touched James's shins and he scooted forward in the seat and beamed down at me. "Fuck me, baby," I said softly.

"No. Don't tell him what to do," Deida said. I stood back up, stymied. I took another deep breath and began running my hands along my hips.

"Do you see how her energy is stuck?" Deida asked the room. "This is what men call a cold fish. It's why they cheat. She's the kind of woman who needs to be slapped, and I don't mean that offensively. She really needs her energy moved."

I turned to Deida in all seriousness and said, "All right, so slap me."

"I can't," he said. For legal reasons, I presumed.

"Then help me. Tell me what to do."

"I don't know." He shrugged. "Act like a porn star?"

My eyes widened. A thousand bucks and three thousand miles to hear the man who wrote *Finding God Through Sex* tell me to act like a porn star.

"Really? Just let loose on him?"

"Yes. You can't kiss him or touch him sexually, but anything else is fine."

I straddled James's lap, pulled the elastic from my ponytail, and began running my nose and lips along his neck. He was about thirty-five and sternly handsome. I squeezed his biceps, ran my fingers through his hair, pushed my chest up against his collarbone, tilted his chin back and hovered my mouth above it. He held me by the hips. I ground them into his, making the circles I liked when I was on top during sex, ran my hands over my breasts, moaned, threw my head back, then tossed all my hair over his face and growled at him, making use of the aggression Deida's comments had engendered. When I finally sat up, I was panting and the room was applauding. Deida looked only slightly more satisfied than before. I got up from James's lap and a man in the front row raised his hand. Deida called on him.

"So, speaking for myself, that was a lot," the man said, and a few others laughed and nodded. "I'd personally prefer something between what she was doing at first and what she ended up doing."

"Right," Deida said. "Every man needs a different variety and level of feminine energy."

It occurred to me that I had Nicole in one ear preaching slow sex and the harm of the porn model, and Deida in the other preaching, at least on some level, the opposite.

"Cold fish my ass," Val whispered as I returned to my spot beside her.

In the final exercise of the weekend, the men took seats and the women had to choose a man and sit astride him. Precisely because he intimidated me, I walked straight up to a muscular blond in his late twenties whom Val and I had jokingly nick-named Hollywood for his leading-man looks. Loud, tribal drum music began playing. Deida directed us to follow the man's breath and gaze while moving in his lap. Hollywood was a good breather. Following his lengthy inhales and exhales dizzied me. His hands went around my lower waist, fingers pressed to my sacrum. I held on to the back of the chair and rocked my hips in his lap. We began sweating. The music got faster and louder. Several woman were making noise now—ahhh, oooh, ohhh. Some flailed their arms wildly and threw their heads back, building up to what looked and sounded like fully clothed tantric orgasms.

Could breathing really do that? Perhaps if you had a transparent body made of light and held your hands and spine correctly, or if you truly believed that the way you moved could ever trump the things you said. But not, let's face it, if you were a bookie's daughter from Scranton, a melancholy ballbuster whose sexual response was as capricious as her unrelenting consciousness.

32

The Brutal, Slippery Truth

HAVING SPENT MY CHILDHOOD DENYING—quite naturally and without a thought—the fact that someone was hurting me, it proved easy to fall back on denial when I started hurting Scott. I told myself I was lying to protect his feelings, leaving unspoken the fact that my main impetus was to protect myself: protect my options, keep them open. But it didn't work that way. The longer I lied, the more my options closed. Deception, I found out, adheres to its own metaphysical rules, as stable as the laws of gravity. Scott and I were so deeply connected that hurting him had to hurt me, even if a sheen of self-delusion kept me from feeling it at first. My lies buried themselves like slow-growing tumors. I wouldn't feel the full extent of them until years later, when they woke me up at night, haunted my waking hours, forced me to sit down on a busy curb and cry.

And yet, as loaded as adultery is with sorrow and guilt, there's a reason people continue to practice it. It was so incredibly satisfying to find myself regularly traveling the two poles that rounded out my life—stability and passion—instead of withering away in the cold security of one or burning to dust in the flames of the other. How fully they balanced me. How often I daydreamed of having two husbands, of letting each of them also have two wives. Not an endless polyamorous supply, just two. Would that work logistically? Doubtful. But in the several weeks during which I lived in the gray area, I came to think of the Golden Gate Bridge as a long hallway in my ideal mansion, a bedroom at each end of it where I could finally express both the tenderness and the ferocity in my heart. It was that very combination I'd once hoped Ruby would help manifest.

Ruby. A baby to cement a relationship, fill in its weak spots. Talk about a daydream. Babies don't improve sex lives, they kill them. They don't complete marriages, they stress them. Babies don't even complete women, or at least not women like me. Right?

Then what to make of the clipping I stumbled upon one afternoon? Scott was gone camping, Alden was out of town, and I spent the day sitting in my kitchen with Cleo, sorting through old letters and cards. Poking from a folder dated 1988, a yellowed page of *The New York Times*. I slid it out and opened it, recalling at once how I'd stowed it away when I was only twenty-four, before I'd ever harbored a single conscious thought of motherhood. In it, Anna Quindlen announces she will stop writing her *Times* column because she has just birthed her third child, a girl named Maria, and some experiences should simply be lived, not pondered.

I remembered where I was the day I read it, a sunny, rundown apartment in Midtown Sacramento where I lived with the boyfriend who preceded Scott. I'd painted the walls gray and sewn lace curtains for the bay windows. I was sitting near one of those windows reading the paper, and when I finished I sat looking at Quindlen's words, fingering the newsprint encoding this dual symbol of womanhood—mother and writer, a life encompassing children *and* self—as if I'd never seen anything like it. I walked to the kitchen, took scissors from the drawer, snipped around the even borders of the text, folded it in thirds, and stowed it away like a secret.

Biology. Fast-forward a few years from my affair with Alden, around the time I find myself waking up at night crying, recounting my lies, experiencing physically their steely, loveless edges, as if they have the power to fray my insides. My joy has circumnavigated to focus once again on the kitchen, the fireplace, the dinner with girlfriends, the engrossing novel. I'm reading an interview with a gynecologist about the hormonal changes women endure in their forties. She describes how estrogen, which she calls "the hormone that makes us want to look pretty, have lots of sex, and make babies," surges in a woman's early forties, one last hurrah before trailing off into perimenopause. The body's final chance to do what it came to earth to do. "You can always tell a woman has passed into perimenopause when all she wants to do is stay home, wear yoga pants, and read." I look down at my yoga pants. I marvel that this doctor just summed up the most event-filled years of my life in one sentence. But no functioning adult can get away with blaming her behavior on hormones.

Right?

"Truth is often not simple," George was fond of saying when I would press us to land on some conclusion regarding my childhood's effect on me. "As you turn inward and dig through the layers, notice how at some point, you become a mystery even to yourself."

Back when we first arrived in San Francisco, before Scott and I bought our house, before the positive pregnancy test and the vasectomy, we lived in a one-bedroom apartment in Pacific Heights. Each morning before I started in on my freelance writing, I went to the café across the street and sunk into an old red leather couch with the newspaper or a book. I was reading *On Mexican Time* when a tall, well-built man sat down next to me and said, "Love Mexico. Love the Mexican people. Such a gentle, graceful people. Hi there, I'm Jake, great to meet you." He leaned forward and reached out his hand to shake mine. "Look at those sandals. You must be a real girly girl."

"Not really," I replied, closing the book and looking into his slate blue eyes. "My husband and I are driving down to Baja next week in our RV."

"Derrriving an arrrrveeee," he exclaimed, dropping his dimpled jaw in mock fascination and holding it there a second. "Love that idea."

Several times a week for the next many months, I had coffee with Jake and listened to him talk about his youthful adventures abroad and his simple quest for a warm, nurturing girlfriend—with whom he could eventually have a family—in a city of fleece-wearing, ambitious career women. Because I was a writer, worked from home, wore girly sandals, and loved to cook, Jake thought of me as the exception, and I did nothing to counter this assumption. Jake was my age and Scott's height. He reminded me of the Italian boys I'd grown up with: athletic, outgoing, confident almost to the point of aggression.

One day he came into the coffee shop straight from a run in a pair of shorts, waved at me, and got in line to order. I was sitting on the couch, our usual meeting spot. The line was long, and as I looked up from the paper a minute later, my eyes happened to land on his perfectly formed knee, midway between the long stretch of his thigh and the taut runner's muscle of his calf. Something slipped between my shoulder blades. There were no words attached to it, just a skipped heartbeat, a sense of some small thing reviving itself. I went back to the paper and tried to ignore it.

A few weeks later, Jake sat in our living room in navy blue dress slacks and a white business shirt, the collar of which he'd unbuttoned. He'd come straightaway from his job downtown. Scott was kitty-corner to Jake in a big armchair, barefoot in jeans and a T-shirt. They were talking politics—Bush, Iraq, Afghanistan. I wasn't listening closely, just noting the balance between the two. Jake made passionate, sweeping statements about Republican ethics and Scott responded with budget details and Iraq casualty statistics. "Dude, you are blowing my mind," Jake said. "You're on a whole other level."

Eventually, Jake put down his coffee and placed his big hands on his knees, preparing to leave. "Oh my god," he said, "what an incredible meal, what amazing conversation. You two are the warm, thoughtful couple this cold neighborhood needs. I am so impressed. So impressed." He slipped on his navy blue suit jacket, shoved his loose tie into its pocket, and said goodnight.

Scott and I walked back over to the couch and sat down.

"He's a character," Scott said.

"I think I want to sleep with him," I said, the words erupting from me unbidden, an underground jolt rupturing a fault line.

Scott got up from the couch, paced, then turned to face me. "While I'm out in a cubicle earning money, you're here at your café finding guys to sleep with?" He went to the closet, put on running shoes and a coat, and left. He was gone several hours.

"Where did you go?" I asked when he came to bed around 2:00 a.m.

"Walking through the Presidio. I was thinking of how I dated Rosemary all those years and her husband gave his blessing."

He paused and I waited. He didn't often delve into the emotional details of that relationship.

"He had no choice. All he could do was watch while he slowly lost her. And now it's coming back to bite me. This feels like the first symptom of a disease that's going to kill me."

We drove a hundred miles to Sacramento to see our old counselor George. He suggested we up the romance. He told me to greet Scott at the door when he got home, show him I was glad to see him. He told Scott to plan dates for us, look at that book of romantic weekend destinations I'd given him years ago. "The feminine is the soul and center of life," George told Scott. "A man who doesn't recognize that and nurture it will be left in the far outer reaches, alone."

Then George turned to me, cautioning against my urge to go outside the marriage for any kind of intimacy. "Nonmonogamy creates a kind of fracturing that's just the opposite of integration. And I know you, Robin. You seek integration. If you want to sleep with others, I advise you to end the marriage first."

The idea was unthinkable. I loved Scott too much to leave him. I just wanted him to show more passion because I didn't know how to show less. Just a little more passion, Scott, just enough that I won't become unglued at the sight of another man's knee. I can see now in hindsight how much easier it was to keep believing he was holding something back than to conclude the obvious: He was giving it his all, and his all wasn't enough.

I thought: I will do my part. I'll take the feeling Jake rouses in me and give it to Scott instead. I'll keep practicing all those skills I learned at the school of womanly arts: flirting with Scott, focusing on pleasure, wearing bright colors, keeping my own juices flowing. I'll sign up for those pole dancing lessons.

Later, at home, I said, "Scott, when I was younger and at my most vulnerable, and you were calm and steady, I felt so close to you. But that can't be our only way to connect. And you don't really need me like I needed you. So we have to find a new way."

Scott listened. Perhaps he was thinking about the time he handed me condoms and a weekend pass to do whatever I liked in New Orleans, and I came home with them unopened. Perhaps he was wondering about all those years when I was sick or depressed and he was the rock, when I needed him to be slow and sensitive to my sadness, not forceful and penetrating. Maybe he was riddling over my nagging to get engaged, then moving out after he proposed. Quite possibly he was wondering, *Why am I with this woman when I know I can never win?*

"When we met, there was a wildness in you," I said. "Where has that gone?"

He looked at me in exasperation, as if I'd pried out something he'd rather not say.

"I had to kill that in order to remain faithful to you."

If I could bring myself to forgive my father his violence, you'd think I could have forgiven my husband a vasectomy. If I could drum up empathy for my father's addiction, for other members of my family or friends in need, why not for my own husband? For a long time I blamed Scott's lack of expression, his understatedness, as George would call it, for conveniently blinding me to his suffering. If I'm honest, however, there was also a more germane barrier to my empathy: the fact that unlike the other people in my life, Scott had needs that interfered with my own.

I could understand why one or two friends had asked whether the project's main impetus was revenge. But the truth was uglier than that, as revenge at least implies blind emotion. Vengeance may have helped fuel my initial reckless impulse to knock on Paul's door that first night, but it did not fuel a whole year's worth of open marriage, and it certainly didn't fuel my affair with Alden, which was leaden with guilt the moment it began. My approach was tactical. When I realized I couldn't prevent the vasectomy, I used it as a bargaining chip to get something I wanted: a little freedom to explore the burgeoning sexuality that time and again came up against the walls of the marriage. I had begged Scott to nail me down the way men had been doing for ages—get me barefoot and pregnant, hold me fast under his roof, bind us by blood. Spare me the responsibility of choice. Fulfill my maternal desires in order to save me from other, less sanctioned ones. Those are my sins against my husband: abdicating responsibility, failing to empathize with him, cheating and lying. In the end, I was the one who needed to ask forgiveness.

33

The Crossroads

WHEN I GOT HOME from Miami, I told Scott about the rage exercise, the dance contest, the full moon. I didn't tell him about my question to Deida.

"He called me a cold fish."

"Are you kidding me?" He laughed. "Is he nuts?"

"He said my energy was stuck and I needed to be slapped."

"If your energy is stuck I'd hate to see energy that's moving."

"Are you sure you don't want to come to the San Diego workshop with me?" A ridiculous question at this point.

I stood next to him at the stove as he stirred a batch of mead. "Yeah, I'm sure, kitty. It's your thing, not mine."

"And you don't mind me going alone?" I employed this volley as a vague meter of his detachment. "I mean, I look into other men's eyes, I cry, they say I'm beautiful. It's pretty intimate."

He stopped stirring and looked at me measuredly. "I'm not worried. But when you get back, let's plan a trip, okay? We haven't been on a real vacation since Paris."

The second Deida workshop had a much lesser impact on me than the first. What affected me most was the drive down the coast to San Diego and especially the return trip back home. I drove through beachside towns, orchards, wineries, and long stretches of windblown grassland. A taco stand in Santa Barbara. A cookie-cutter strip mall where I bought a pair of comfortable pants. All the while I kept hitting repeat on Bon Iver's "Skinny Love": *And I told you to be patient and I told you to be fine . . . And now all your love is wasted and then who the hell was I?*

I needed the music to take up all the space in the front of my mind while in back, I clawed my way through a thicket of urge and reasoning. The good girl was long dead but the smart girl was not. She made her case. *Enough of these antics*, she said. *This is your future on the line. Don't let desire outsmart you. It's a shape-shifter, a charlatan. Alden looks like some beacon, but it's going to circle right back around to you. Wherever you go, there you are.*

In the opposite corner, the rumblings of the body. My body craved Alden irrefutably, and in that craving I felt real hope for the first time in years. The body said, *You have one shot at this life. One.* It didn't elaborate. While ideas like spiritual advancement, transcendence of self, goodness, and growth swirled through my head, my gut kept throbbing with the same repetitive message: one life, one shot.

In one ear I heard Deida's promise of integrating spirit and flesh through polarity, and also the harsh truth of how I hindered that polarity with my own melancholy, not to mention my clumsily expressed demands, all of which probably emasculated my husband more than inspired him. In the other ear, Nicole and my OneTaste friends expounded the merits of delving deeper into orgasmic meditation. They were reporting layers of emotional and sexual blocks giving way, moments of breakthrough and even physical healing, all as a result of consistent OMing. Noah had said he was breaking his "addiction" to long-term partnership and Margit was taking on new lovers even as she became engaged to Oden. But I wasn't built like them and didn't want to keep up this level of breathless flux forever. My life was neither infinite nor a game.

I'd confided in Susan and Ellen. I didn't want to put either of them in a sticky situation with Scott, but I desperately needed advice. Knowing me as well as they did, what would they suggest I do? Susan said, "I love Scott so much, and I love you two together, but Rob, I honestly think the marriage died when you saw how he responded to that positive pregnancy test." Ellen had a different outlook. "I vote for Scott," she said. "We all know how this story ends. After two years of passion you'll want your steady, loving husband back."

And then there was Scott himself, waiting, on some level possibly even knowing, standing firm as always in his commitments and his principles. Next to him stood Alden, saying I was the only woman he wanted, and that he would wait for me to decide until it became too painful to wait. And far in the distance, framing them both, lurked the shadow of my parents' marriage, the way it sent me reeling for safety with Scott only to be sabotaged in the long run by hunger; the walls it built in me against both solitude and commitment, leaving me to wander the cramped and sterile space between them; and the fact that it had finally ended when my mother was forty-five—the age I was now.

The last big vacation Scott and I had taken was to Paris, a full year and a half before the project started. It came right on the heels of the positive pregnancy test and his announcing, that December day in Delphyne's office, that he was going to get a vasectomy. The week between Christmas and New Year's found the city cloudy and bristling cold, the sky lowering to evening by 5:00 p.m. We stayed in a small hotel in Saint-Germain and walked the streets each day with other tourists, mostly European couples and families. In the dark afternoons we sat in cafés drinking hot mulled wine and perusing guidebooks. The couples around us were so good-looking and well dressed that I couldn't stop staring as they lifted their coffee cups, lit cigarettes, leaned in to talk quietly. The strollers parked next to their tables inevitably held a sleeping or otherwise silent infant.

We walked beneath the bare, wintry branches of the Luxembourg Gardens, through the endless hallways of the Louvre and Musée D'Orsay, climbed the steps to the top of Notre-Dame and the cobbled streets leading up to Montmartre. On our last day in town, Scott went to visit another museum while I headed off to shop. I took the Metro to the Marais and browsed the boutiques, practicing my few mangled French phrases with each proprietor, until I found the perfect blouse, charcoal gray cotton embroidered with eyelets, by a Parisian designer. I headed back to Saint-Germain to find a skirt to match and wandered into a shop where a tall, dark man of about forty with a thick mustache stood smiling behind the counter.

"Bonjour," I said.

"Hello. What can I help you with, young lady?" His English was perfect though thickly accented with what sounded like Spanish.

"I'm looking for a skirt to match this," I said, pulling the edge of the blouse out of its shopping bag.

"Very pretty!" he said. "Let's see what we have." He led me to a rack of beautiful woolen A-line skirts. As I looked through them, he stood behind me chatting. He was from Argentina and had been in Paris twenty years, had a wife and family now, would never dream of living anywhere else.

I picked up a skirt with black paisley swirls on it, reveling in its soft folds. Behind me he asked, "Are you married?"

"Yes," I said, nodding absentmindedly.

"Do you have children?"

"No." I looked up at him.

"No children!" he bellowed good-naturedly. "Why not?" I couldn't help smiling at his Latin-American bluntness, his assumption that we were all one big family who could, and should, talk about anything.

"My husband doesn't want them."

"Then get a new husband!" he yelled, tossing his large hand behind him in the air. We both laughed. I went into the dressing room to try on the skirt, which fit perfectly. I bought it and said goodbye and he wished me good luck and Happy New Year.

The image of his large eyes and laughing face came to me regularly over the years, the impervious surety of his accented words. Get a new husband.

Whom should I listen to, the yogi preaching radiance and softness, telling me to slap myself, get my energy moving, and give my husband a chance, or the Argentine shopkeeper hawking wool skirts and free advice in Saint-Germain?

As I follow 101 North into the city, Bon Iver is on its fourth go-round in the CD player. I pass the Castro and head straight over the Golden Gate Bridge to Alden's, then, a half hour later, return on the bridge's southbound lane, trace the edge of the Presidio to Divisadero, follow its crest through Pacific Heights and down to the Castro, and park in front of my little yellow house. Scott is sitting at the kitchen table, typing on the laptop. I hug and kiss him and sit down.

One final interpretation of the Wild Oats Project: an elaborate attempt to dismantle the chains of love and loyalty holding me so fast to my husband that all else was rendered impossible. They had to be loosened first. It takes time—several years, really—to wreck a marriage.

"We have to talk," I say. How many times has he heard that? The girl who cries wolf.

"I think it's time to part," I say. The hammer is down. The loosened chain slides away.

A word catches in his throat. He barely gets it out. "Divorce?"

I nod yes. I am appalled, in disbelief. How am I doing this? I can't do it, but I have to. It's like the day I walked into the abortion clinic. It's like I'm pointing a gun at his head and just pulled the trigger. No, no, no. Somehow I mouth, "We want different things." I look up and meet his eyes.

Color has drained from his face. This is the moment I will not get over. Two decades—my youth, his prime—half the years I've lived on earth are all swallowed up in his ashen grief, already swirling down into his silent realms of strength, disappearing forever. I don't know what's worse, the pain of hurting him or the black-pit terror of losing him.

We sit for a long time holding hands, crying silently. This is why people pack up and leave while the spouse is at work: a desperate urge to flee the scene of the crime as quickly as possible. Hit and run. But I won't let myself. I will sit here with him for hours, days, weeks, at least until the first shock is absorbed. I owe him that.

Time slows and darkens. We enter the path to grief hand in hand. Two weeks later he comes home drunk, hangs up his coat, and sits down next to me on the couch. "I don't get it. How are you doing this? Are you crazy? I know every inch of your body." For some reason he is whispering, as if the force of the words scares him. "No one's ever going to love you like I do."

"I know," I say. "No one will love me like you do. The most I could hope for is a different kind of love." But what if Scott's kind of love is actually the truest? Charitable agape versus lethal eros. Is it a soul connection and a feminine awakening urging me to throw it away or a maelstrom of hormones, leftover childhood trauma, and middle-aged panic? Or is it all of that? Would you believe me if I told you that I still can't say for sure?

"I've thought about it over and over. It just doesn't make sense. Are you leaving me for someone else?"

Alcohol has softened the lines of communication, created an opening for me to abandon my cowardice and tell him about Alden. Thus far I've convinced myself I'm saving him pain by not divulging the truth, but I've also resolved that if he asks me outright, I can't lie. I brace myself. First I take his hand and ask, "Do you really want to know the answer?"

"No," he says immediately, waving his hand as if to push my words away and shaking his head. "I don't want to know. Don't tell me."

He gets up and goes into the bathroom. The next week, I move out.

34

The New Year

A MONTH LATER, my first Christmas without Scott. I spend it in Pennsylvania, he in Sacramento with his group of lifelong friends. No doubt they hate me at this point, but all I can feel is grateful that he has them.

When I return, Alden picks me up at SFO and drives up the coast to Tomales Bay, where he is cat-sitting for his friend Matt. Matt has recently become engaged. His three-story condo is lined with photos of him and his fiancée embracing Matt's young son. There is a roaring fireplace, a well-stocked kitchen, and a long deck overlooking the water. Oversized bottles of prenatal vitamins line the counter in the master bath.

We spend most of the long New Year's weekend crumpled in the soft white sheets of their king-sized bed. Thick winter light slants through the wooden shades. In the evenings we make it out to the living room to play games and watch movies, and to the kitchen to cook short ribs and drink wine. The world beyond the condo's terrace and the sliver of bay it overlooks has been put on hold, as if the Earth's rotation has paused. In five days I leave the house once, to pick up a few groceries and a pregnancy test. My period is once again a week late.

"No way will it be positive," I say as I sit on the toilet while Alden opens the test. "I'm forty-five, for god's sake." Though my last physical showed that my hormone levels haven't quite abandoned the fertile zone yet.

"Either way, baby," he says. We haven't officially tried to get pregnant, though we definitely haven't tried to prevent it.

"I'm still too nervous to look at it, though," I say, putting the stick down on the sink. "It needs two minutes. Can you look and then come out and tell me?"

"Sure."

I go sit on the bed naked, gathering the comforter around me to ward off the winter chill. Alden comes out with the stick in hand and sits down, putting his arm around me.

"It's negative," he says.

"Yeah, I knew it would be."

"Are you sad?"

"Maybe a little." When I search my feelings, however, I find that the bliss of the past seventy-two hours has made even sadness feel sweet. If it were up to me the Earth would never rotate again. I would live and die in this condo and it would always be 5:00 p.m. on a Sunday in early January.

"Your cycle is probably just changing," he says, leaning back on the bed and taking me down with him. "Who knows, you could be ovulating right now."

"Probably not." I push against him playfully.

"We'll see," he says, pressing down on me so I can't escape.

When we're done, he rolls away, props himself on his right elbow.

"Put your legs up," he says. Something catches in my chest.

I lift them, not completely into plow pose the way I used to after Scott left the room, but straight up. With his long left arm he reaches up and pushes against my ankles, slightly tilting my hips back.

"How long do they need to stay up there to give the little guys a chance?" he asks.

"I'm not sure. I guess about ten minutes."

How many stories begin with a woman striking out into the unknown seeking adventure, wholeness, healing, and end with her marrying, having a baby, or both? I never quite buy it. She may indeed adore her husband and child, yet we know they bring a whole new set of challenges—and if they don't, then time will. The happy ending depends entirely on the quick fade-out. But keep the eye pinned to the frame, unfurl a few flash-forwards, and you'll see a different kind of happiness—wiser, less dependent on circumstance, and, even in the midst of beloved others, unfolding inside a deepening solitude.

A year after I leave Scott, I'm living with Alden in Potrero Hill, in an apartment furnished almost completely with his belongings. Apart from my clothes, books, a nightstand, a desk, and a stained glass lamp that was my first adult purchase back in Sacramento, I've left nearly everything behind in the house with Scott. I stop by Sanchez Street every few months to either pick up or drop off Cleo, and when I do, I find that I can't catch my breath. Sometimes, upon entering the front door, I simply walk into his arms and sob. He tears up too. Then he leads me back to the kitchen, past the stripper's pole, and pours me a glass of homemade strawberry wine.

Even as Scott fills the house with more wine and art and equipment to use in the classes he's begun teaching, and even though I've left nearly all of our marital possessions in place, the once-cozy rooms somehow appear empty. Even when his new roommate brings in her cookbooks and photos, the fully stocked kitchen looks bereft. In fact, the house doesn't start coming back to life in my eyes until two years later, when Scott finds a girl-friend whose hobbies are biking and craft beer instead of tantra and therapy.

By that time, when I quit my magazine job to begin work on this book, the grief has landed hard. What I couldn't foresee is how even an amicable divorce would sever me from almost all aspects of my previous self, not just Scott and our home and mutual friends but from our entire shared history, which is my history. The list of things I avoid out of pain includes countless daily routines, hundreds of songs I used to love, at least a thousand photos of the girl I used to be. Somehow, the divorce has even weakened my link to my own family, regardless of their uncondi-tional support.

I find myself awake until 2:00 a.m., 4:00 a.m., and when it nears 6:00 a.m. and I still haven't slept, cold black dread fills me. Alden is off in another town working or writing. We find that, in order to sustain itself, our relationship needs regular periods of separation. I drag myself from bed, force down a protein shake in lieu of food, make feeble attempts to leave the house for a few hours. My heavy body trembles; all its exposed surfaces recoil from air, noise, motion, hence walking to the coffee shop be-comes a sensory marathon. To get through the day I must employ a fistful of prayers, texts to Susan and my mother, and a stinging hot bath.

I am able, though, to regularly make it to a park at the top of Potrero Hill that looks west over the city toward Twin Peaks, where Sutro Tower looms above the Castro. The fog flowing in from the Pacific obscures three-fourths of the giant red and white antenna tower, leaving only its two upper spires hovering in the clouds like a masted ship lost at sea. I trace my eyes down to the terra-cotta bell tower of Mission Dolores, then strain them a few blocks north, trying to locate the corner of Sanchez and Market. Somewhere down in that ever-changing city I had my first real home. It took me forty years to find it, and I cherished it for less than two years before I began tearing it down. The arithmetic is unbearable to ponder.

One year later, Alden and I are living in Los Angeles, and as the grief settles and makes itself a permanent part of me, coincidences begin to take shape. How sometimes, when Alden gets upset, I turn focused and reticent, a silent grounding rod to counter his emotion. How adjusting my voice to a slower, calmer register, which at first feels suppressive, begins to feel, after a while, like kindness. How his expressiveness, which fires up our relationship, also requires me to put aside my own needs sometimes. I shake my head at the karmic process by which I've gradually come to understand my marriage only by leaving it.

Expecting marriage to provide passion, in addition to the security and friendship it offered, seems, in the calm wisdom of hindsight, naïve and unfair. And yet, even though I knew that passion and safety don't often commingle, I couldn't give the desire up. On midlife's stark stage of last chances, decisions must be made. In choosing Alden, I had thought I was tossing aside one for the other, but instead I got both—passion with him and security from a new, unexpected source: myself.

This is how desire wound its way around the lessons I failed to learn through self-discipline.

I don't regret going into the dark; I don't regret my wildness. No matter what price I had to pay in guilt and heartbreak—and I wish I'd been the only one to pay—I stopped doubting my decisions early on, back in that bedroom overlooking Tomales Bay in the first days of January. Alden holds my legs aloft. As you might have guessed, baby will not make three. There is no baby; there is instead the book you hold in your hands. As I lie silently with him, my feet dangling in the darkening blue light, the room shifts into focus and suddenly I recognize it as the place that has been calling to me for years, where yearning is honored and everything new is conceived. A sacred place perched halfway between this world and the next, so beautiful I would have given anything to glimpse it, even if only for ten minutes.

Acknowledgments

Thank you first and foremost to Jay O'Rear, my kindred spirit, for leading me in myriad ways to the birth of this book, and for generously supporting it despite the difficulties involved.

Thank you, Scott Mansfield, for encouraging me to write this story on top of everything else, and for your unfailing example of kindness.

Thank you to Chris Bull and Matthew Lore for emphatically stating, "You have to write about this," before I had any intention to do so, and to David Hochman for believing in the book before I did.

Thanks to my agent, Ethan Bassoff, and my editor, Sarah Crichton; I feel very lucky to have landed you both.

Thanks to Sarah Lynch, Leilani Labong, Margaret Jones, and Maraya Cornell for patiently reading drafts and providing invaluable feedback.

Thanks to my dear friends Susan Jarolim, Val Pfahning, and Amy McCall for your continual support and sisterhood in all things. Likewise Stacey Cooper and Maria Torre.

I owe a huge thanks to my family for their unconditional love, and a special debt to my parents for bearing with my telling of some of our most painful moments.

Thank you, Mary Karr, for mercilessly chopping up the first chapter. In fact, thank you to every female writer—and every feminist—who's ever lived.

I deeply thank every teacher, friend, and former lover who appears in this book for what we've shared and what each has taught me. I honor all of it.

A Note About the Author

Robin Rinaldi has worked for newspapers and magazines for seventeen years. She has been the executive editor of *7x7*, a San Francisco lifestyle magazine, and written an award-winning food column for *Philadelphia Weekly*. Her writing has appeared in *The New York Times* and *O, The Oprah Magazine*, among other publications. She lives in Los Angeles.